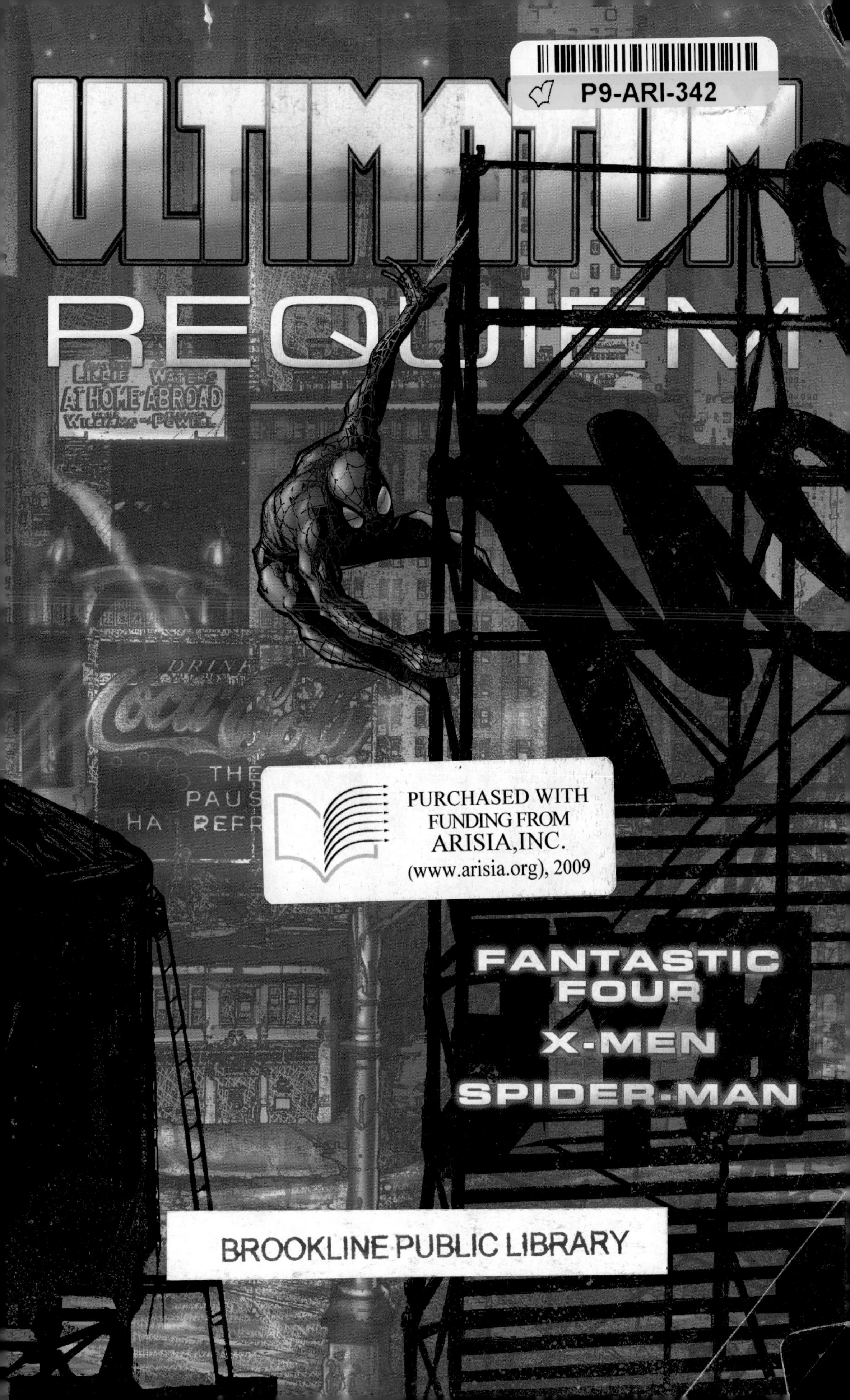
ULTIMATUM
REQUIEM
AT HOME ABROAD
DRINK
THE
FANTASTIC FOUR
X-MEN
SPIDER-MAN

ULTIMATUM REQUIEM

SPIDER-MAN

Writer: Brian Michael Bendis
Pencilers: Mark Bagley & Stuart Immonen
Inkers: Scott Hanna & Wade von Grawbadger
Colorists: Pete Pantazis, Justin Ponsor & Edgar Delgado
Letterer: Virtual Calligraphy's Cory Petit
Cover Art: Stuart Immonen

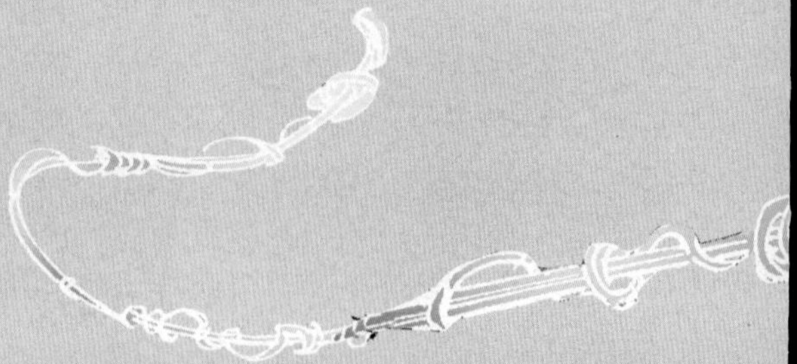

FANTASTIC FOUR

Writer: Joe Pokaski
Penciler: Robert Atkins
Inker: Mark Morales
Colorist: Guru eFX
Letterer: Virtual Calligraphy's Rus Wooton
Cover Art: Pasqual Ferry & Dave McCaig

X-MEN

Writer: Aron E. Coleite
Artist: Ben Oliver
Colorist: Edgar Delgado
Letterer: Comicraft's Albert Deschesne
Cover Art: Mark Brooks

Editor: Lauren Sankovitch
Senior Editor: Mark Paniccia

Collection Editor: Jennifer Grünwald
Assistant Editors: Alex Starbuck & John Denning
Editor, Special Projects: Mark D. Beazley
Senior Editor, Special Projects: Jeff Youngquist
Senior Vice President of Sales: David Gabriel
Production: Jerry Kalinowski
Book Designer: Spring Hoteling

Editor in Chief: Joe Quesada
Publisher: Dan Buckley
Executive Producer: Alan Fine

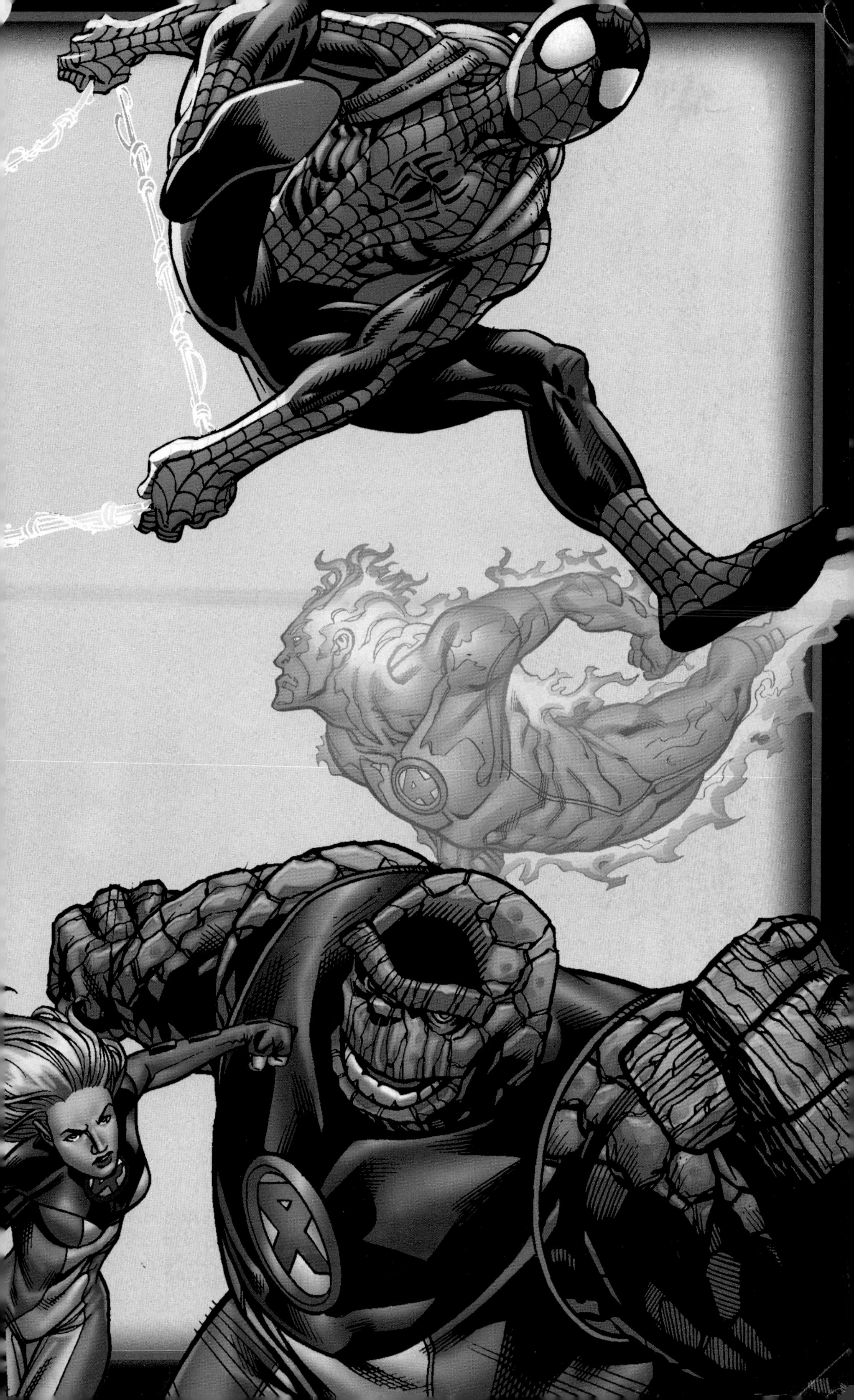

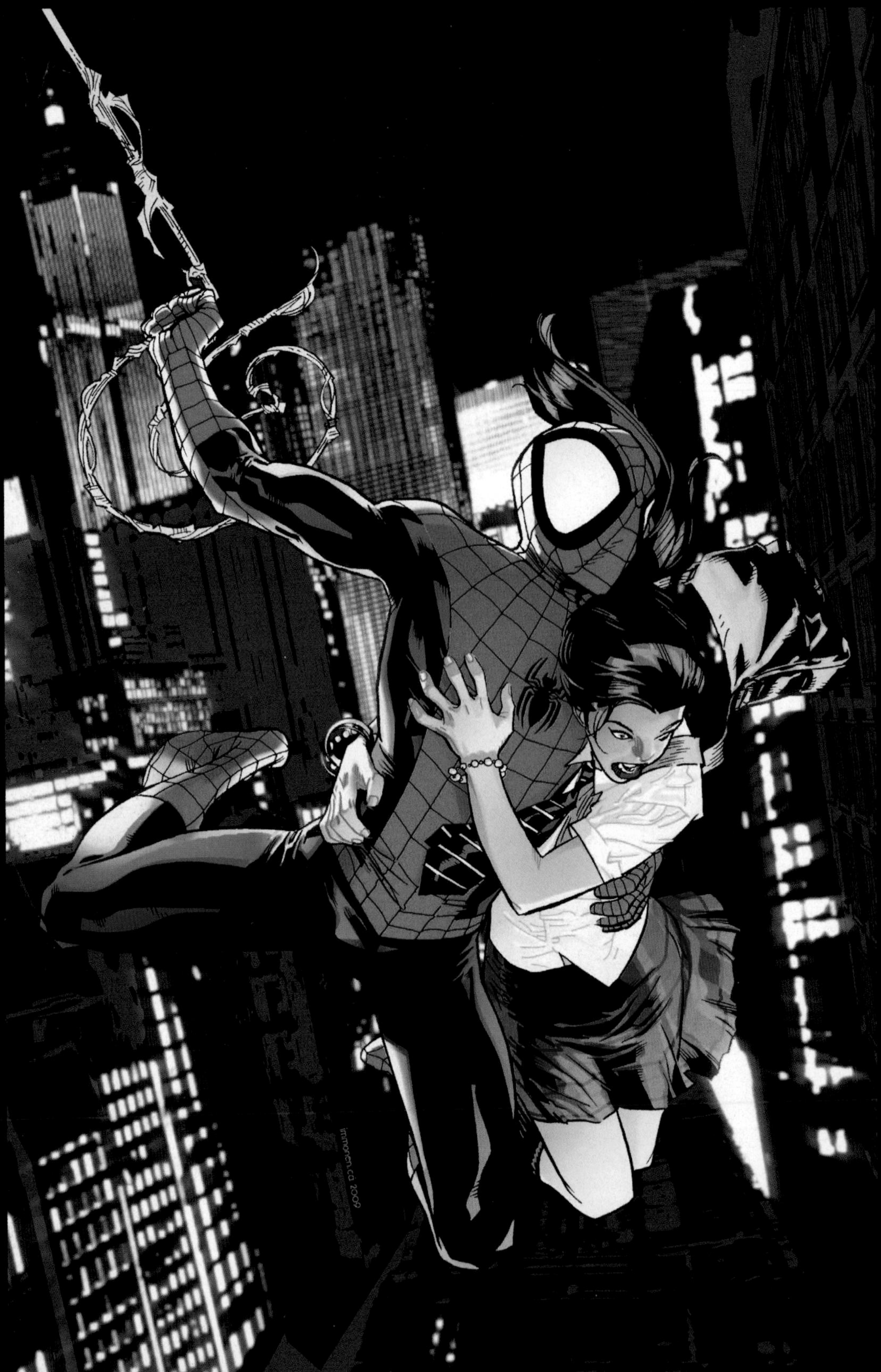

ULTIMATUM: SPIDER-MAN REQUIEM #1

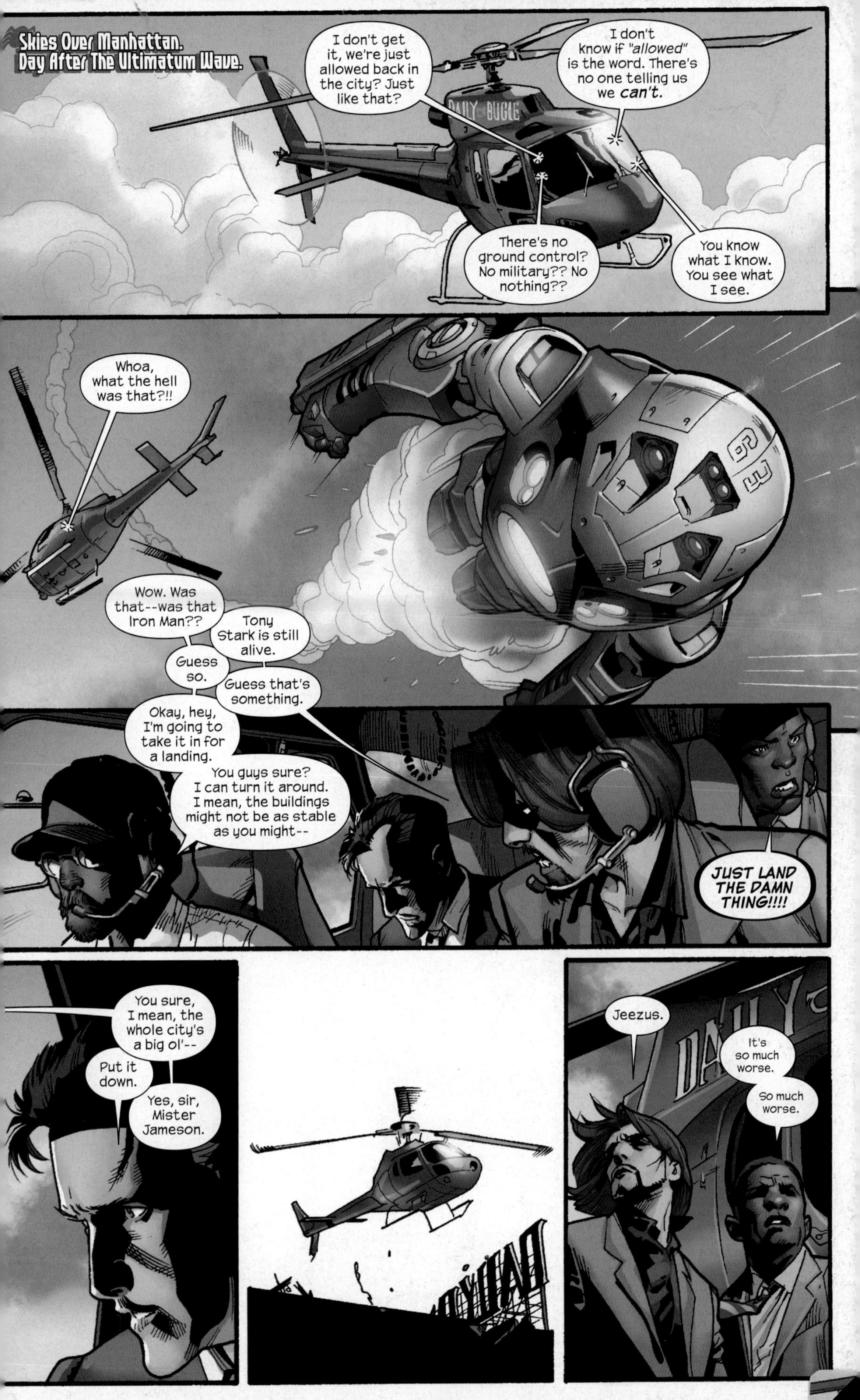
Skies Over Manhattan.
Day After The Ultimatum Wave.
I don't get it, we're just allowed back in the city? Just like that?
I don't know if "allowed" is the word. There's no one telling us we *can't.*
There's no ground control? No military?? No nothing??
You know what I know. You see what I see.
DAILY BUGLE
Whoa, what the hell was that?!!
Wow. Was that--was that Iron Man??
Tony Stark is still alive.
Guess so.
Guess that's something.
Okay, hey, I'm going to take it in for a landing.
You guys sure? I can turn it around. I mean, the buildings might not be as stable as you might--
JUST LAND THE DAMN THING!!!!
You sure, I mean, the whole city's a big ol'--
Put it down.
Yes, sir, Mister Jameson.
Jeezus.
It's so much worse.
So much worse.

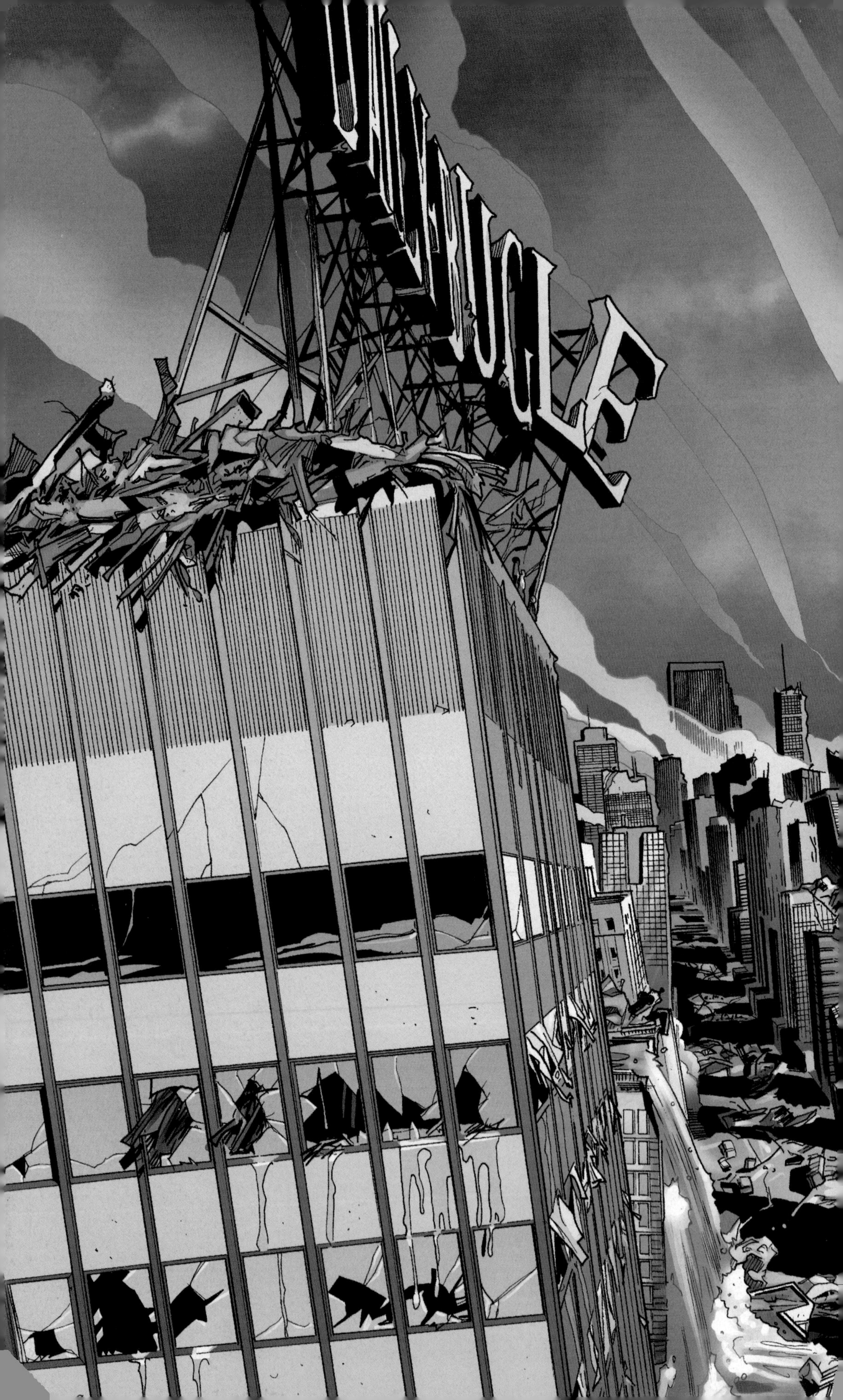

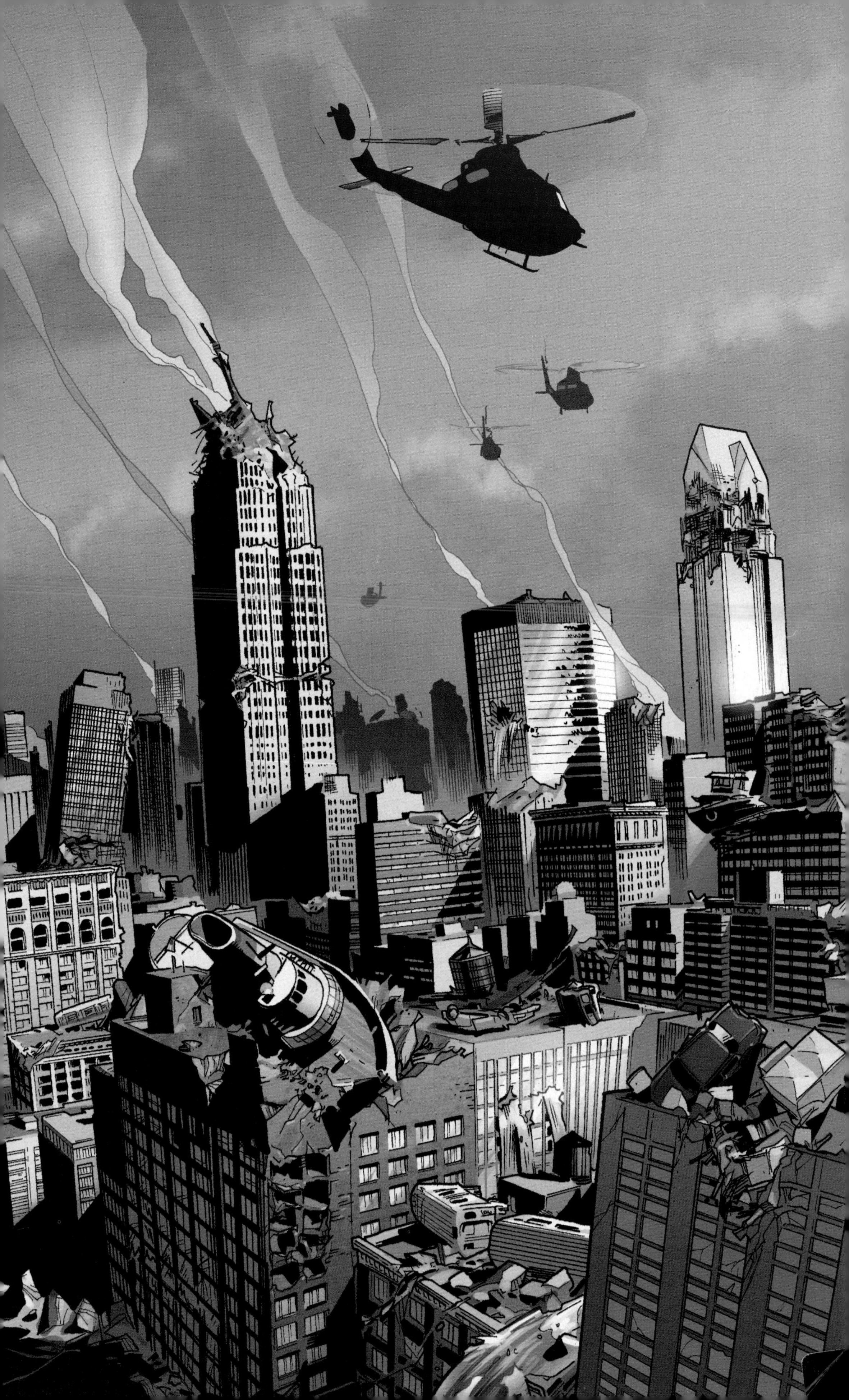

The bite of a genetically altered spider granted high-school student Peter Parker incredible arachnid-like powers! When a burglar killed his beloved Uncle Ben, a grief-stricken Peter vowed to use his amazing abilities to protect his fellow man. He learned the invaluable lesson that with great power there must also come great responsibility!

Now the fledgling super hero tries to balance a full high school curriculum, a night job as a web designer for the Daily Bugle tabloid, a relationship with the beautiful Mary Jane Watson, and swing time as the misunderstood, web-slinging Spider-Man!

PREVIOUSLY IN ULTIMATE SPIDER-MAN...

The Ultimatum wave has destroyed New York City. With no warning a massive tidal wave crashed down on the island of Manhattan, killing millions of people in the blink of an eye.

When the tidal wave subsided, Spider-Man helped search for survivors in the watery hell that was Midtown. He then found himself face-to-face with the Incredible Hulk.

Spider-Man seemed to not survive the encounter.

Kitty Pryde and Spider-Woman searched for Peter but only found his torn mask. MJ, Gwen Stacy and Aunt May all survived the attack but are horrified when Kitty brings them the horrible news.

J. Jonah Jameson, publisher of the Daily Bugle, was witness to Spider-Man's last day of heroics. After months of bashing Spider-Man because it sold newspapers, the event profoundly changed him.

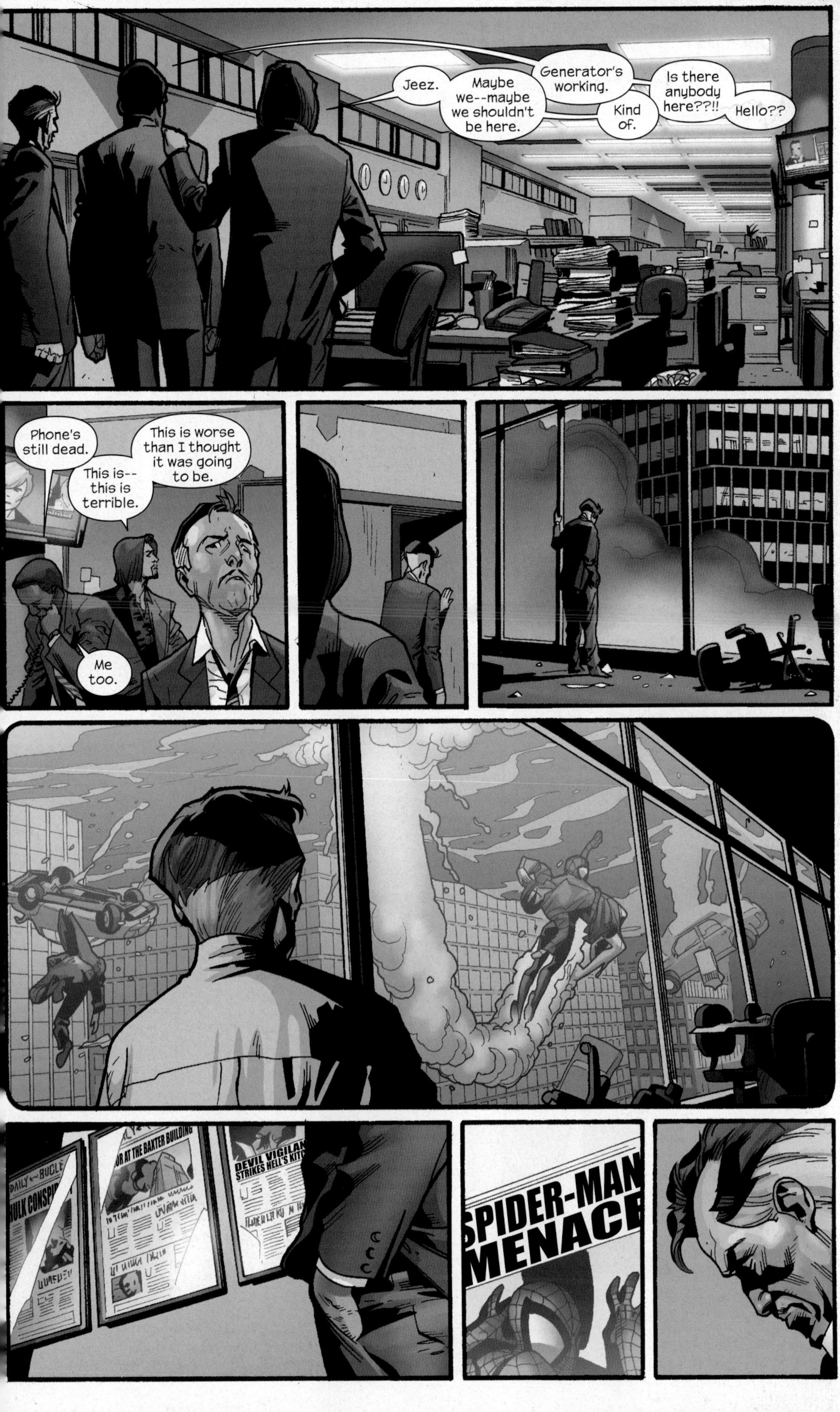
Jeez.
Maybe we--maybe we shouldn't be here.
Generator's working.
Kind of.
Is there anybody here??!!
Hello??
Phone's still dead.
This is-- this is terrible.
This is worse than I thought it was going to be.
Me too.
DAILY BUGLE
HULK CONSPI
AT THE BAXTER BUILDING
DEVIL VIGILAN
STRIKES HELL'S KITC
SPIDER-MAN
MENACE

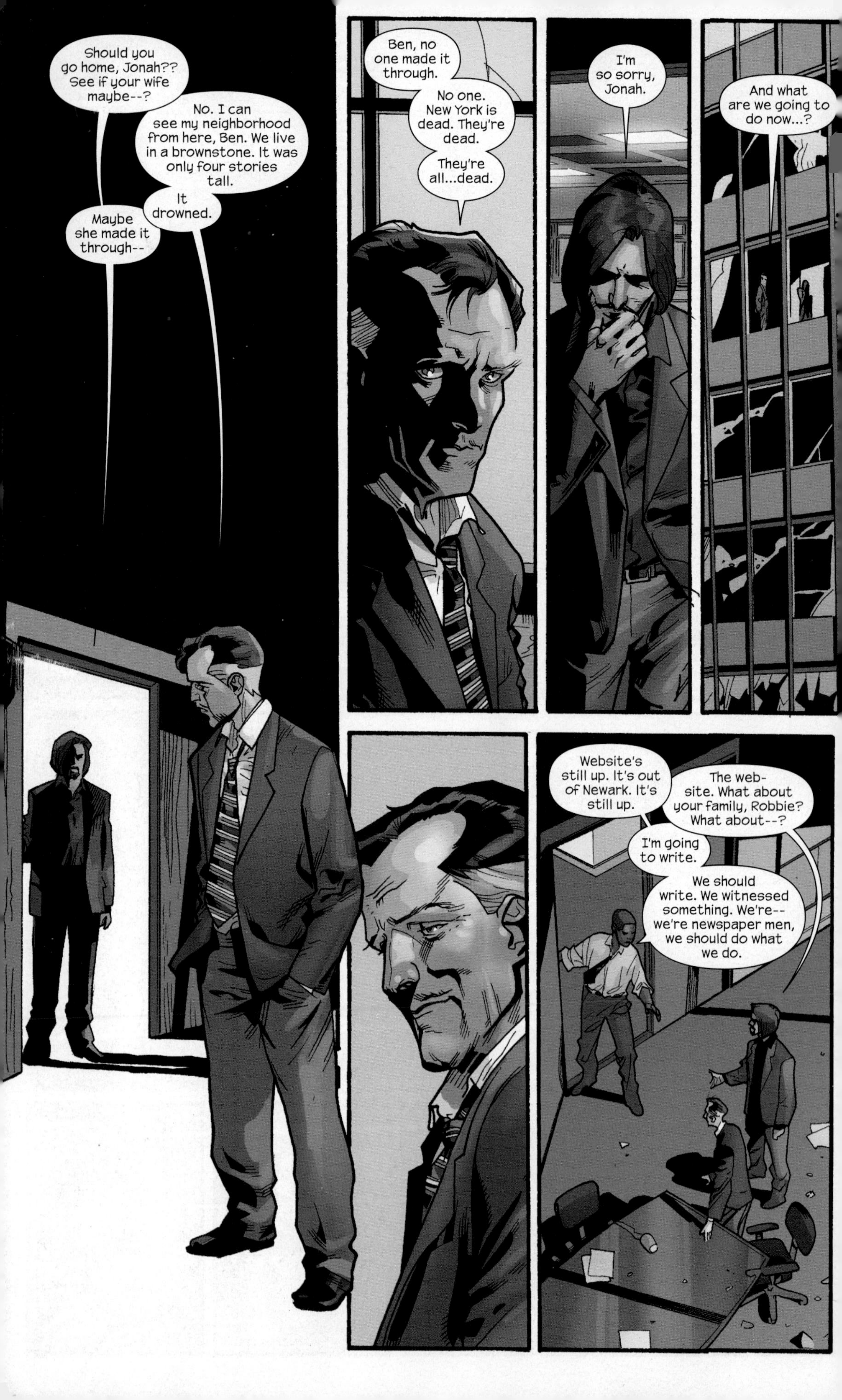

Should you go home, Jonah?? See if your wife maybe--?
No. I can see my neighborhood from here, Ben. We live in a brownstone. It was only four stories tall.
It drowned.
Maybe she made it through--
Ben, no one made it through.
No one. New York is dead. They're dead.
They're all...dead.
I'm so sorry, Jonah.
And what are we going to do now...?
Website's still up. It's out of Newark. It's still up.
The web-site. What about your family, Robbie? What about--?
I'm going to write.
We should write. We witnessed something. We're--we're newspaper men, we should do what we do.

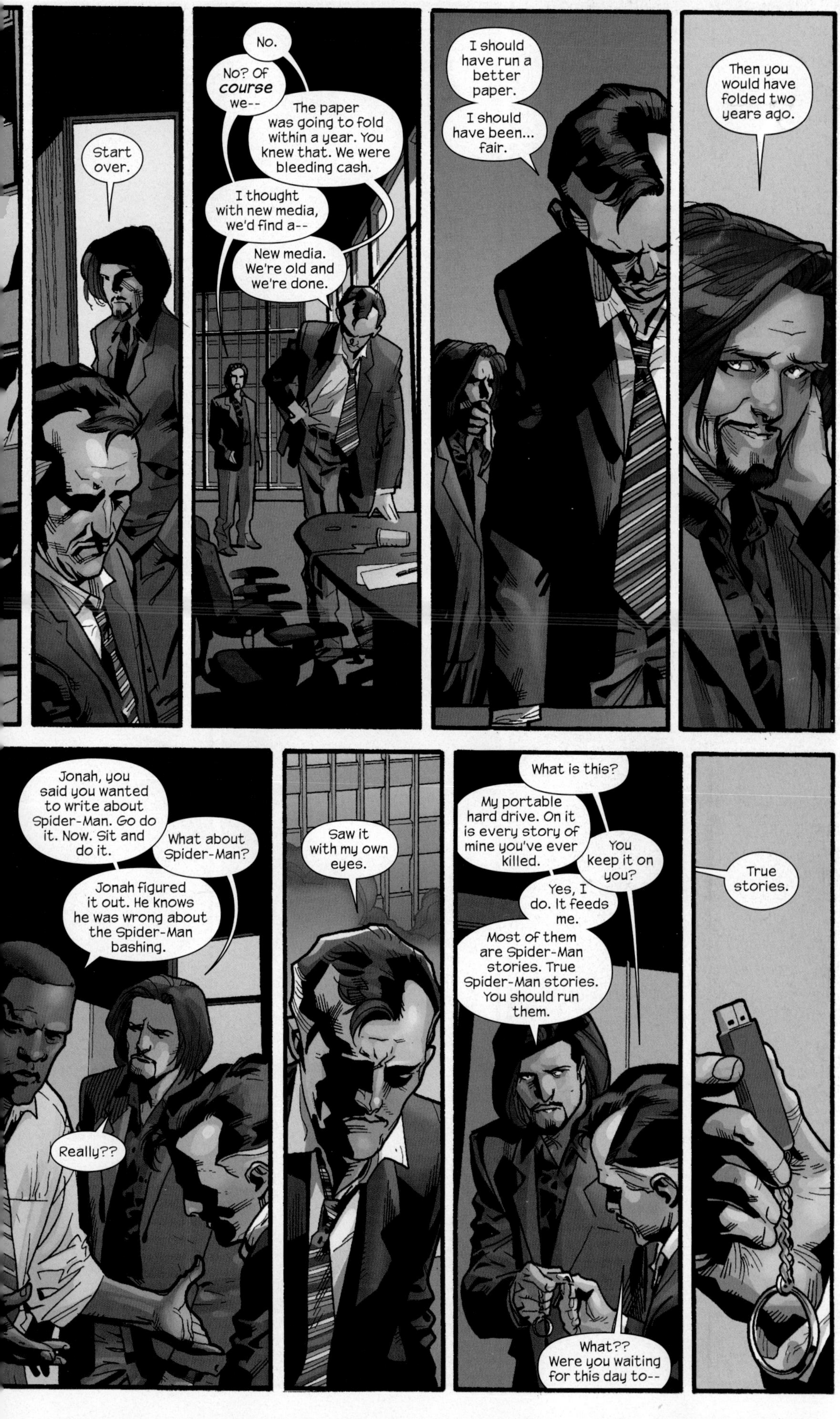

Start over.
No.
No? Of *course* we--
The paper was going to fold within a year. You knew that. We were bleeding cash.
I thought with new media, we'd find a--
New media. We're old and we're done.
I should have run a better paper.
I should have been... fair.
Then you would have folded two years ago.
Jonah, you said you wanted to write about Spider-Man. Go do it. Now. Sit and do it.
What about Spider-Man?
Jonah figured it out. He knows he was wrong about the Spider-Man bashing.
Really??
Saw it with my own eyes.
What is this?
My portable hard drive. On it is every story of mine you've ever killed.
You keep it on you?
Yes, I do. It feeds me.
Most of them are Spider-Man stories. True Spider-Man stories. You should run them.
What?? Were you waiting for this day to--
True stories.

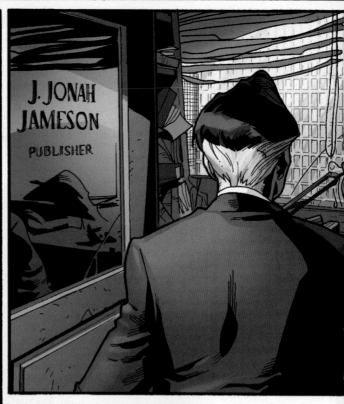

J. JONAH
JAMESON

PUBLISHER

KILLED STORIES

MOB
SPIDER-MAN   SPIDER-MAN

SPIDER-MAN VAMPIRE
SPIDER-MAN GIANT LIZARD
SPIDER-MAN HULK QUEENS
SPIDER TERRORIST THREAT/ SPIDER-MAN
STARK ATTACK ON COMIC COMPANY
ALIEN ATTACK ON COMIC COMPANY
SPIDER-MAN GORES TO HIGH SCHOOL
SPIDER-MAN TAKES DOWN KINGPIN
SPIDER-MAN IS GOVERNMENT SANCTIONED
SPIDER-MAN'S TOP HEROIC MOMENTS...

CLIK

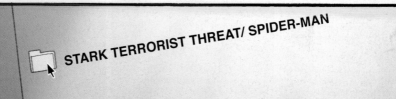

📁 STARK TERRORIST THREAT/ SPIDER-MAN

STARK INDUSTRIES VICTIM OF TERRORISM- SPIDER-MAN SAVES DAY

A story wrapped in mystery, conspiracy and shadow. That is the word coming from Stark Industries Midtown headquarters in New York City where the life of Tony Stark may or may not have been in great jeopardy in a fight that may or may not Spider-Man.

I remember this one...

STARK INDUSTRIES VICTIM OF TERRORISM- SPIDER-MAN SAVES DAY

A story wrapped in mystery, conspiracy
That is the word coming

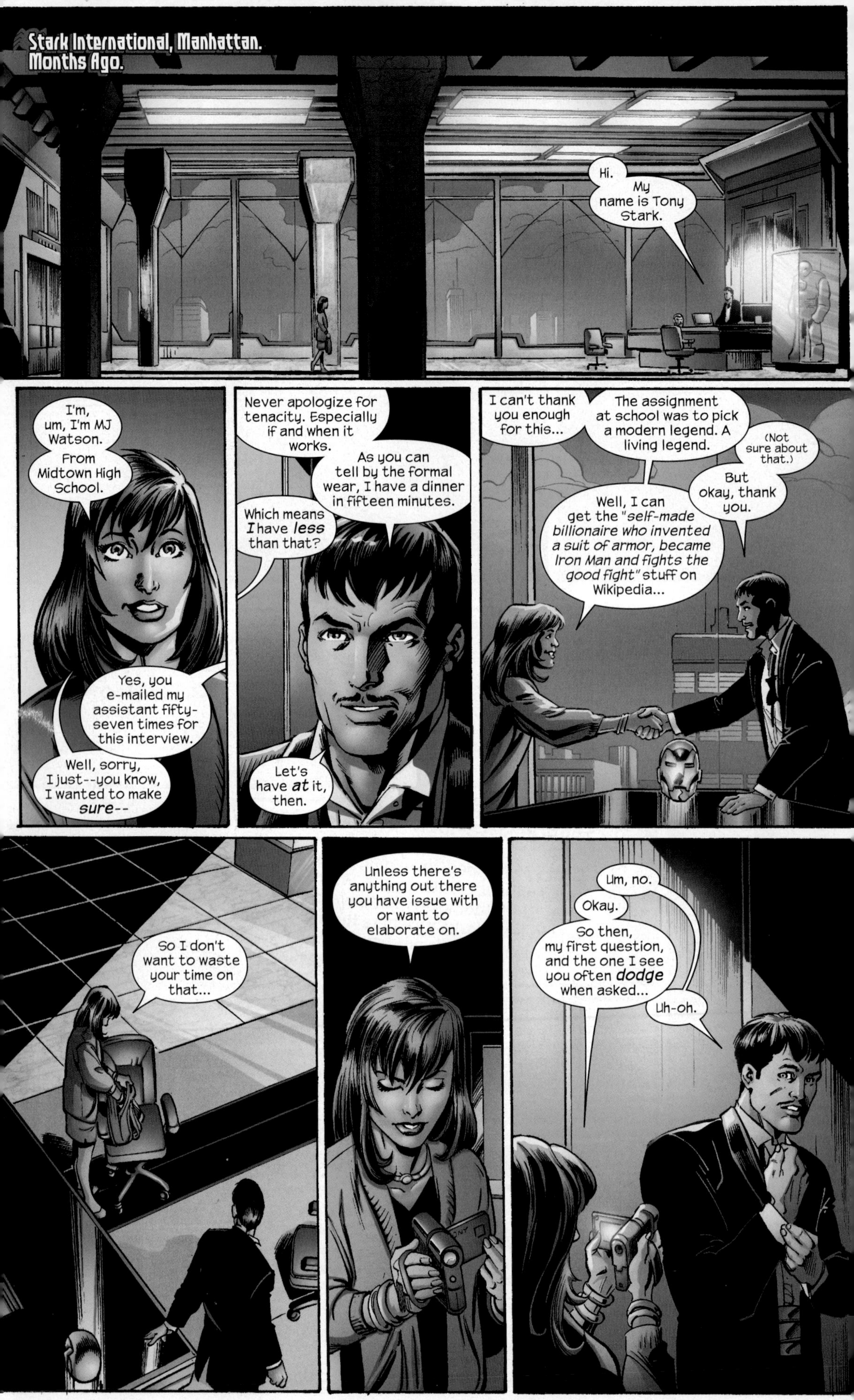

Stark International, Manhattan.
Months Ago.
Hi.
My name is Tony Stark.
I'm, um, I'm MJ Watson.
From Midtown High School.
Yes, you e-mailed my assistant fifty-seven times for this interview.
Well, sorry, I just--you know, I wanted to make *sure*--
Never apologize for tenacity. Especially if and when it works.
As you can tell by the formal wear, I have a dinner in fifteen minutes.
Which means *I* have *less* than that?
Let's have *at* it, then.
I can't thank you enough for this...
The assignment at school was to pick a modern legend. A living legend.
(Not sure about that.)
But okay, thank you.
Well, I can get the *"self-made billionaire who invented a suit of armor, became Iron Man and fights the good fight"* stuff on Wikipedia...
So I don't want to waste your time on that...
Unless there's anything out there you have issue with or want to elaborate on.
Um, no.
Okay.
So then, my first question, and the one I see you often *dodge* when asked...
Uh-oh.

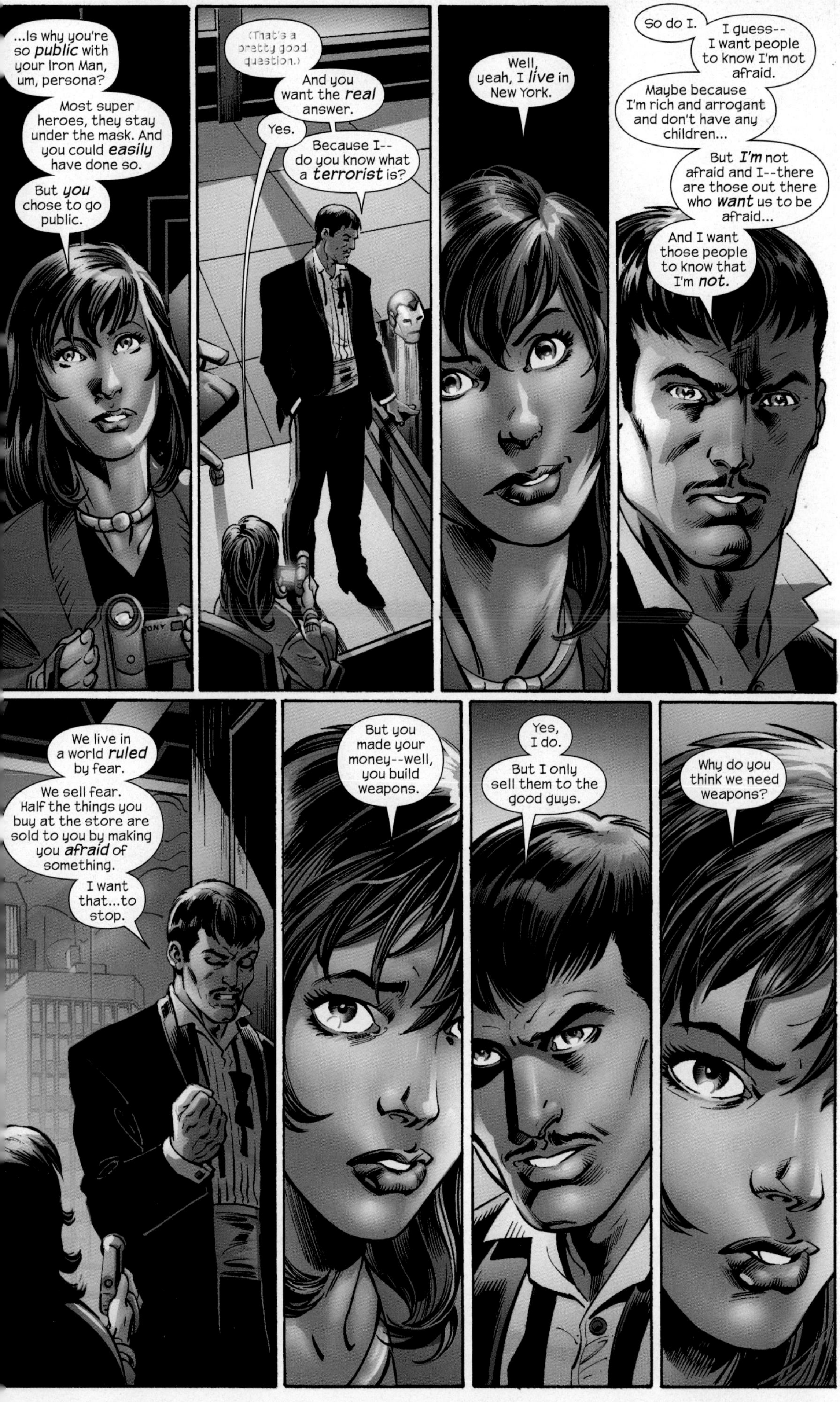
...Is why you're so public with your Iron Man, um, persona?
Most super heroes, they stay under the mask. And you could easily have done so.
But you chose to go public.
(That's a pretty good question.)
And you want the real answer.
Yes.
Because I-- do you know what a terrorist is?
SONY
Well, yeah, I live in New York.
So do I.
I guess-- I want people to know I'm not afraid.
Maybe because I'm rich and arrogant and don't have any children...
But I'm not afraid and I--there are those out there who want us to be afraid...
And I want those people to know that I'm not.
We live in a world ruled by fear.
We sell fear. Half the things you buy at the store are sold to you by making you afraid of something.
I want that...to stop.
But you made your money--well, you build weapons.
Yes, I do.
But I only sell them to the good guys.
Why do you think we need weapons?

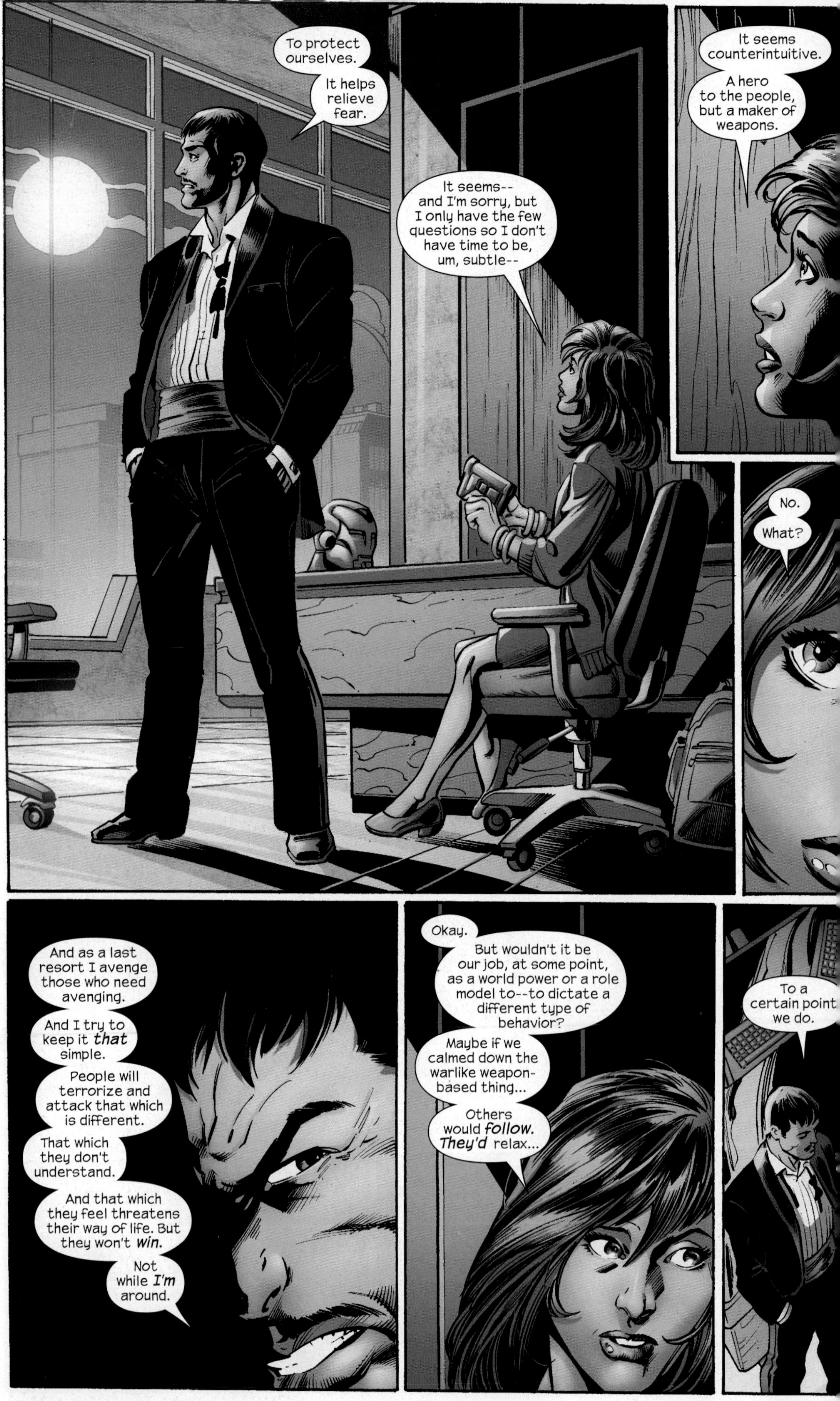
To protect ourselves.
It helps relieve fear.
It seems-- and I'm sorry, but I only have the few questions so I don't have time to be, um, subtle--
It seems counterintuitive.
A hero to the people, but a maker of weapons.
No.
What?
And as a last resort I avenge those who need avenging.
And I try to keep it *that* simple.
People will terrorize and attack that which is different.
That which they don't understand.
And that which they feel threatens their way of life. But they won't *win.*
Not while *I'm* around.
Okay.
But wouldn't it be our job, at some point, as a world power or a role model to--to dictate a different type of behavior?
Maybe if we calmed down the warlike weapon-based thing...
Others would *follow.* *They'd* relax...
To a certain point we do.

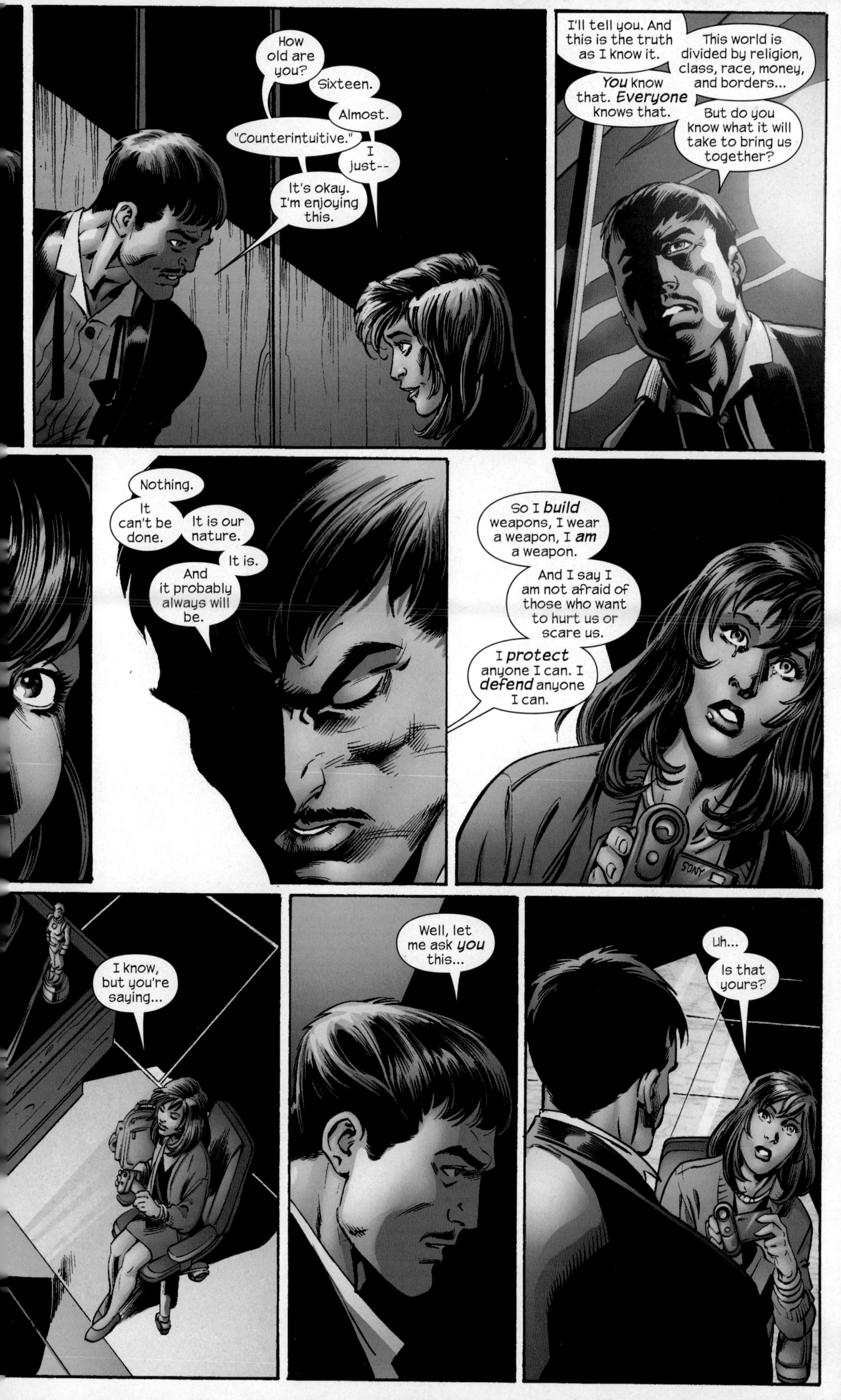
How old are you?
Sixteen.
Almost.
"Counterintuitive."
I just--
It's okay. I'm enjoying this.
I'll tell you. And this is the truth as I know it.
This world is divided by religion, class, race, money, and borders...
You know that. Everyone knows that.
But do you know what it will take to bring us together?
Nothing.
It can't be done.
It is our nature.
It is.
And it probably always will be.
So I build weapons, I wear a weapon, I am a weapon.
And I say I am not afraid of those who want to hurt us or scare us.
I protect anyone I can. I defend anyone I can.
SONY
I know, but you're saying...
Well, let me ask you this...
Uh...
Is that yours?

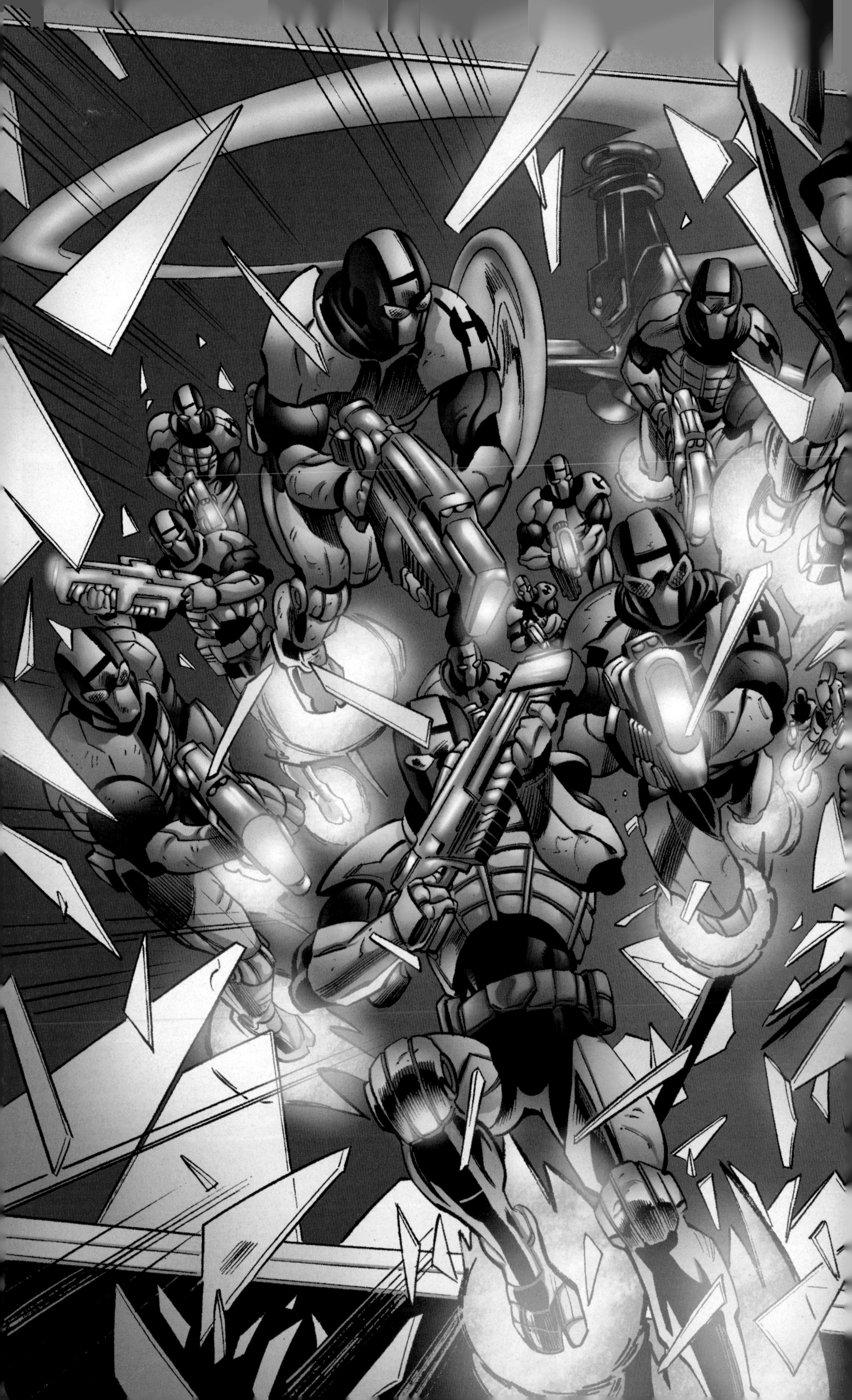

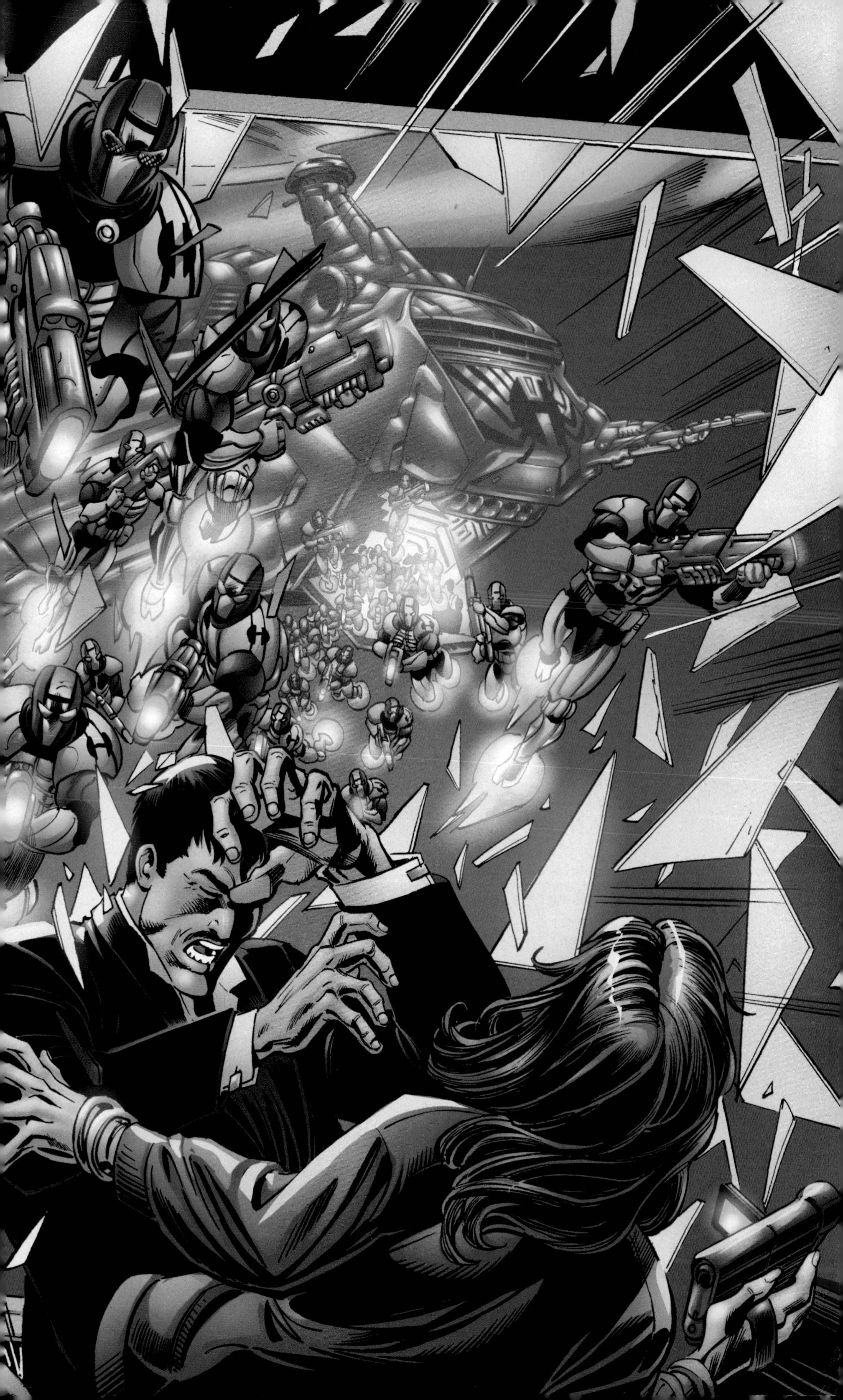

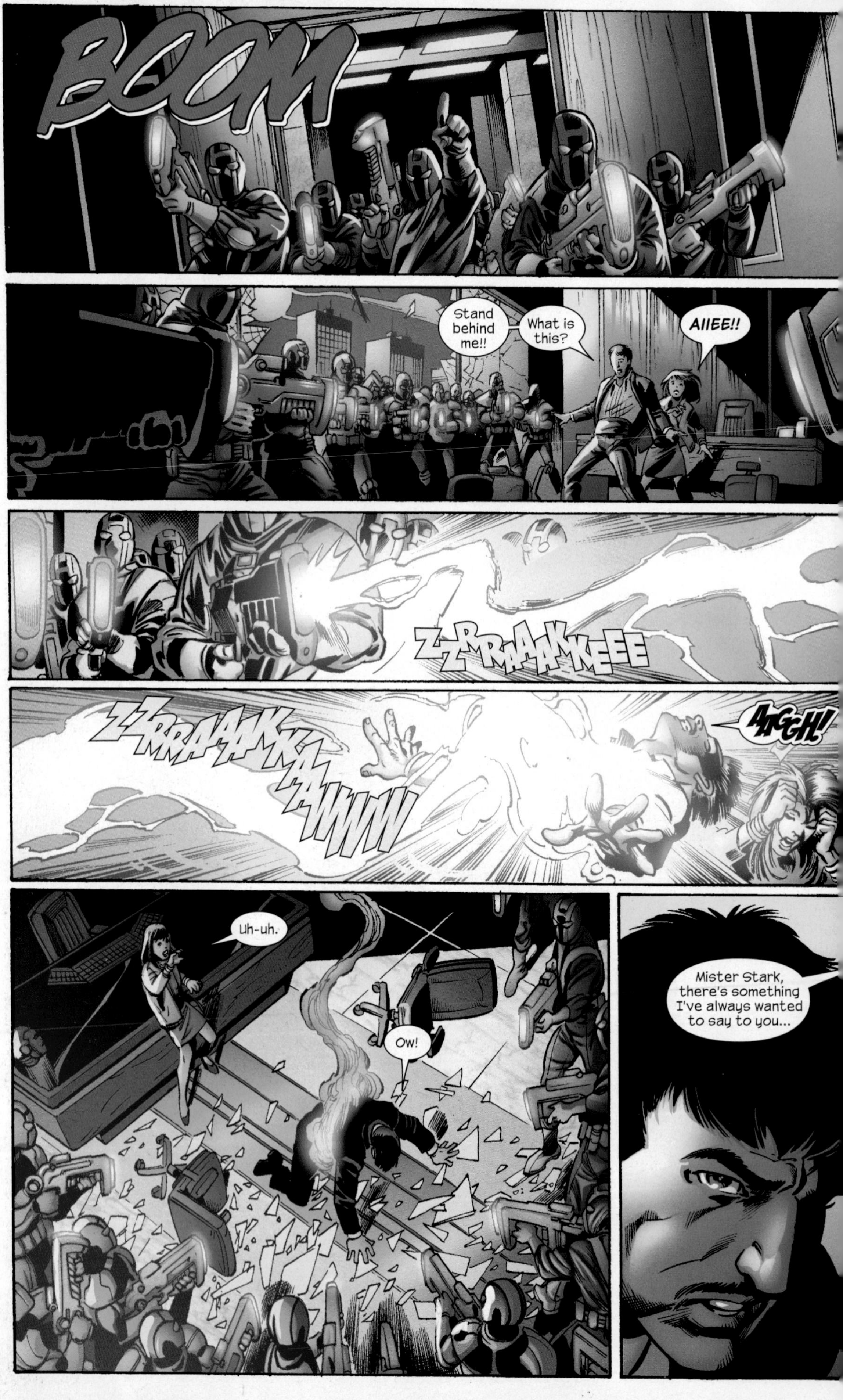
BOOM
Stand behind me!!
What is this?
AIIEE!!
ZZRRAAAKKEEE
ZZRRAAAKKAAWWW
AAGGH!
Uh-uh.
Ow!
Mister Stark, there's something I've always wanted to say to you...

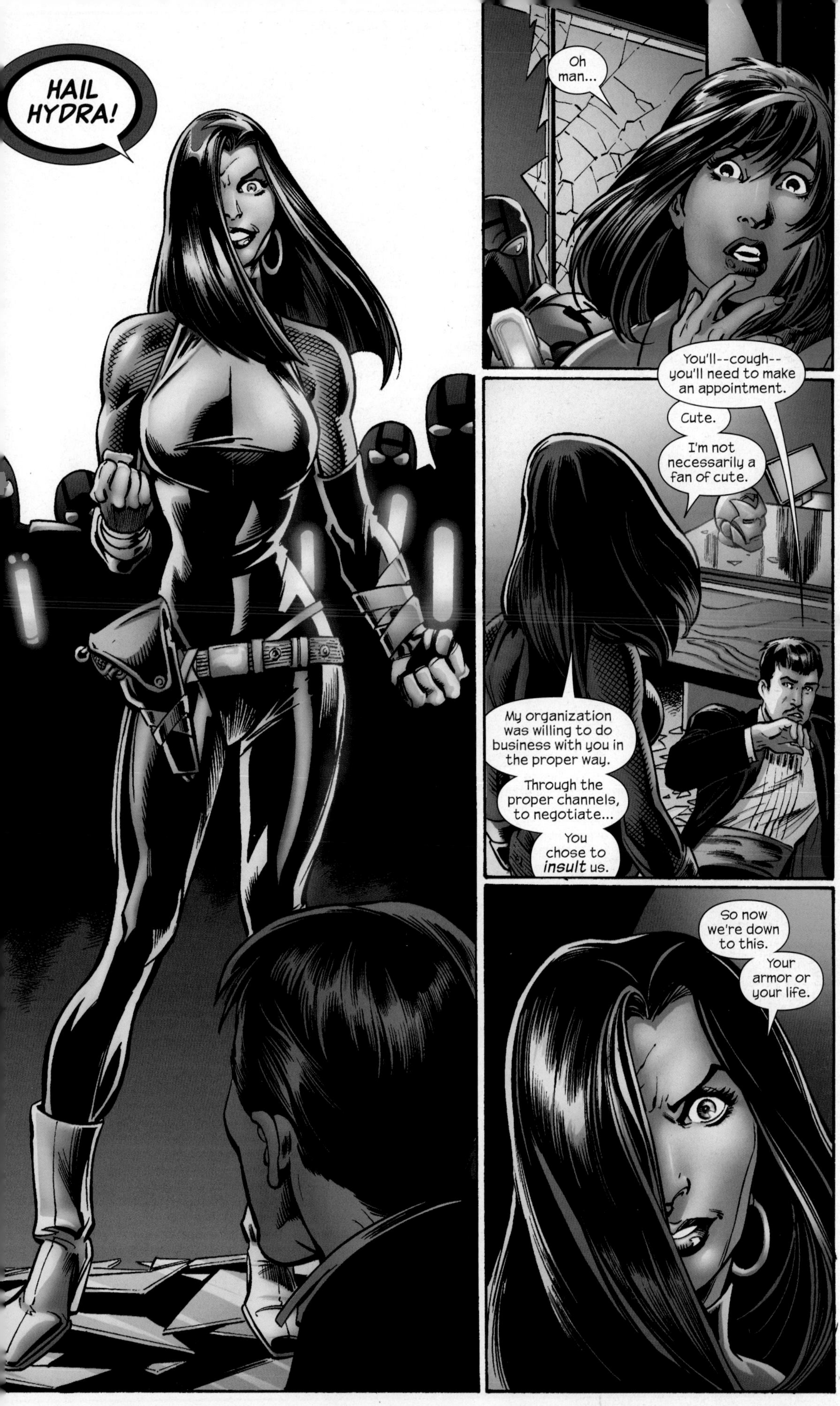
HAIL HYDRA!
Oh man...
You'll--cough--you'll need to make an appointment.
Cute.
I'm not necessarily a fan of cute.
My organization was willing to do business with you in the proper way.
Through the proper channels, to negotiate...
You chose to *insult* us.
So now we're down to this.
Your armor or your life.

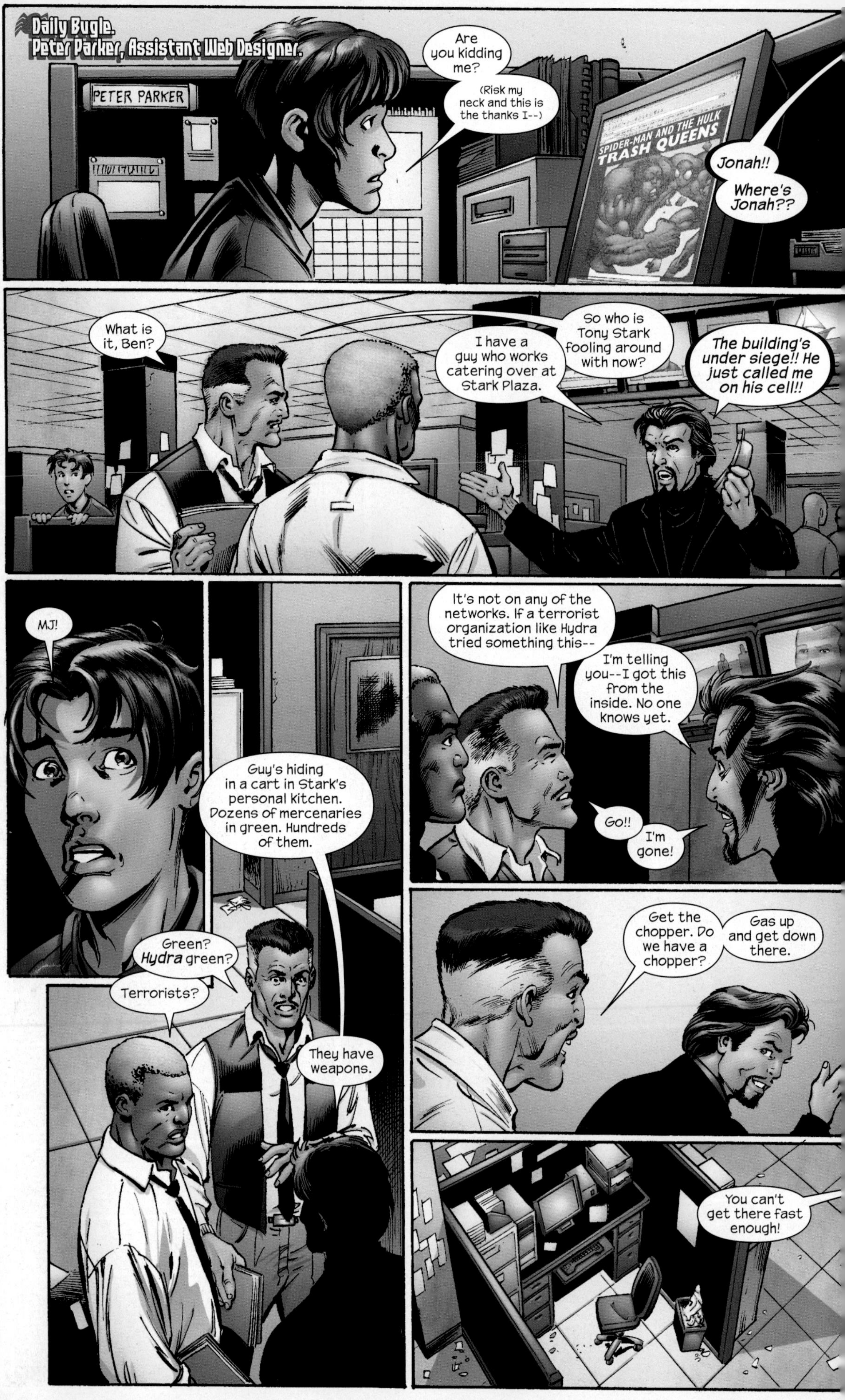
Daily Bugle.
Peter Parker, Assistant Web Designer.
PETER PARKER
Are you kidding me?
(Risk my neck and this is the thanks I--)
SPIDER-MAN AND THE HULK TRASH QUEENS
Jonah!!
Where's Jonah??
What is it, Ben?
I have a guy who works catering over at Stark Plaza.
So who is Tony Stark fooling around with now?
The building's under siege!! He just called me on his cell!!
MJ!
Guy's hiding in a cart in Stark's personal kitchen. Dozens of mercenaries in green. Hundreds of them.
Green? Hydra green?
Terrorists?
They have weapons.
It's not on any of the networks. If a terrorist organization like Hydra tried something this--
I'm telling you--I got this from the inside. No one knows yet.
Go!!
I'm gone!
Get the chopper. Do we have a chopper?
Gas up and get down there.
You can't get there fast enough!

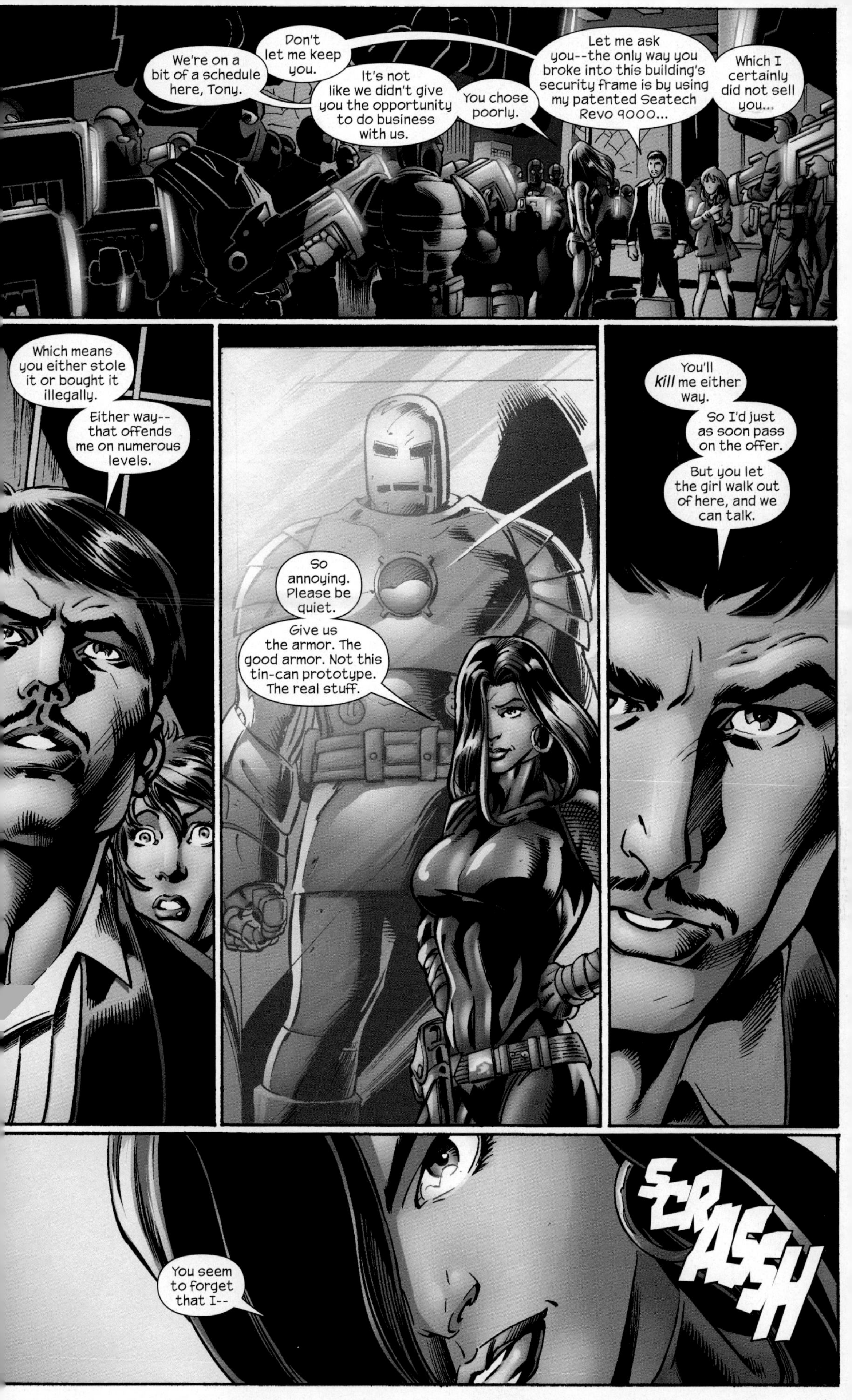
We're on a bit of a schedule here, Tony.
Don't let me keep you.
It's not like we didn't give you the opportunity to do business with us.
You chose poorly.
Let me ask you--the only way you broke into this building's security frame is by using my patented Seatech Revo 9000...
Which I certainly did not sell you...
Which means you either stole it or bought it illegally.
Either way--that offends me on numerous levels.
So annoying. Please be quiet.
Give us the armor. The good armor. Not this tin-can prototype. The real stuff.
You'll *kill* me either way.
So I'd just as soon pass on the offer.
But you let the girl walk out of here, and we can talk.
You seem to forget that I--
SCRASSH

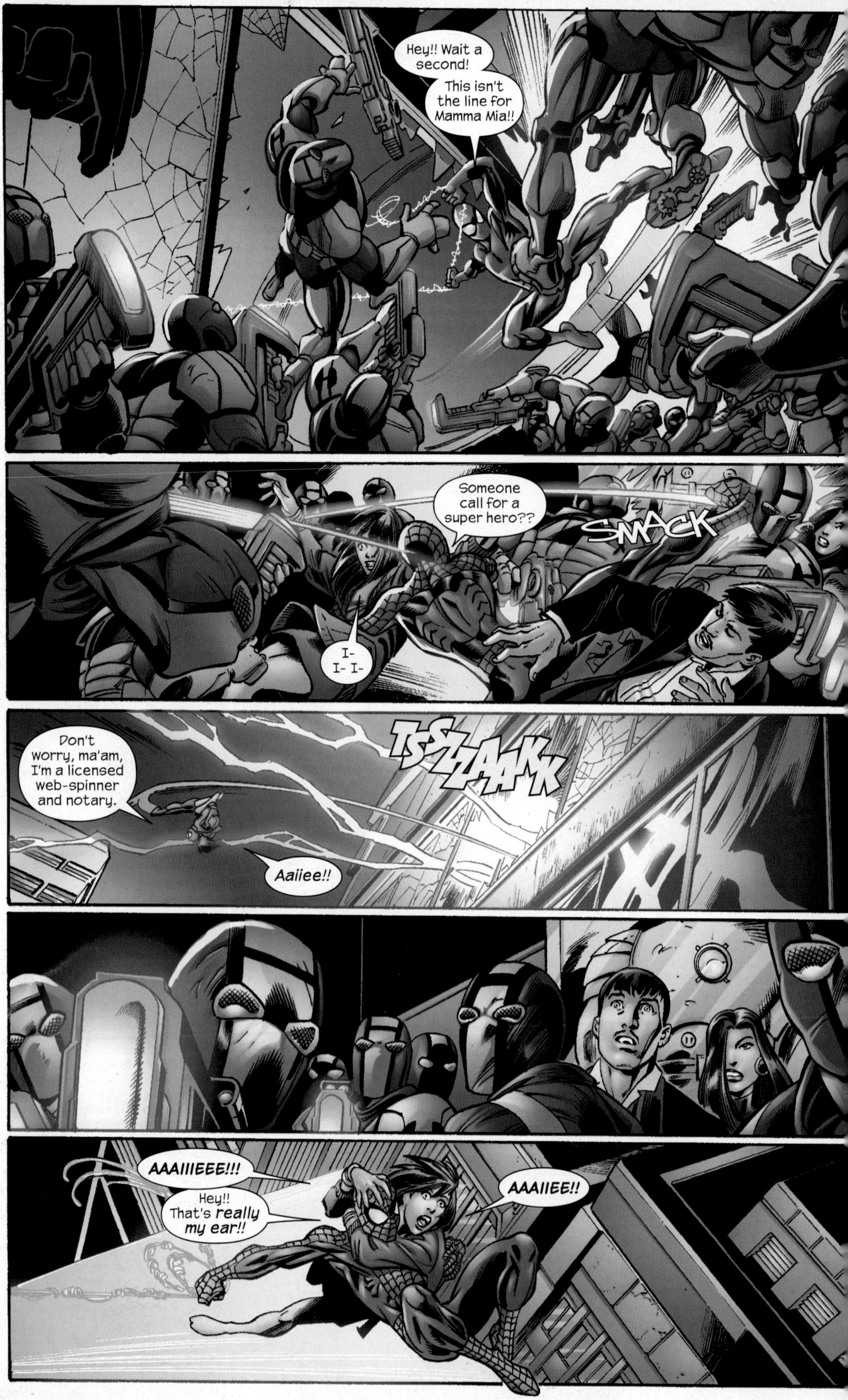

Hey!! Wait a second!
This isn't the line for Mamma Mia!!
Someone call for a super hero??
SMACK
I- I- I-
TSSZAAKK
Don't worry, ma'am, I'm a licensed web-spinner and notary.
Aaiiee!!
AAAIIIEEE!!!
Hey!! That's really my ear!!
AAAIIEE!!

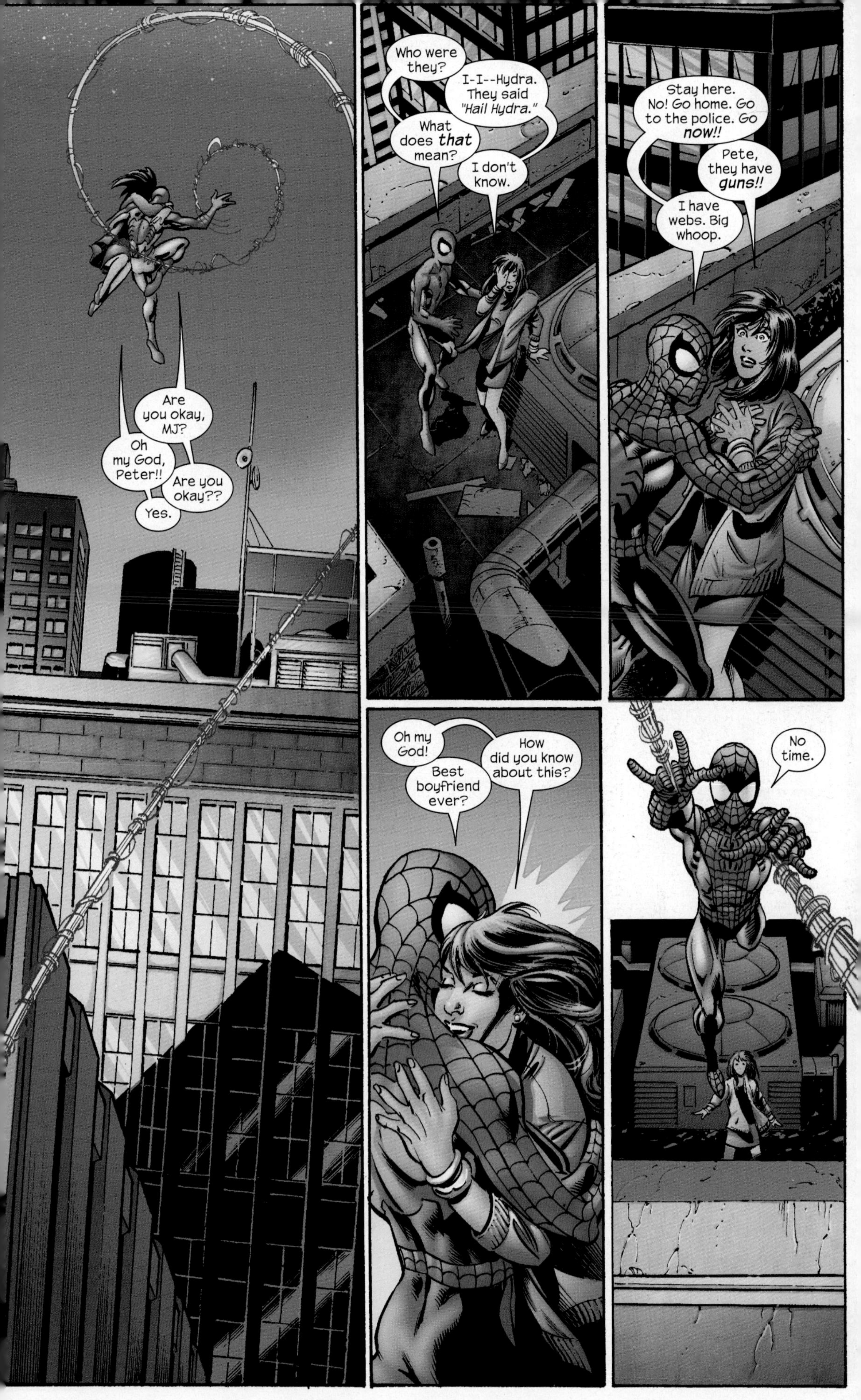
Are you okay, MJ?
Oh my God, Peter!!
Are you okay??
Yes.
Who were they?
I-I--Hydra. They said "Hail Hydra."
What does *that* mean?
I don't know.
Stay here. No! Go home. Go to the police. Go ***now!!***
Pete, they have ***guns!!***
I have webs. Big whoop.
Oh my God!
How did you know about this?
Best boyfriend ever?
No time.

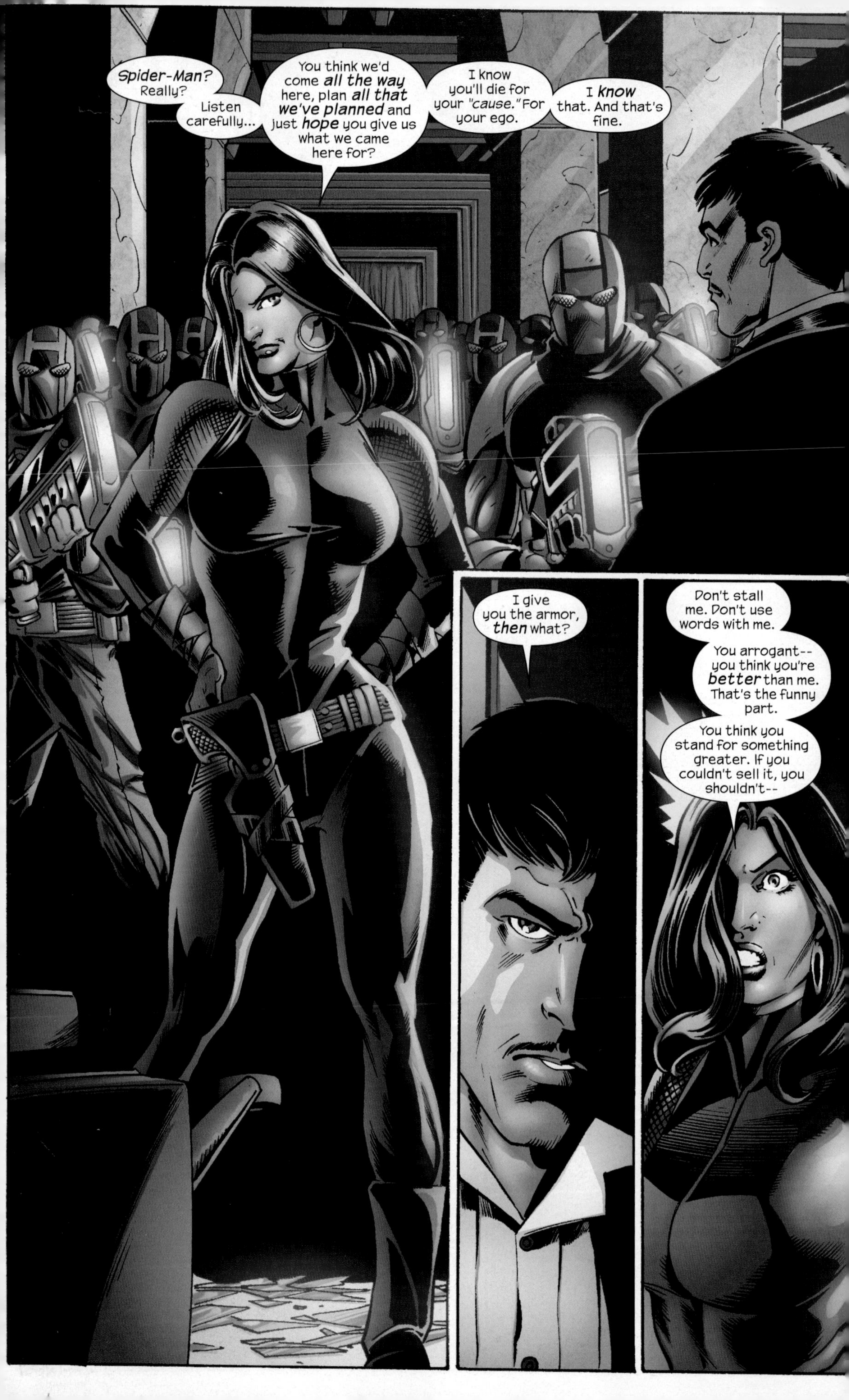

Spider-Man? Really?
Listen carefully...
You think we'd come all the way here, plan all that we've planned and just hope you give us what we came here for?
I know you'll die for your "cause." For your ego.
I know that. And that's fine.
I give you the armor, then what?
Don't stall me. Don't use words with me.
You arrogant-- you think you're better than me. That's the funny part.
You think you stand for something greater. If you couldn't sell it, you shouldn't--

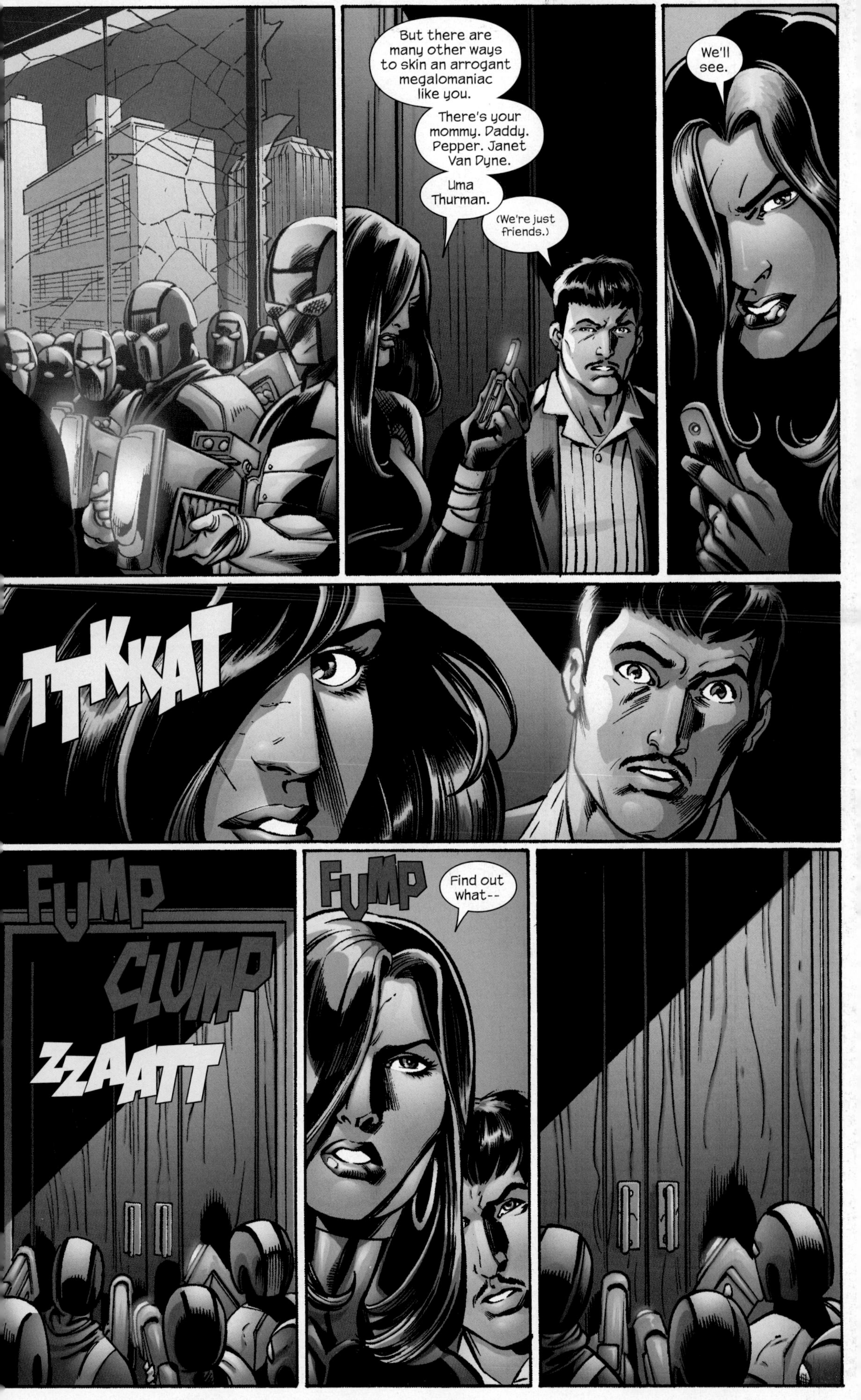

But there are many other ways to skin an arrogant megalomaniac like you.
There's your mommy. Daddy. Pepper. Janet Van Dyne.
Uma Thurman.
(We're just friends.)
We'll see.
TTKKAT
FUMP
CLUMP
ZZAATT
FUMP
Find out what--

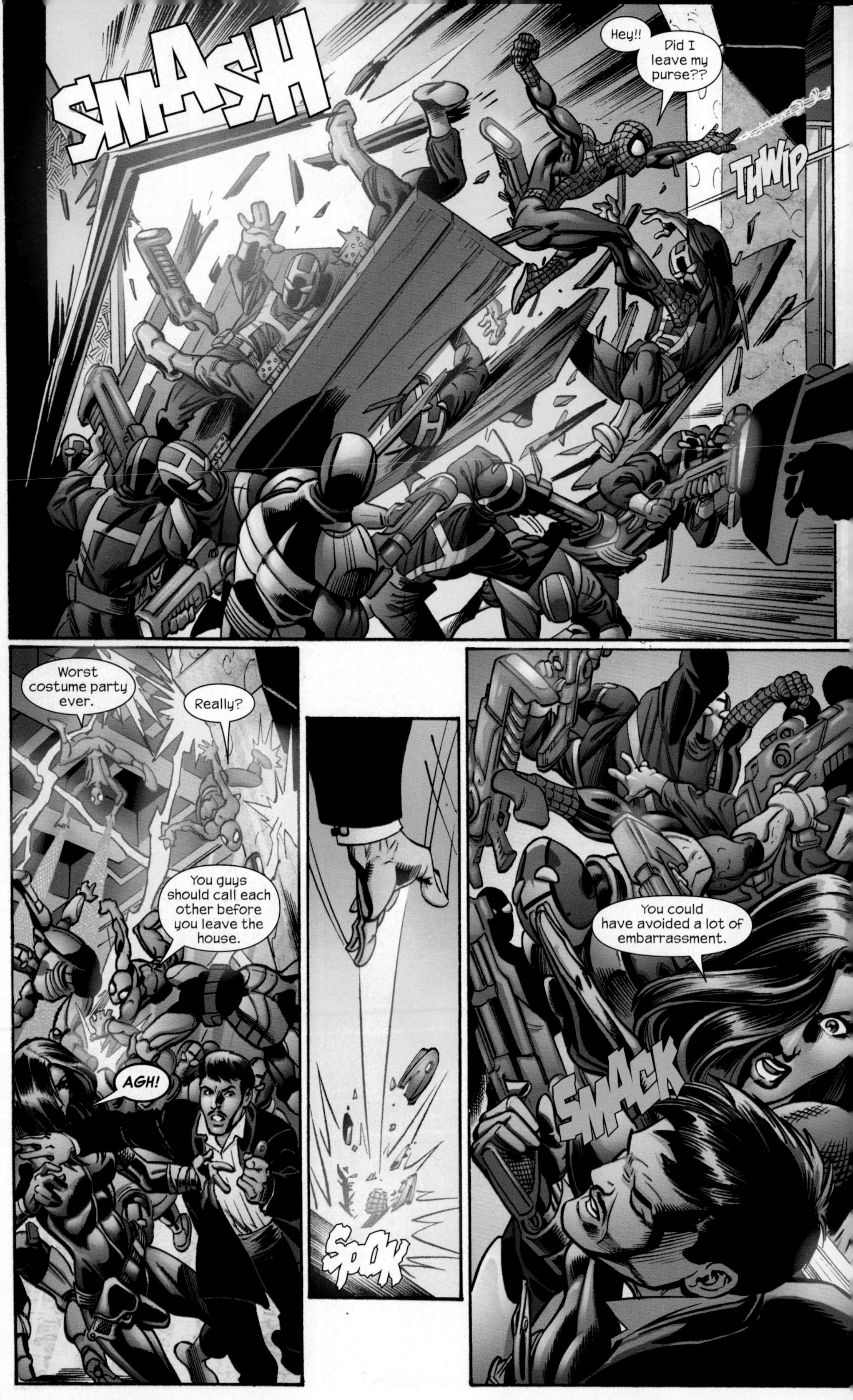
SMASH
Hey!!
Did I leave my purse??
THWIP
Worst costume party ever.
Really?
You guys should call each other before you leave the house.
AGH!
SPOK
You could have avoided a lot of embarrassment.
SMACK

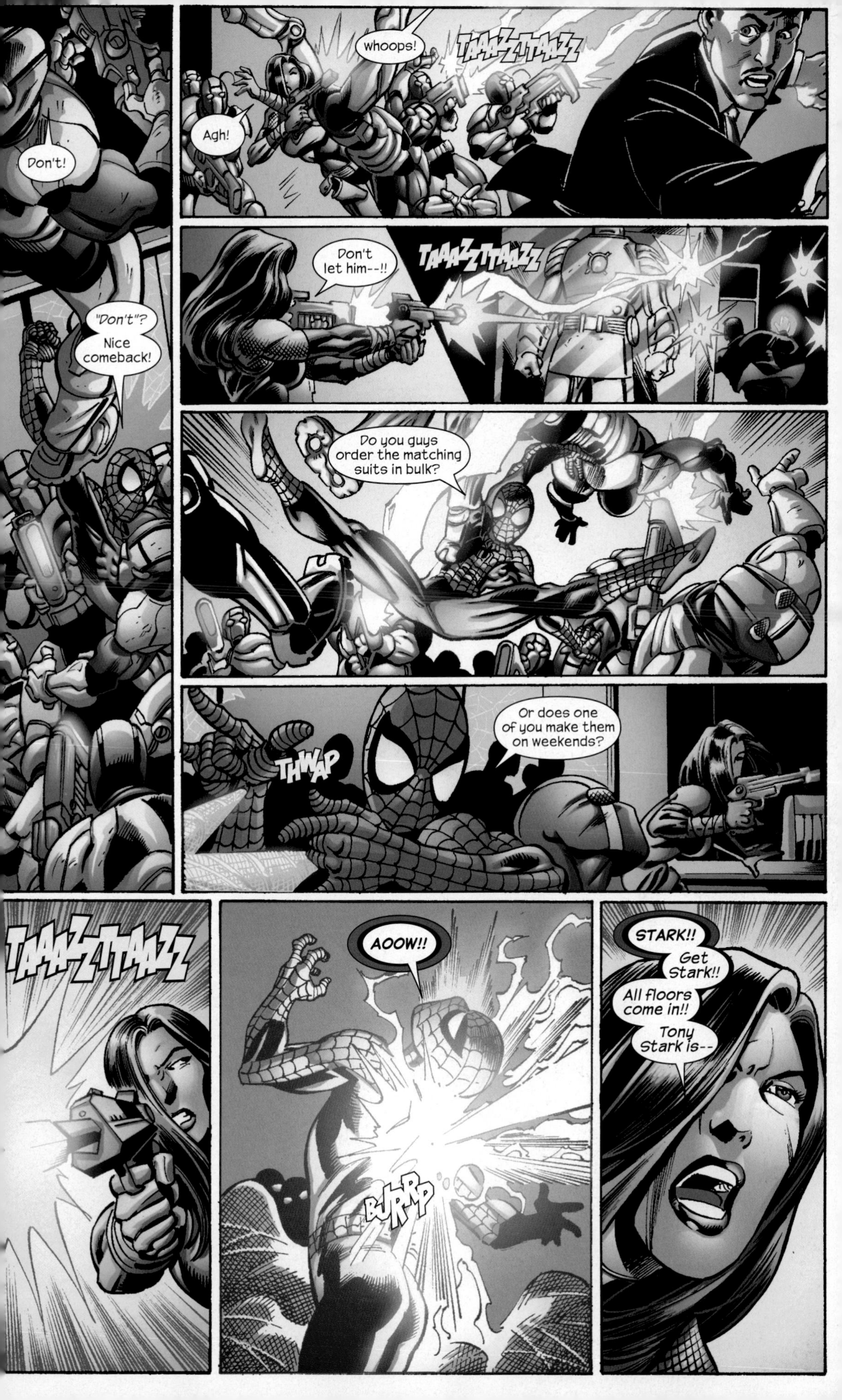
Don't!
"Don't"? Nice comeback!
whoops!
Agh!
TAAAZZTTAAZZ
Don't let him--!!
TAAAZZTTAAZZ
Do you guys order the matching suits in bulk?
Or does one of you make them on weekends?
THWAP
TAAAZZTTAAZZ
AOOW!!
BURRP
STARK!!
Get Stark!!
All floors come in!!
Tony Stark is--

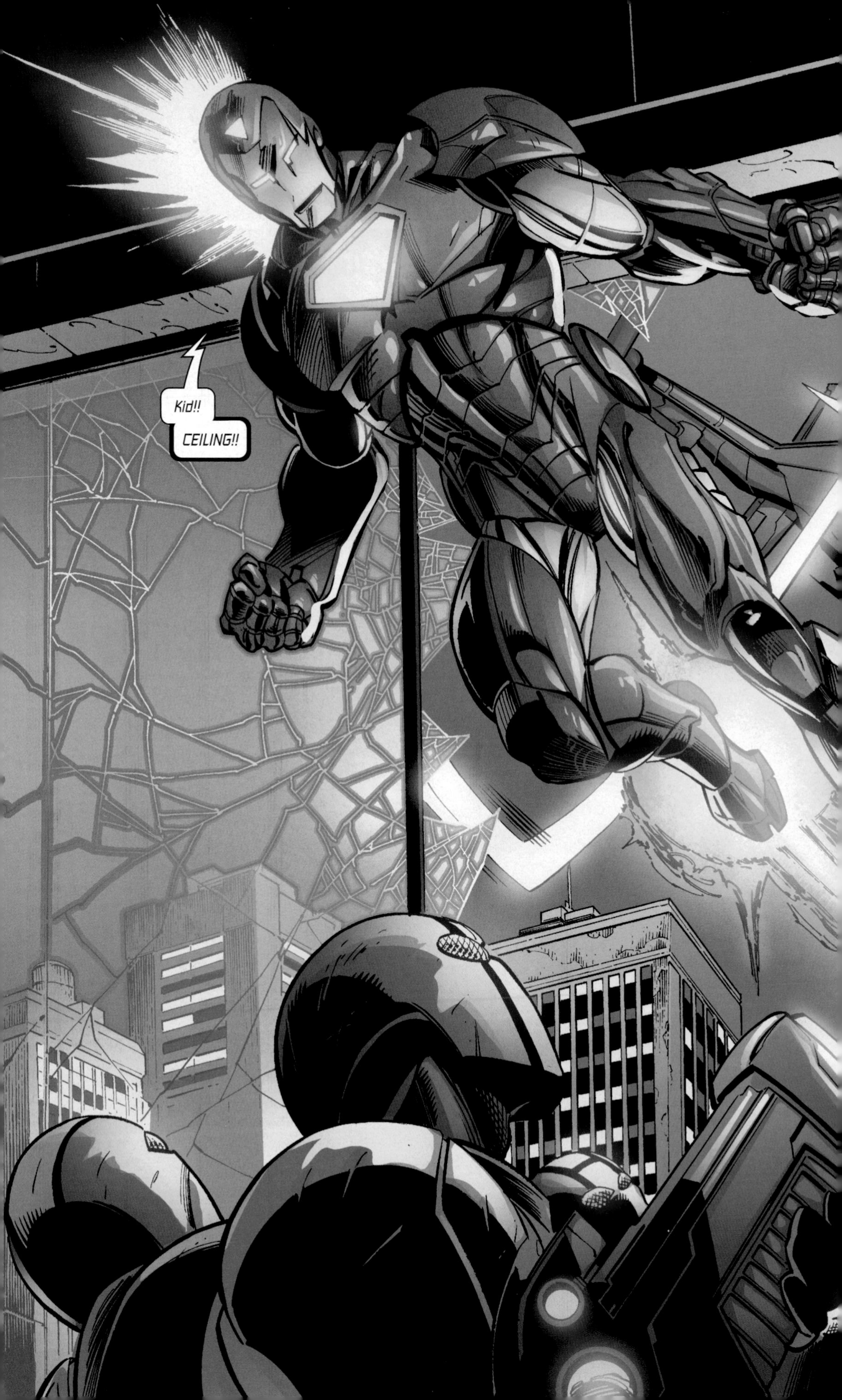
Kid!!
CEILING!!

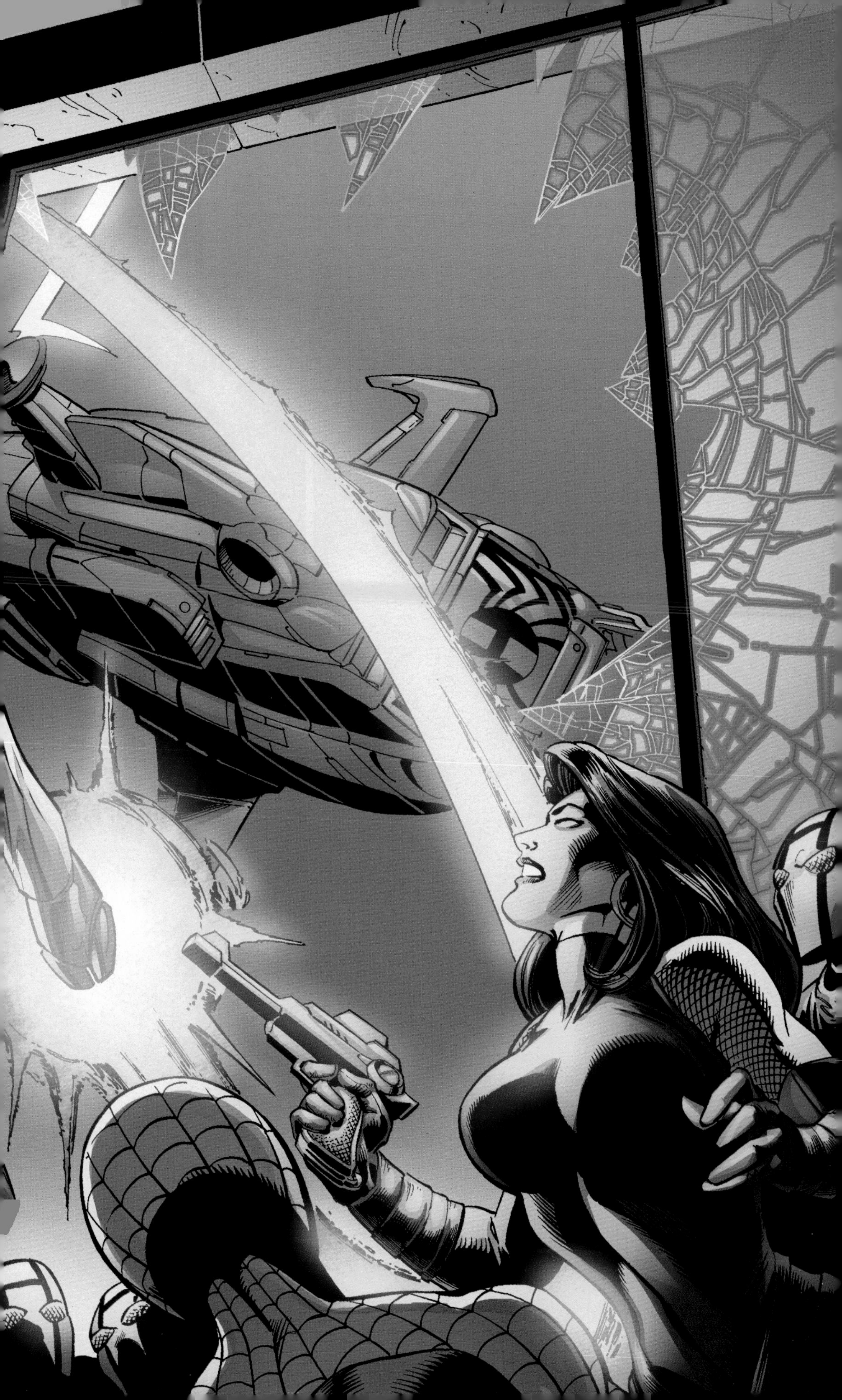

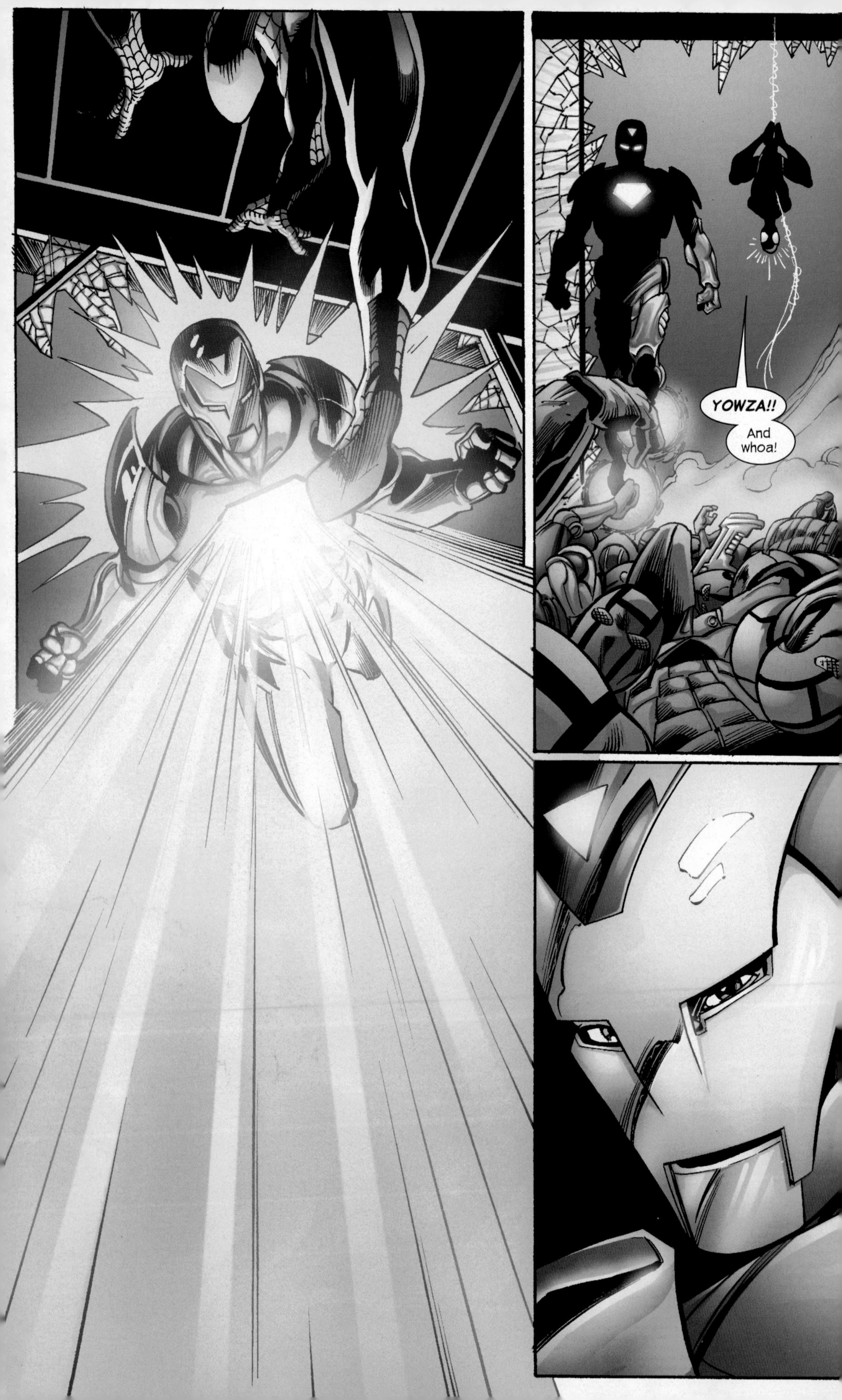
YOWZA!!
And whoa!

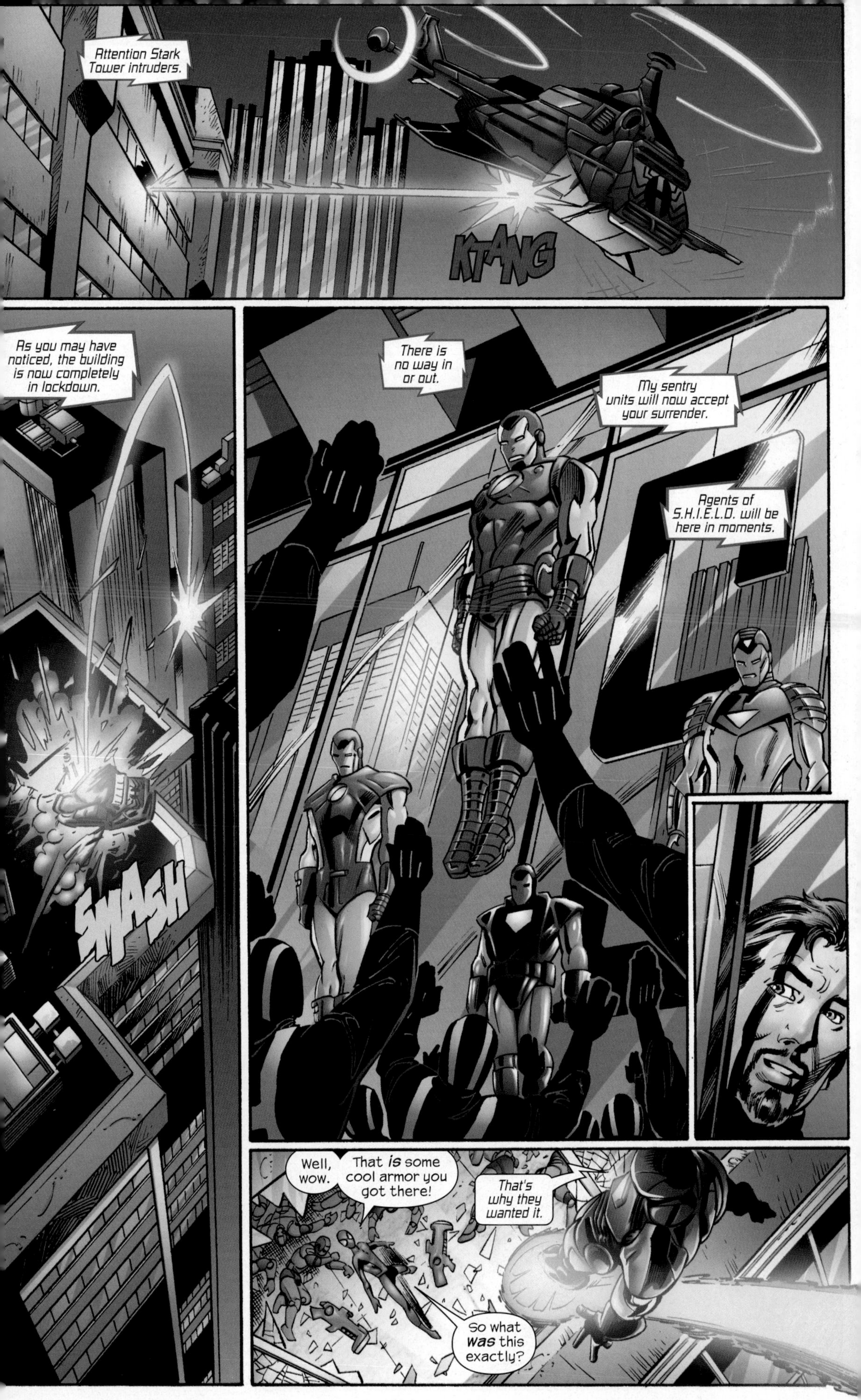
Attention Stark Tower intruders.
KTANG
As you may have noticed, the building is now completely in lockdown.
SMASH
There is no way in or out.
My sentry units will now accept your surrender.
Agents of S.H.I.E.L.D. will be here in moments.
Well, wow.
That *is* some cool armor you got there!
That's why they wanted it.
So what *was* this exactly?

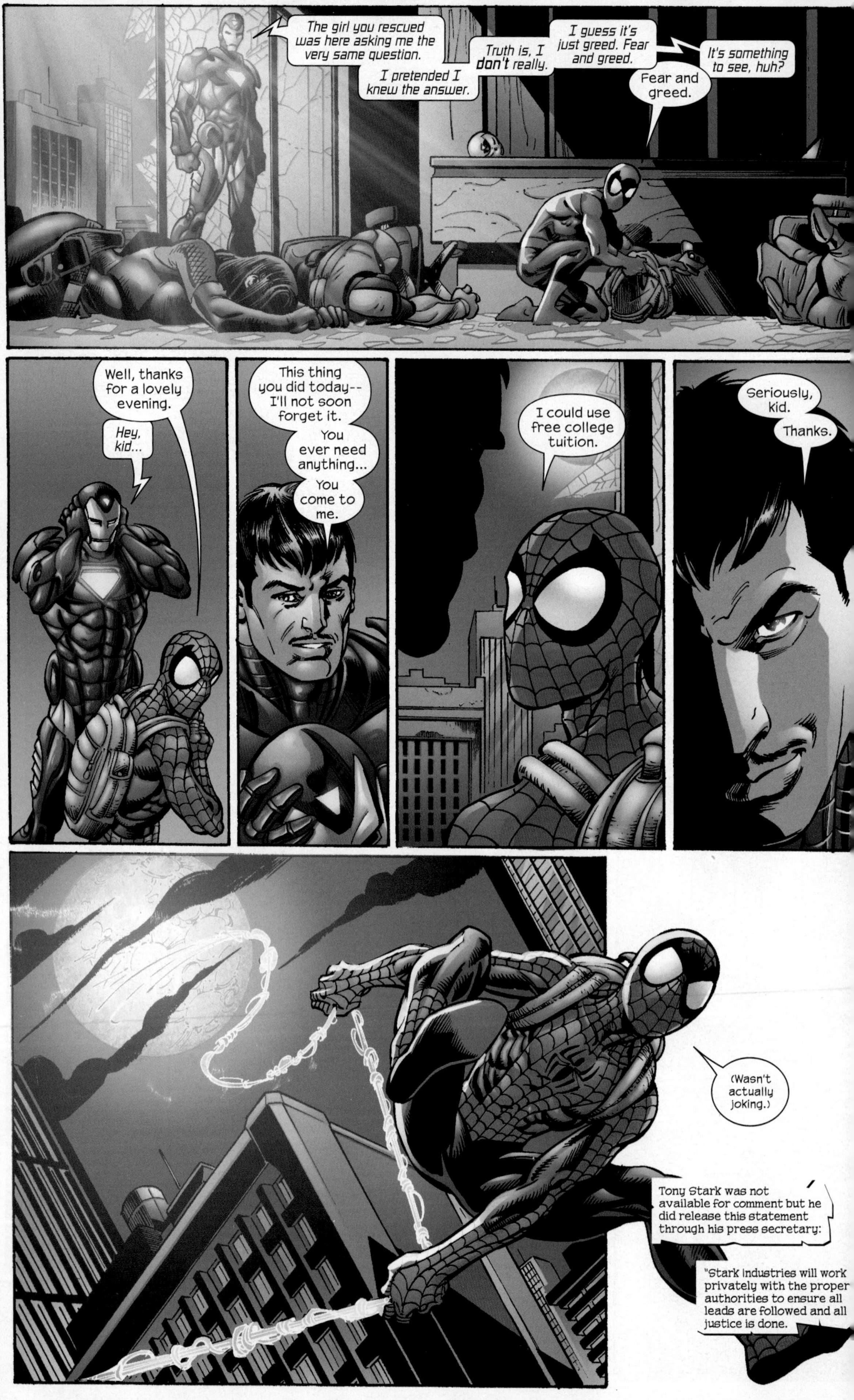
The girl you rescued was here asking me the very same question.
I pretended I knew the answer.
Truth is, I don't really.
I guess it's just greed. Fear and greed.
It's something to see, huh?
Fear and greed.
Well, thanks for a lovely evening.
Hey, kid...
This thing you did today-- I'll not soon forget it.
You ever need anything...
You come to me.
I could use free college tuition.
Seriously, kid.
Thanks.
(Wasn't actually joking.)
Tony Stark was not available for comment but he did release this statement through his press secretary:
"Stark Industries will work privately with the proper authorities to ensure all leads are followed and all justice is done.

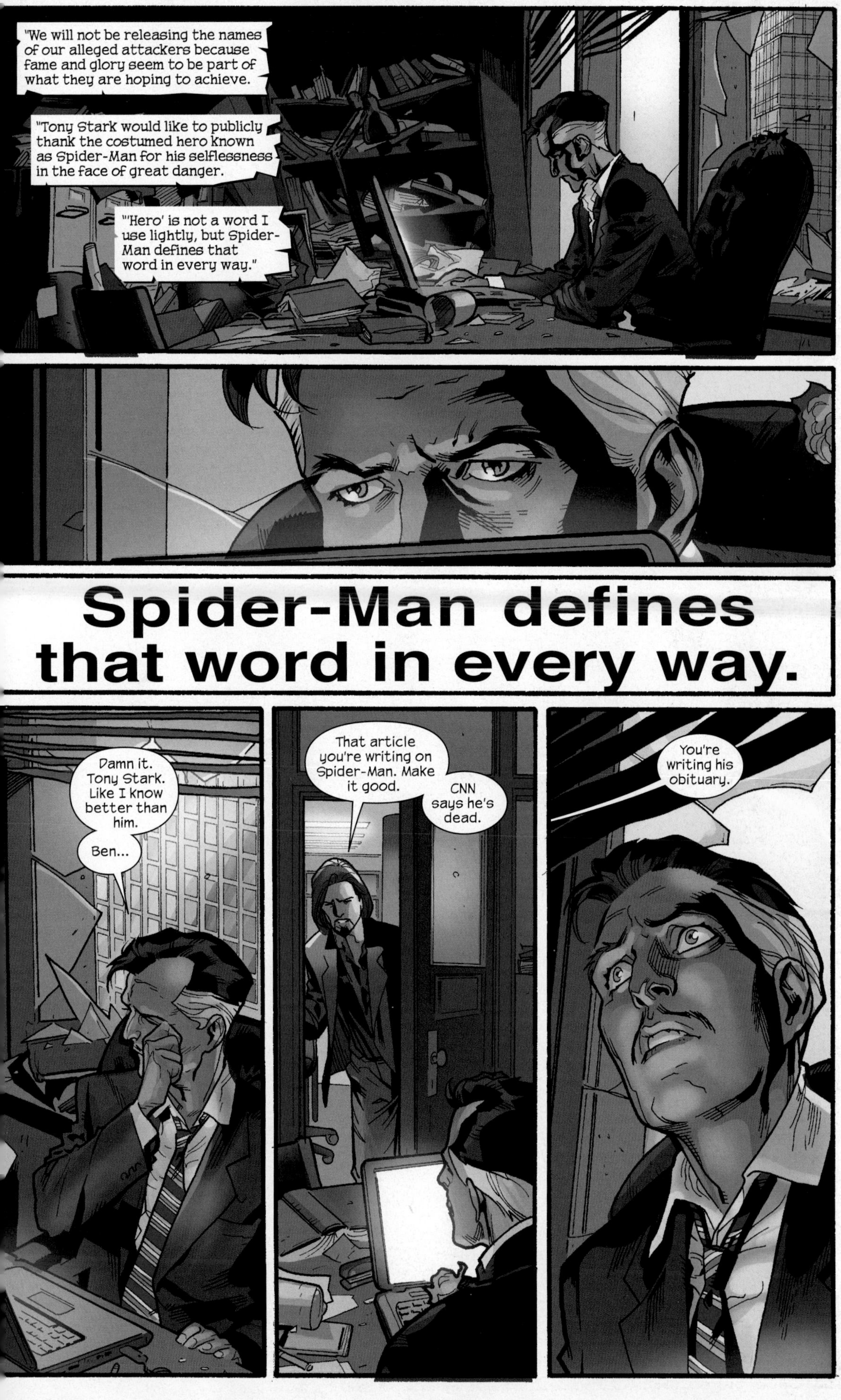
"We will not be releasing the names of our alleged attackers because fame and glory seem to be part of what they are hoping to achieve.
"Tony Stark would like to publicly thank the costumed hero known as Spider-Man for his selflessness in the face of great danger.
"'Hero' is not a word I use lightly, but Spider-Man defines that word in every way."
Spider-Man defines that word in every way.
Damn it. Tony Stark. Like I know better than him.
Ben...
That article you're writing on Spider-Man. Make it good.
CNN says he's dead.
You're writing his obituary.

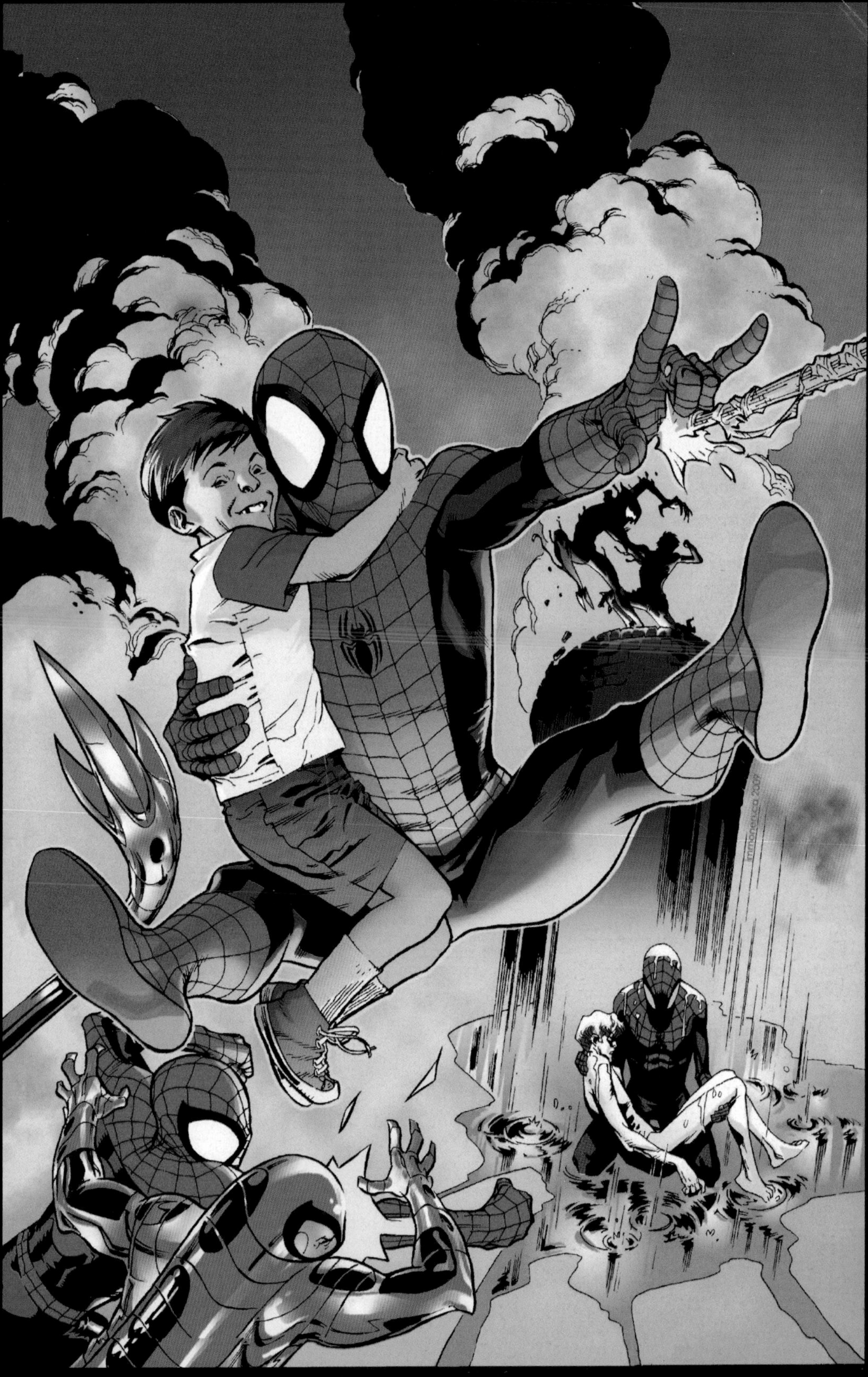

ULTIMATUM: SPIDER-MAN REQUIEM #2

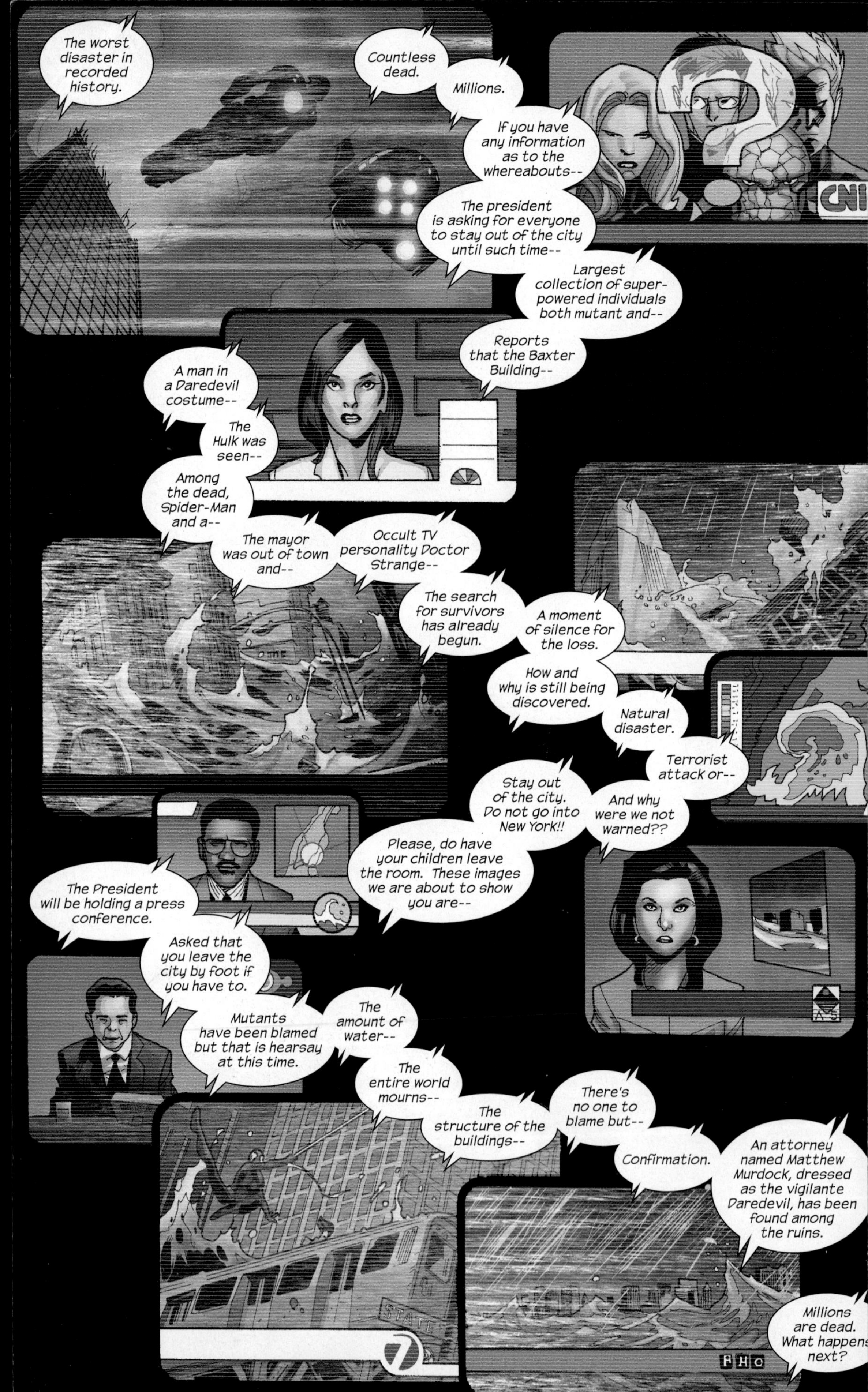

The worst disaster in recorded history.
Countless dead.
Millions.
If you have any information as to the whereabouts--
The president is asking for everyone to stay out of the city until such time--
Largest collection of super-powered individuals both mutant and--
Reports that the Baxter Building--
A man in a Daredevil costume--
The Hulk was seen--
Among the dead, Spider-Man and a--
The mayor was out of town and--
Occult TV personality Doctor Strange--
The search for survivors has already begun.
A moment of silence for the loss.
How and why is still being discovered.
Natural disaster.
Terrorist attack or--
Stay out of the city. Do not go into New York!!
And why were we not warned??
Please, do have your children leave the room. These images we are about to show you are--
The President will be holding a press conference.
Asked that you leave the city by foot if you have to.
Mutants have been blamed but that is hearsay at this time.
The amount of water--
The entire world mourns--
The structure of the buildings--
There's no one to blame but--
Confirmation.
An attorney named Matthew Murdock, dressed as the vigilante Daredevil, has been found among the ruins.
Millions are dead. What happens next?

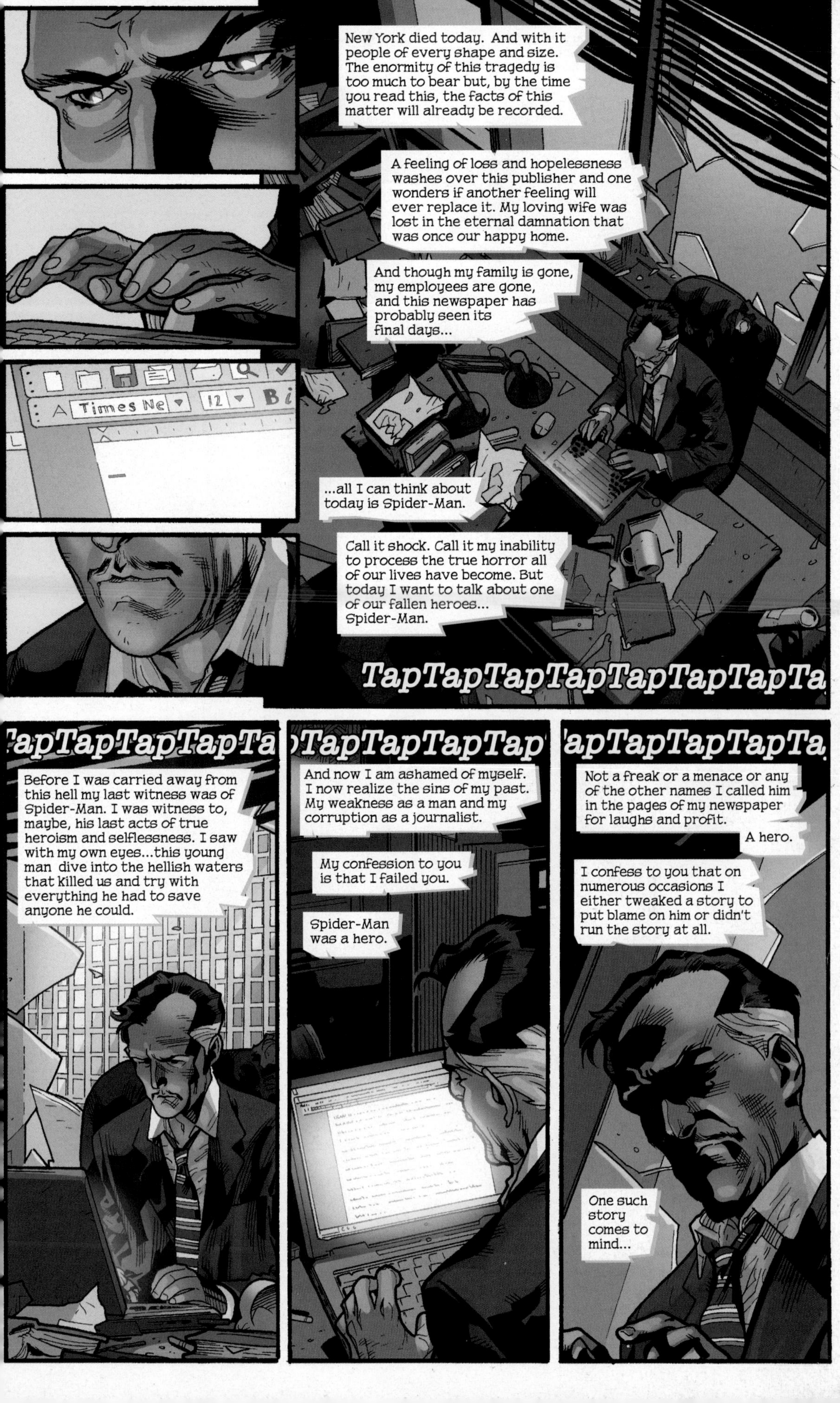
New York died today. And with it people of every shape and size. The enormity of this tragedy is too much to bear but, by the time you read this, the facts of this matter will already be recorded.
A feeling of loss and hopelessness washes over this publisher and one wonders if another feeling will ever replace it. My loving wife was lost in the eternal damnation that was once our happy home.
And though my family is gone, my employees are gone, and this newspaper has probably seen its final days...
Times Ne
12
...all I can think about today is Spider-Man.
Call it shock. Call it my inability to process the true horror all of our lives have become. But today I want to talk about one of our fallen heroes... Spider-Man.
TapTapTapTapTapTapTapTa
TapTapTapTapTa
TapTapTapTap
apTapTapTapTa
Before I was carried away from this hell my last witness was of Spider-Man. I was witness to, maybe, his last acts of true heroism and selflessness. I saw with my own eyes...this young man dive into the hellish waters that killed us and try with everything he had to save anyone he could.
And now I am ashamed of myself. I now realize the sins of my past. My weakness as a man and my corruption as a journalist.
My confession to you is that I failed you.
Spider-Man was a hero.
Not a freak or a menace or any of the other names I called him in the pages of my newspaper for laughs and profit.
A hero.
I confess to you that on numerous occasions I either tweaked a story to put blame on him or didn't run the story at all.
One such story comes to mind...

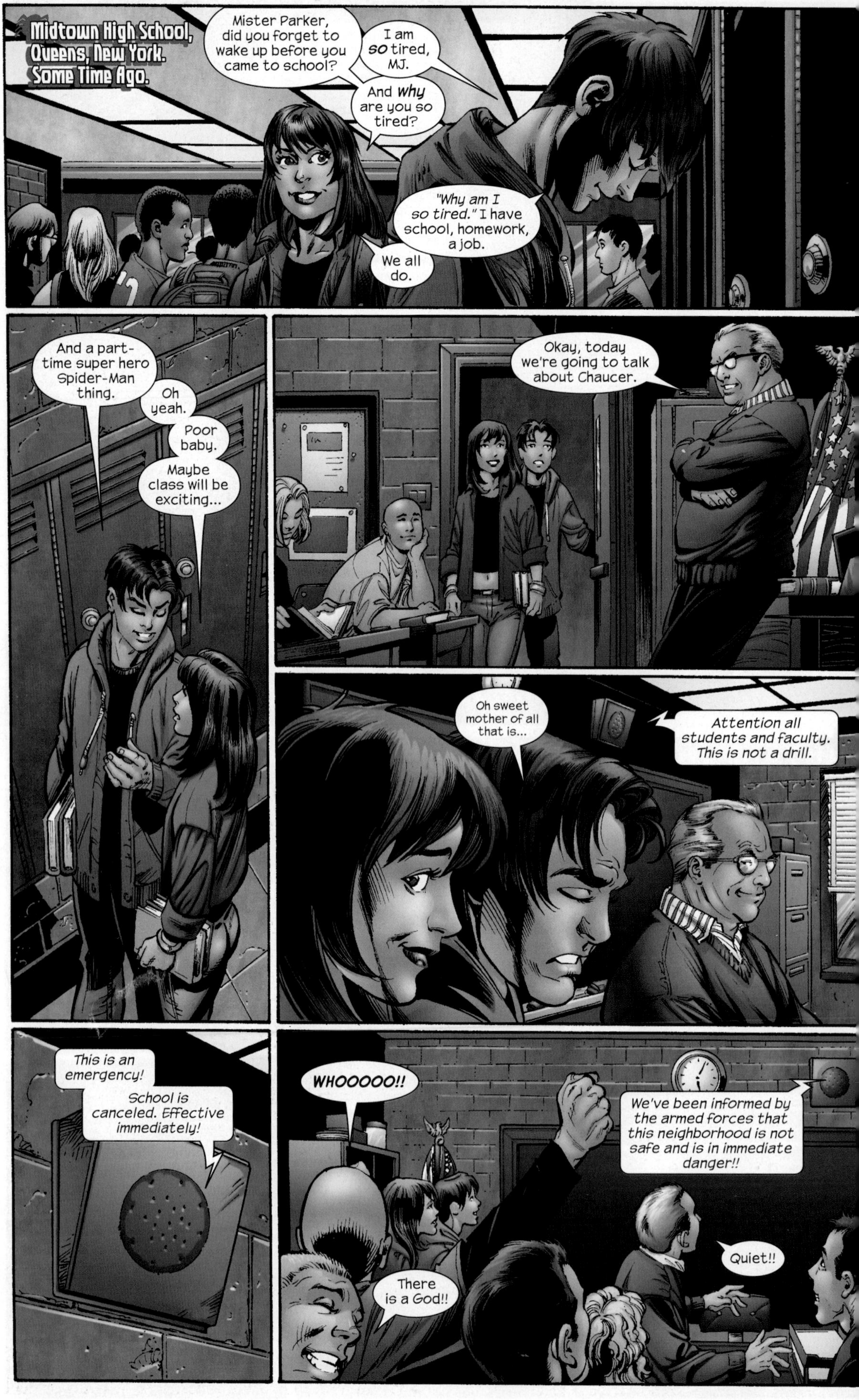

Midtown High School, Queens, New York. Some Time Ago.
Mister Parker, did you forget to wake up before you came to school?
I am so tired, MJ.
And why are you so tired?
"Why am I so tired." I have school, homework, a job.
We all do.
And a part-time super hero Spider-Man thing.
Oh yeah.
Poor baby.
Maybe class will be exciting...
Okay, today we're going to talk about Chaucer.
Oh sweet mother of all that is...
Attention all students and faculty. This is not a drill.
This is an emergency!
School is canceled. Effective immediately!
WHOOOOO!!
We've been informed by the armed forces that this neighborhood is not safe and is in immediate danger!!
Quiet!!
There is a God!!

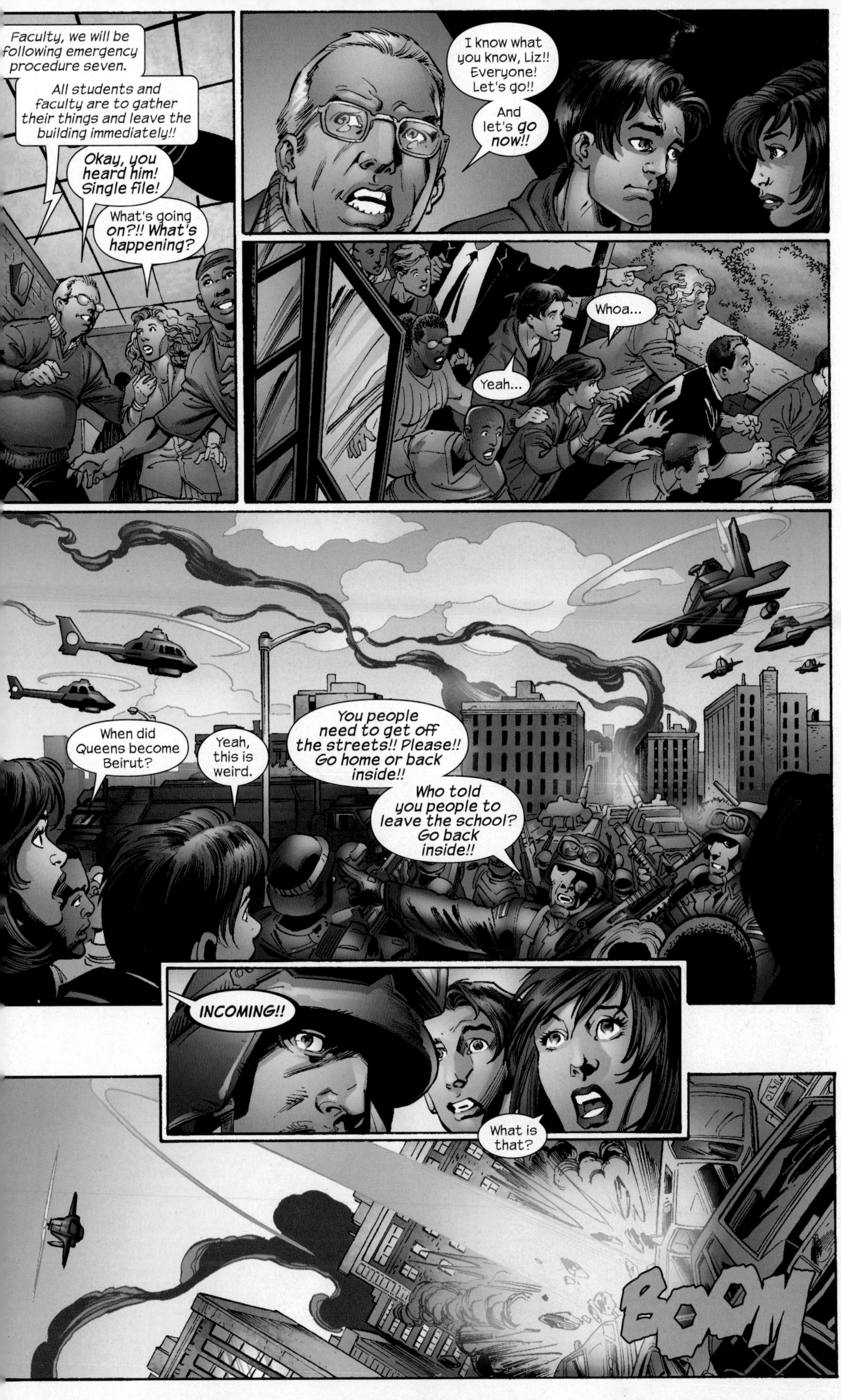

Faculty, we will be following emergency procedure seven.
All students and faculty are to gather their things and leave the building immediately!!
Okay, you heard him! Single file!
What's going on?!! What's happening?
I know what you know, Liz!! Everyone! Let's go!!
And let's go now!!
Whoa...
Yeah...
When did Queens become Beirut?
Yeah, this is weird.
You people need to get off the streets!! Please!! Go home or back inside!!
Who told you people to leave the school? Go back inside!!
INCOMING!!
What is that?
BOOM

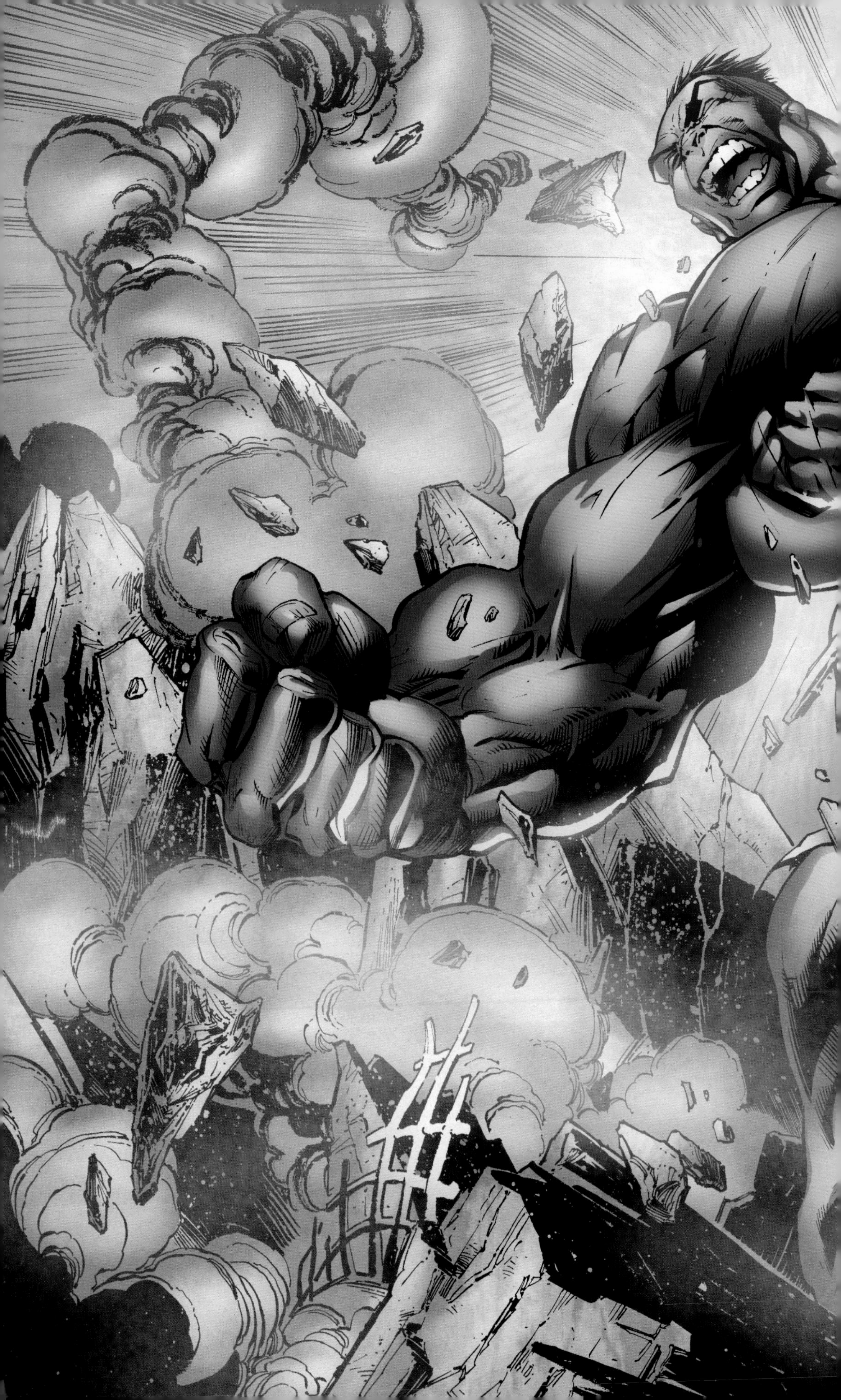

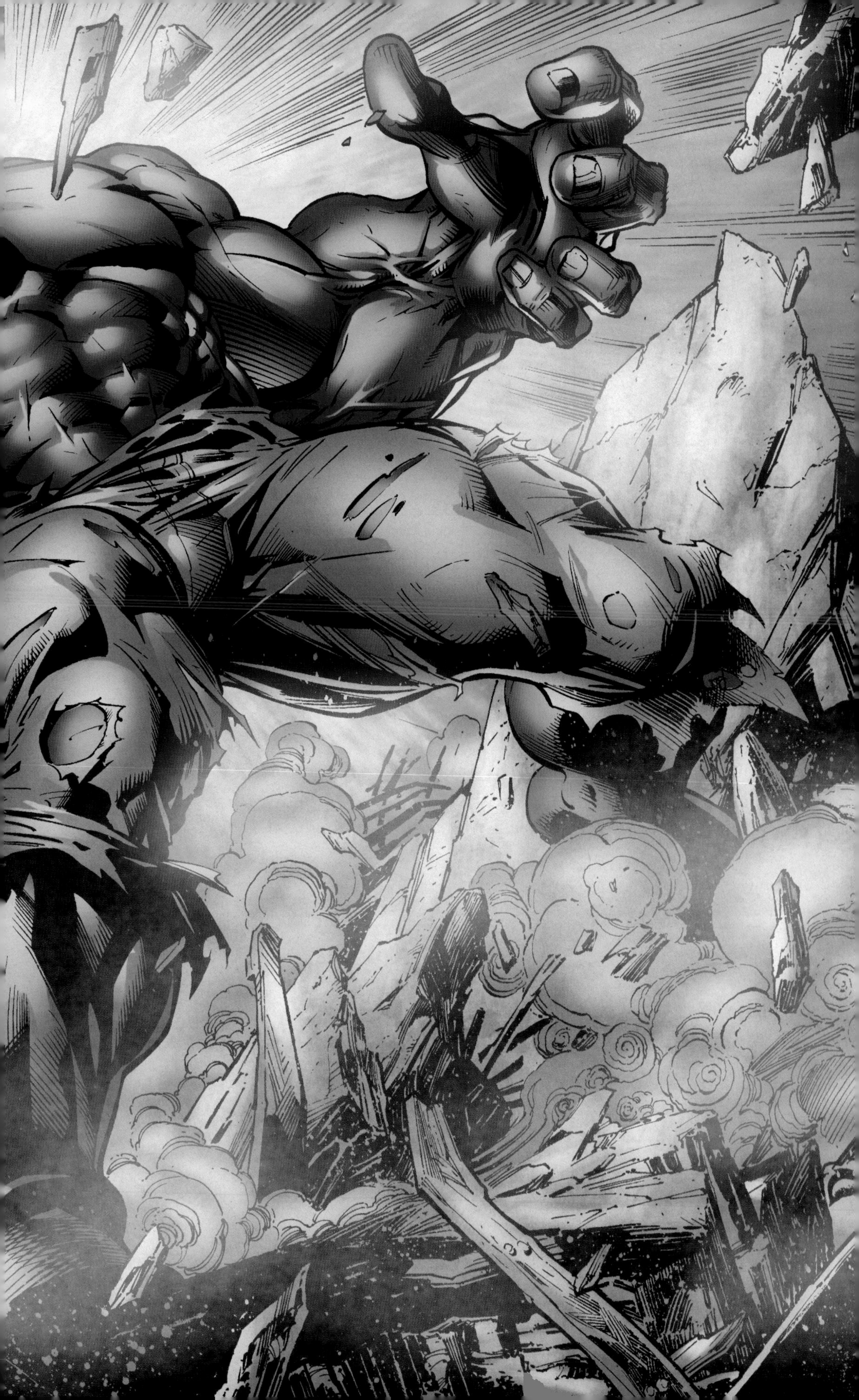

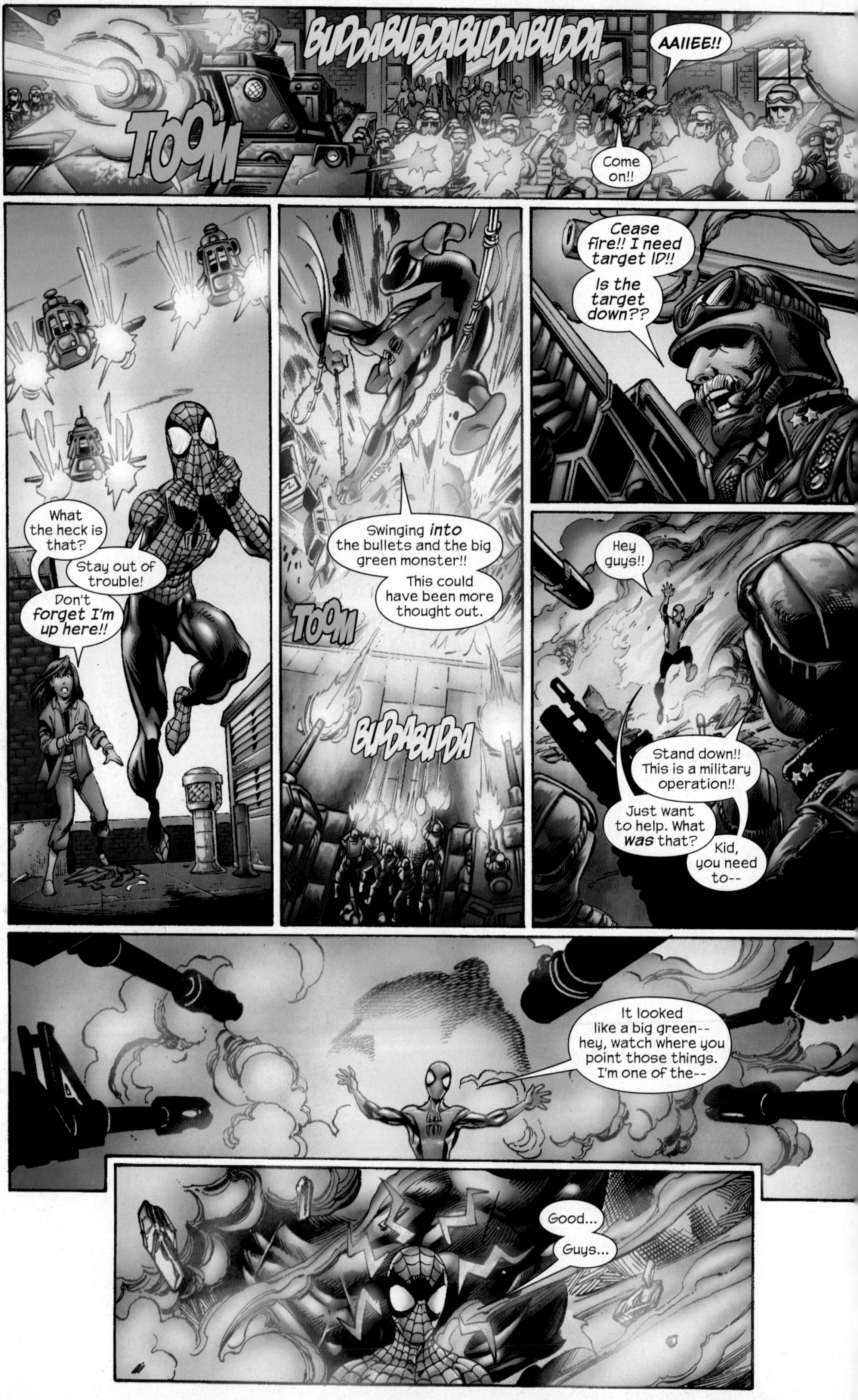
BUDDABUDDABUDDABUDDA
AAIIEE!!
TOOM
Come on!!
What the heck is that?
Stay out of trouble!
Don't forget I'm up here!!
Swinging into the bullets and the big green monster!!
This could have been more thought out.
TOOM
BUDDABUDDA
Cease fire!! I need target ID!!
Is the target down??
Hey guys!!
Stand down!! This is a military operation!!
Just want to help. What was that?
Kid, you need to--
It looked like a big green-- hey, watch where you point those things. I'm one of the--
Good...
Guys...

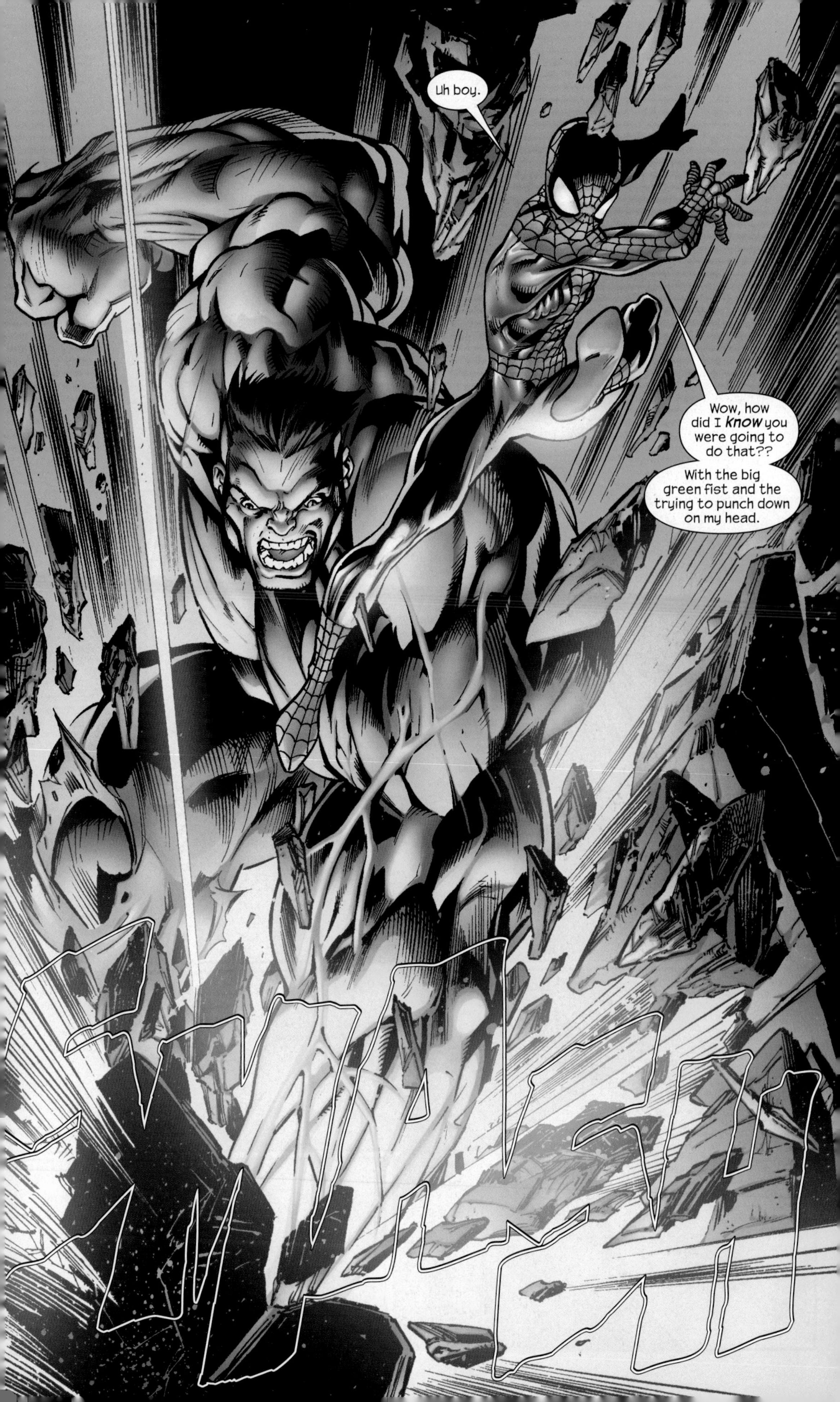
Uh boy.
Wow, how did I *KNOW* you were going to do that??
With the big green fist and the trying to punch down on my head.

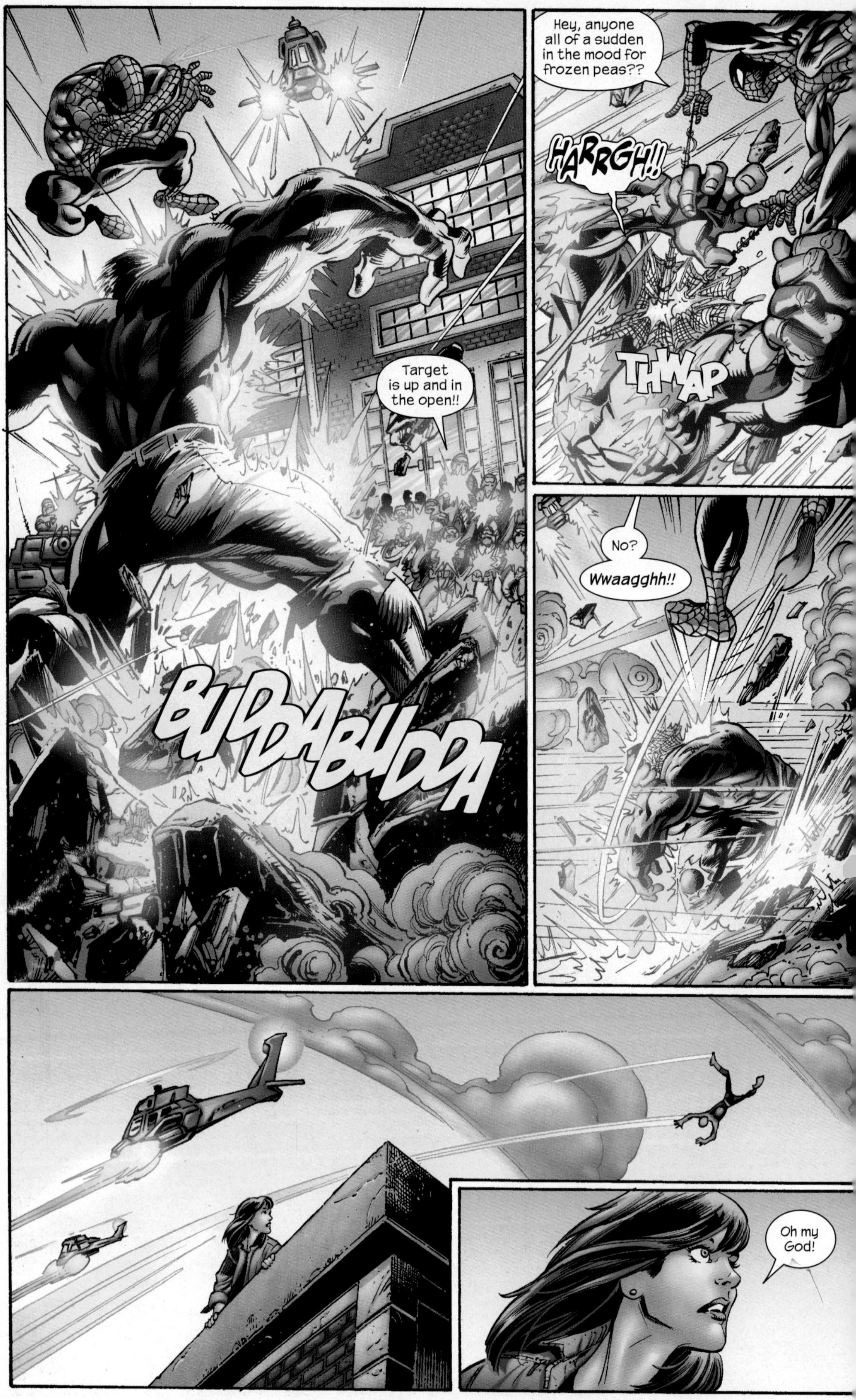
Target is up and in the open!!
BUDABUDDA
Hey, anyone all of a sudden in the mood for frozen peas??
HARRGH!!
THWAP
No?
Wwaagghh!!
Oh my God!

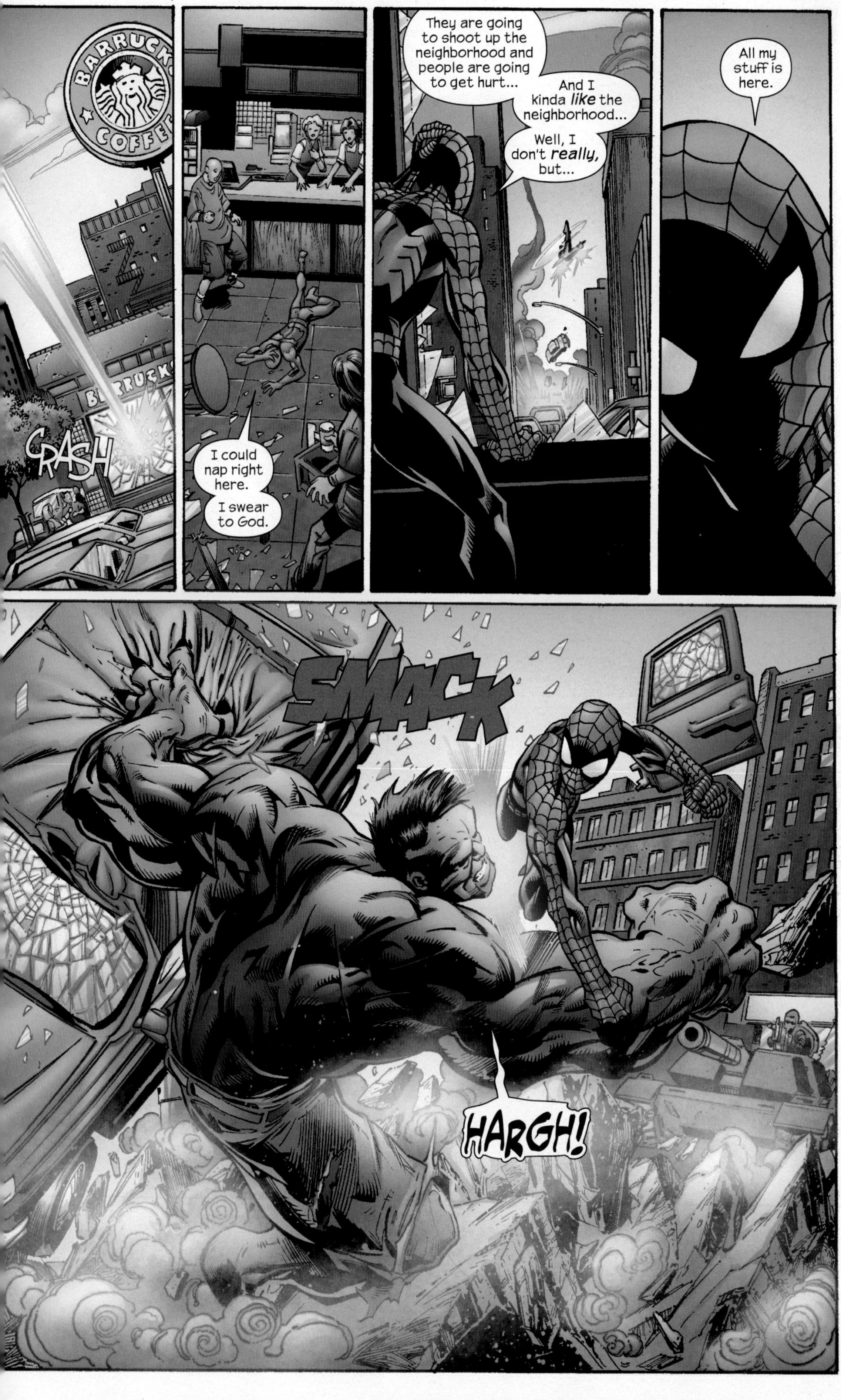

BARRUCKS COFFEE
BARRUCKS
CRASH
I could nap right here.
I swear to God.
They are going to shoot up the neighborhood and people are going to get hurt...
And I kinda *like* the neighborhood...
Well, I don't *really*, but...
All my stuff is here.
SMACK
HARGH!

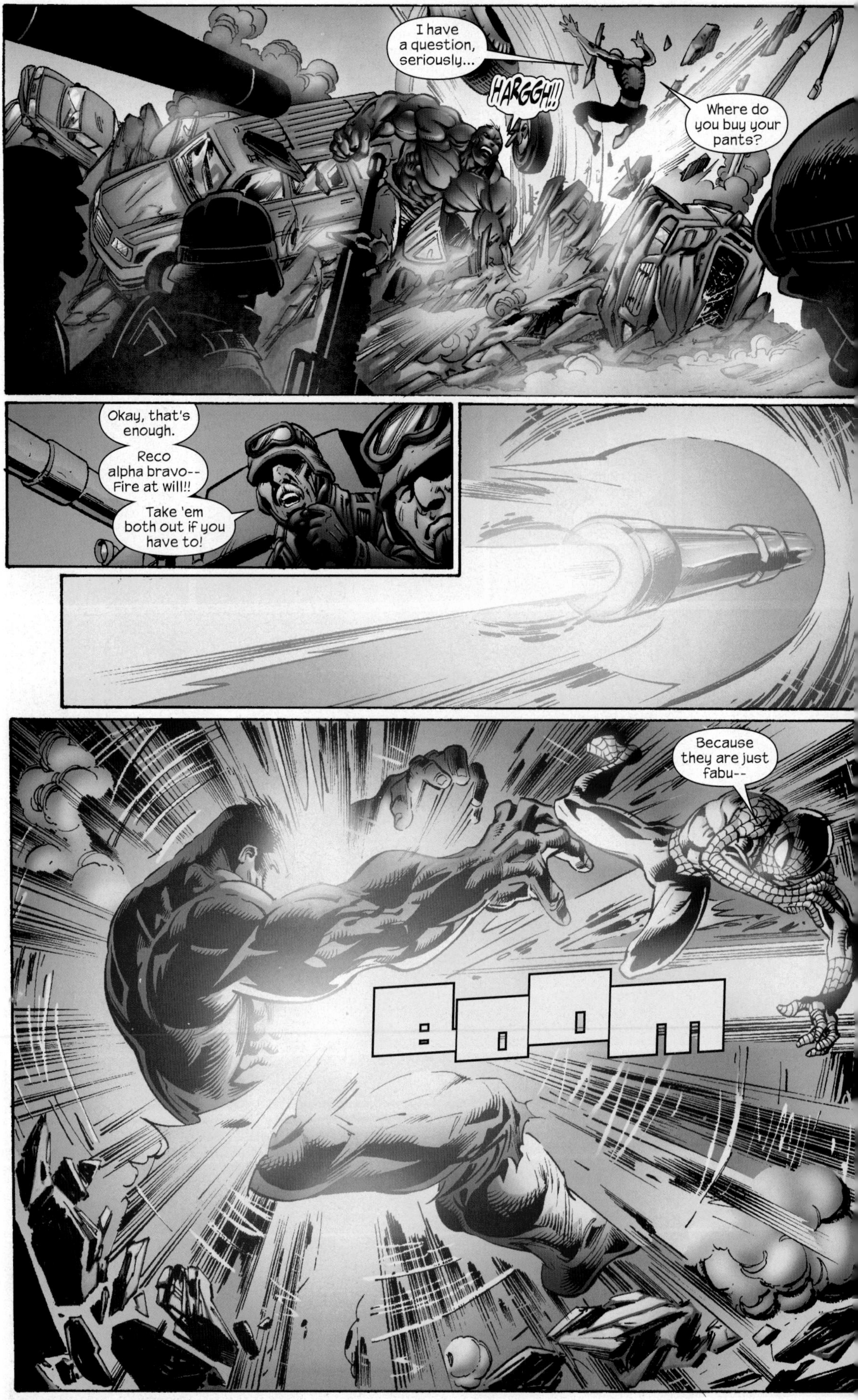
I have a question, seriously...
HARGGH!!!
Where do you buy your pants?
Okay, that's enough.
Reco alpha bravo-- Fire at will!!
Take 'em both out if you have to!
Because they are just fabu--
BOOM

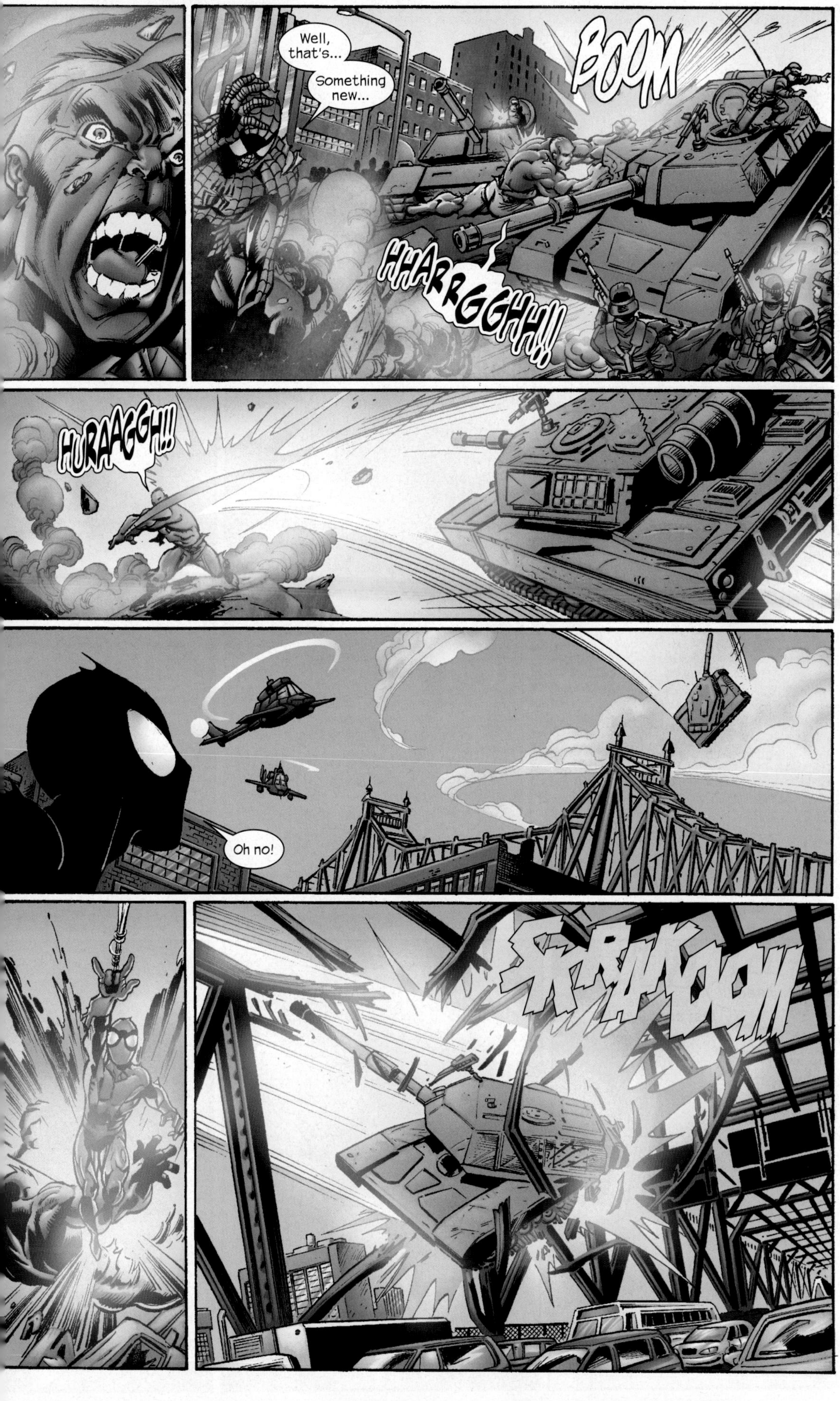
Well, that's...
Something new...
BOOM
HHARRGGHH!!
HURAAGGH!!
Oh no!
SKRUKOOM

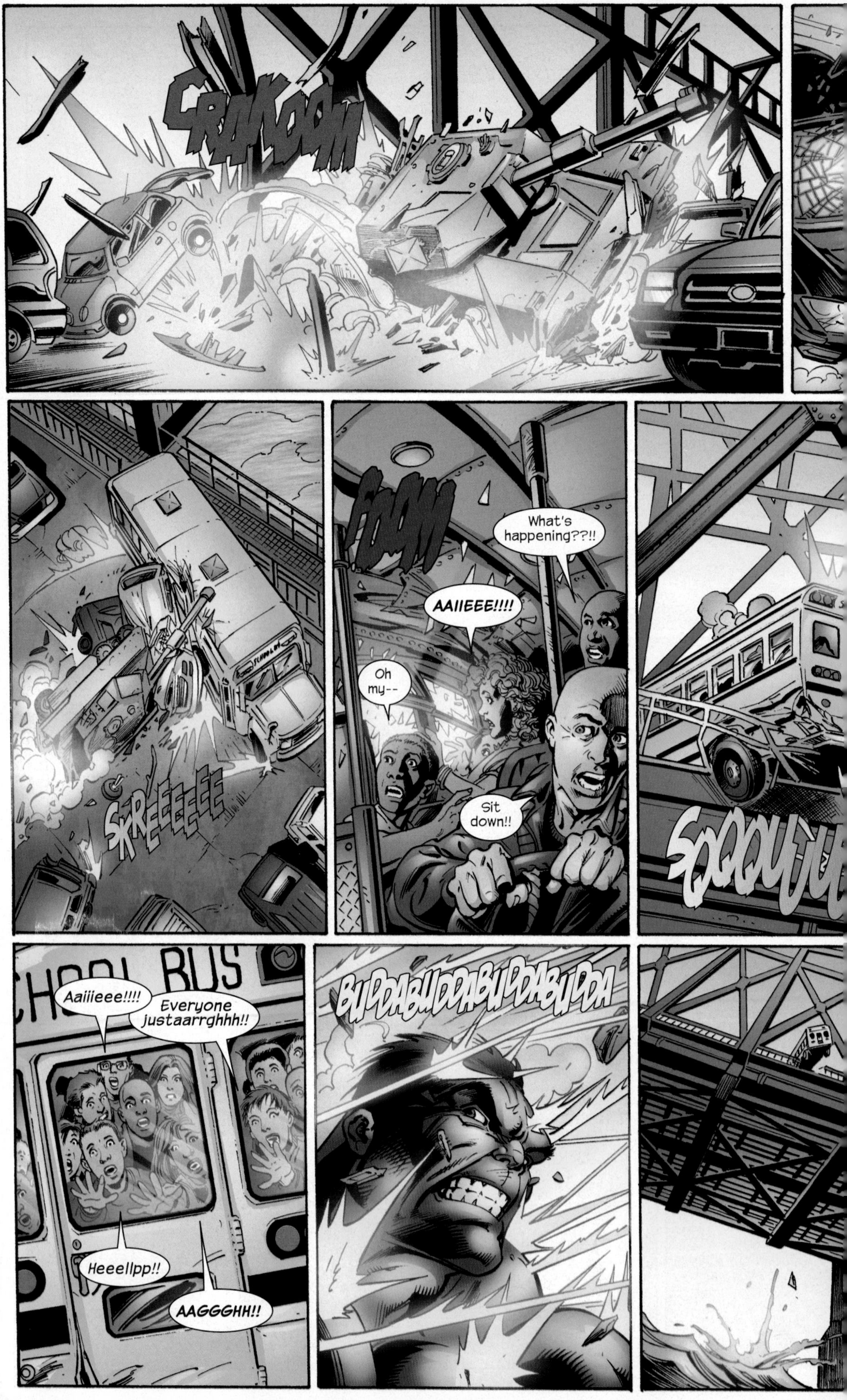

CRAKOOM
SKREEEEEEE
FOOM
What's happening??!!
AAIIEEE!!!!
Oh my--
Sit down!!
SPOOUUU
SCHOOL BUS
Aaiiieee!!!!
Everyone justaarrghhh!!
Heeellpp!!
AAGGGHH!!
BUDDABUDDABUDDABUDDA

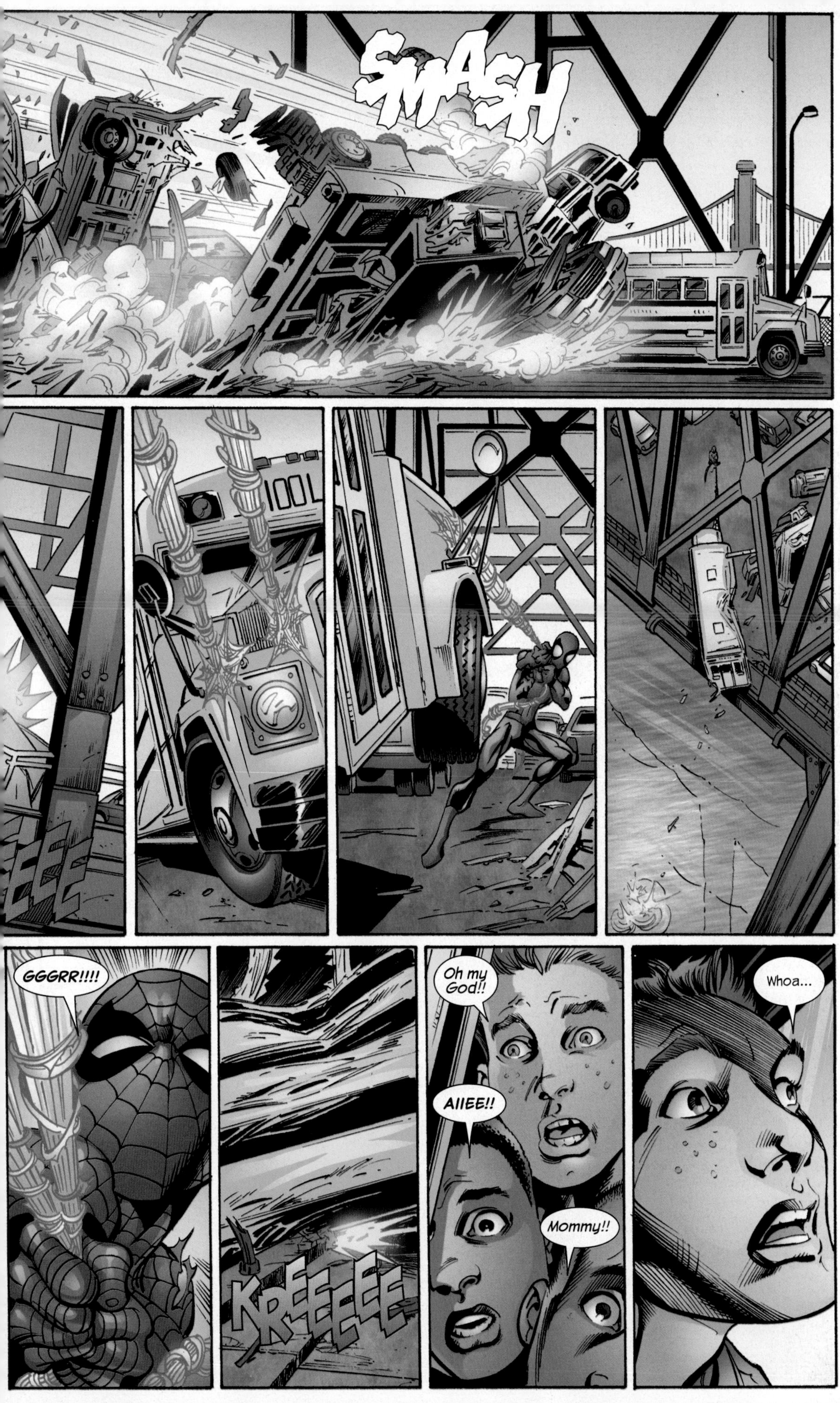
SMASH
SCHOOL
EEEE
GGGRR!!!!
KREEEEEE
Oh my God!!
AIIEE!!
Mommy!!
Whoa...

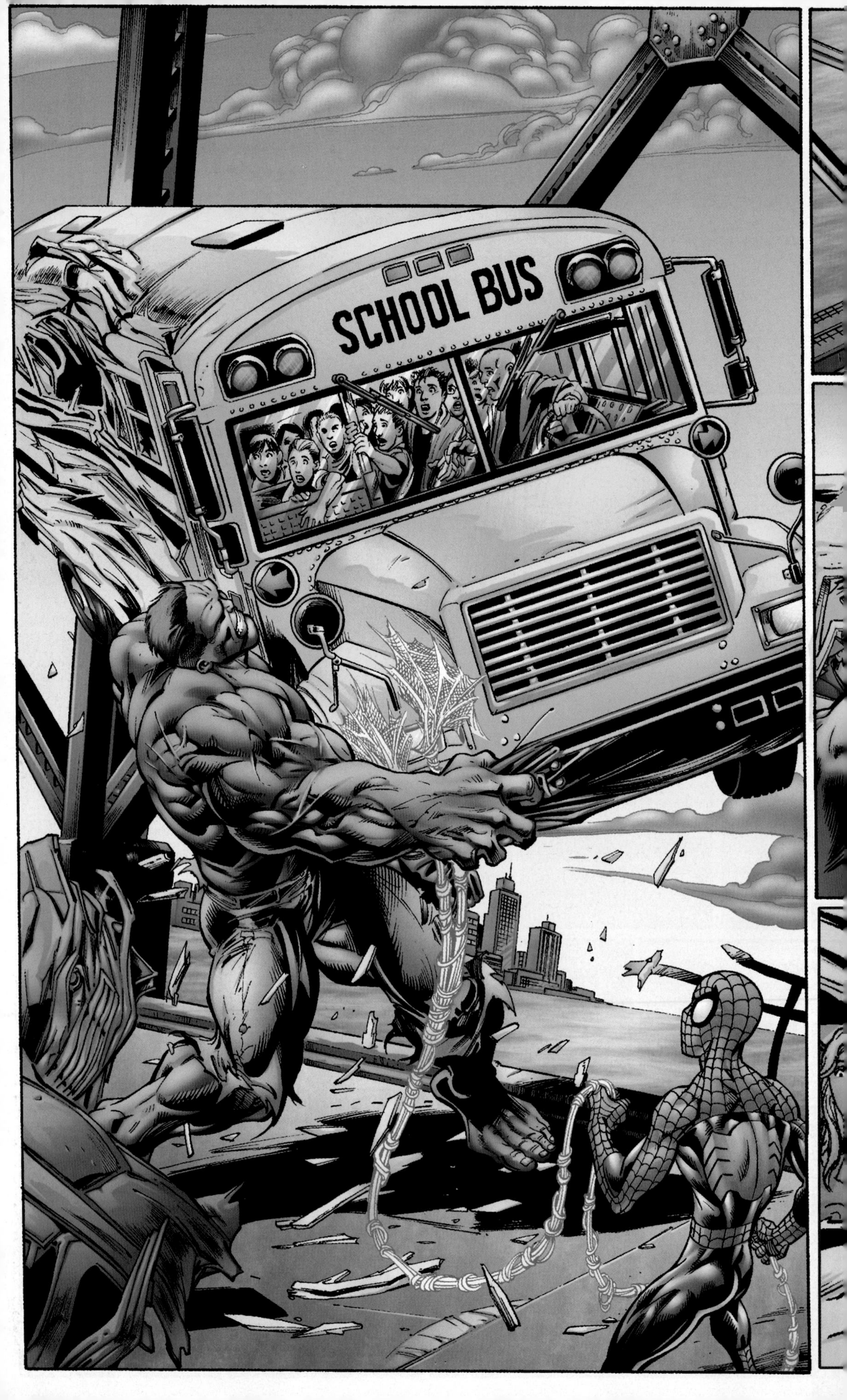
SCHOOL BUS

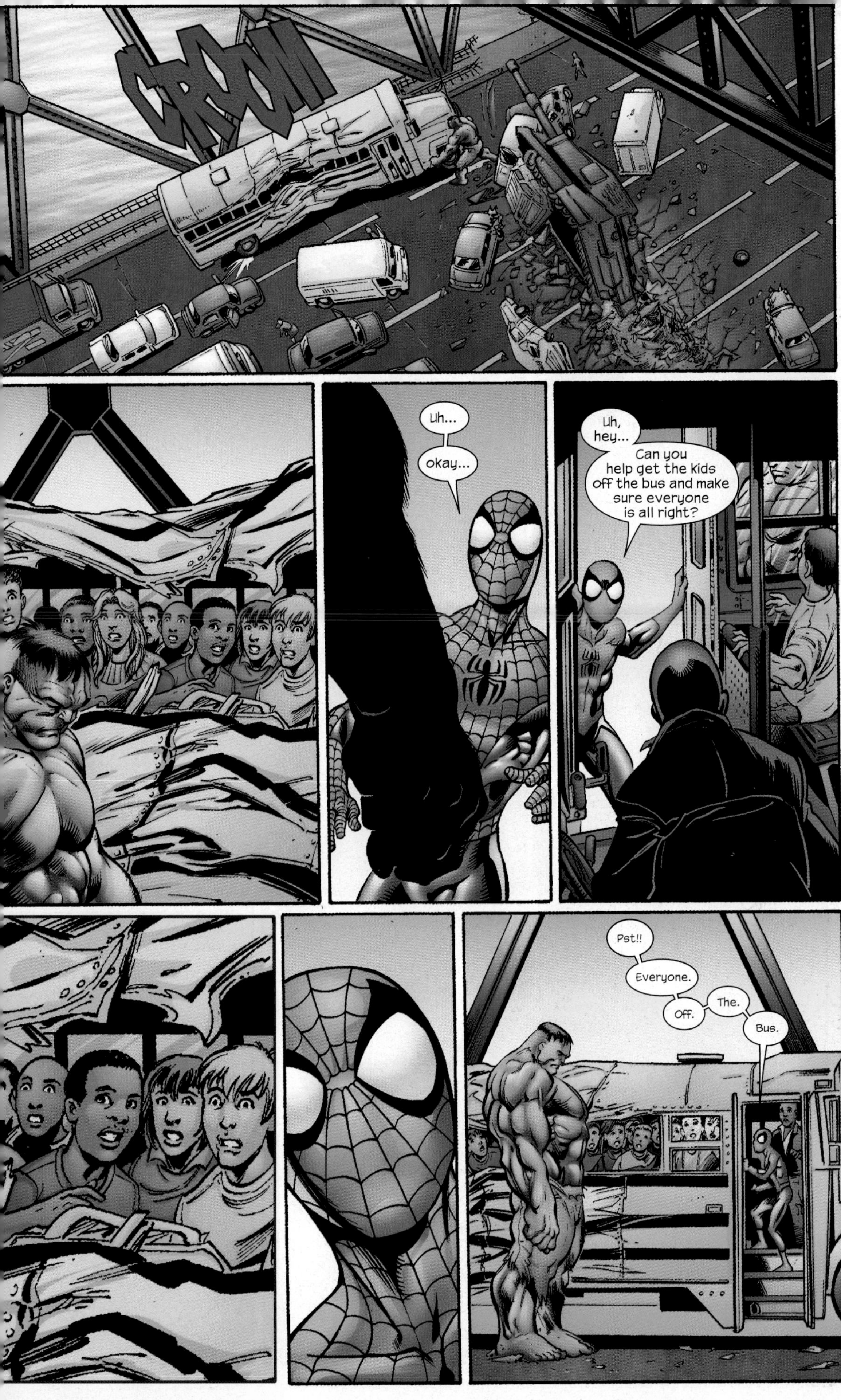
CROOM
Uh...
okay...
Uh, hey...
Can you help get the kids off the bus and make sure everyone is all right?
Pst!!
Everyone.
Off.
The.
Bus.

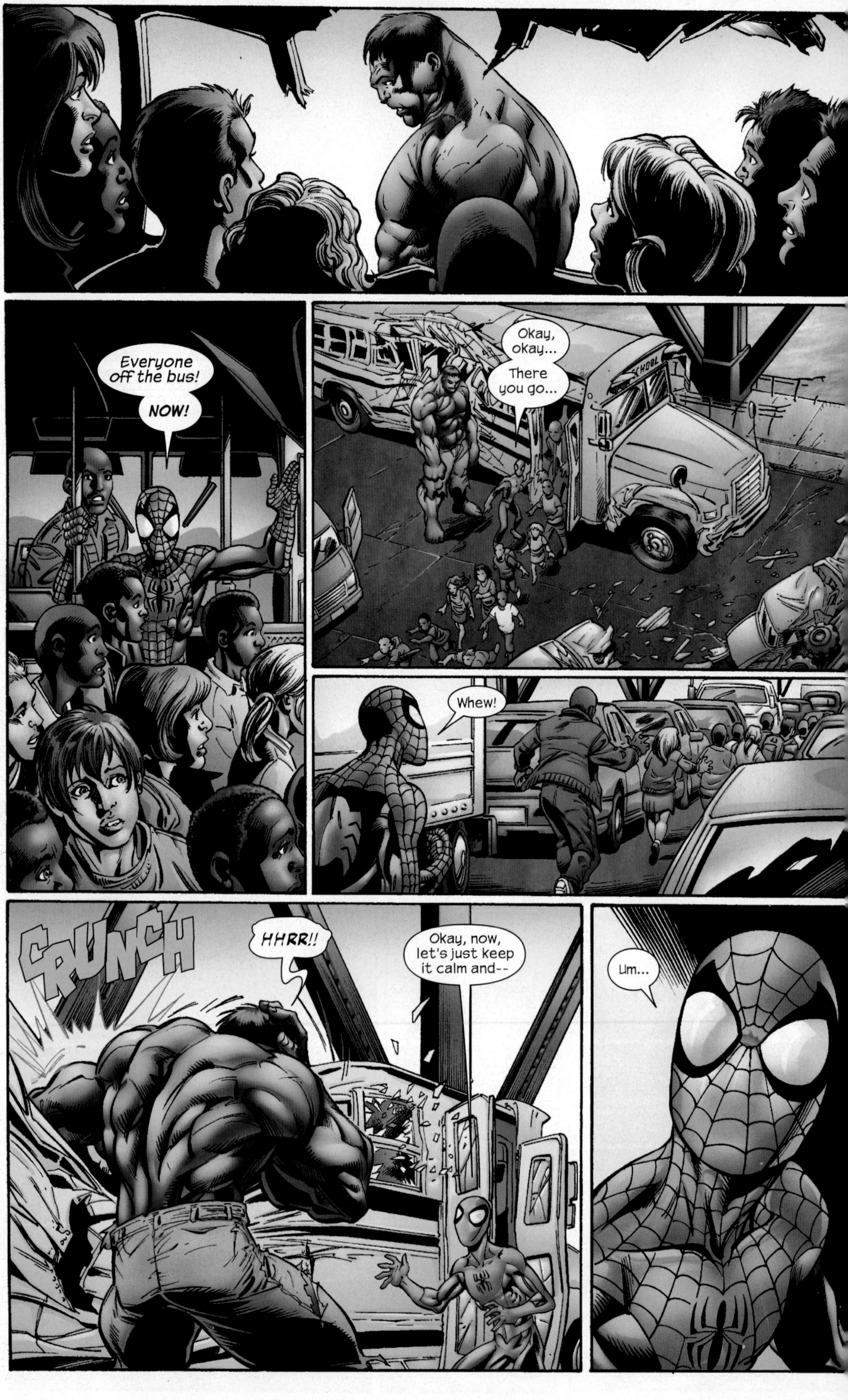
Everyone off the bus!
NOW!
Okay, okay...
There you go...
Whew!
CRUNCH
HHRR!!
Okay, now, let's just keep it calm and--
Um...

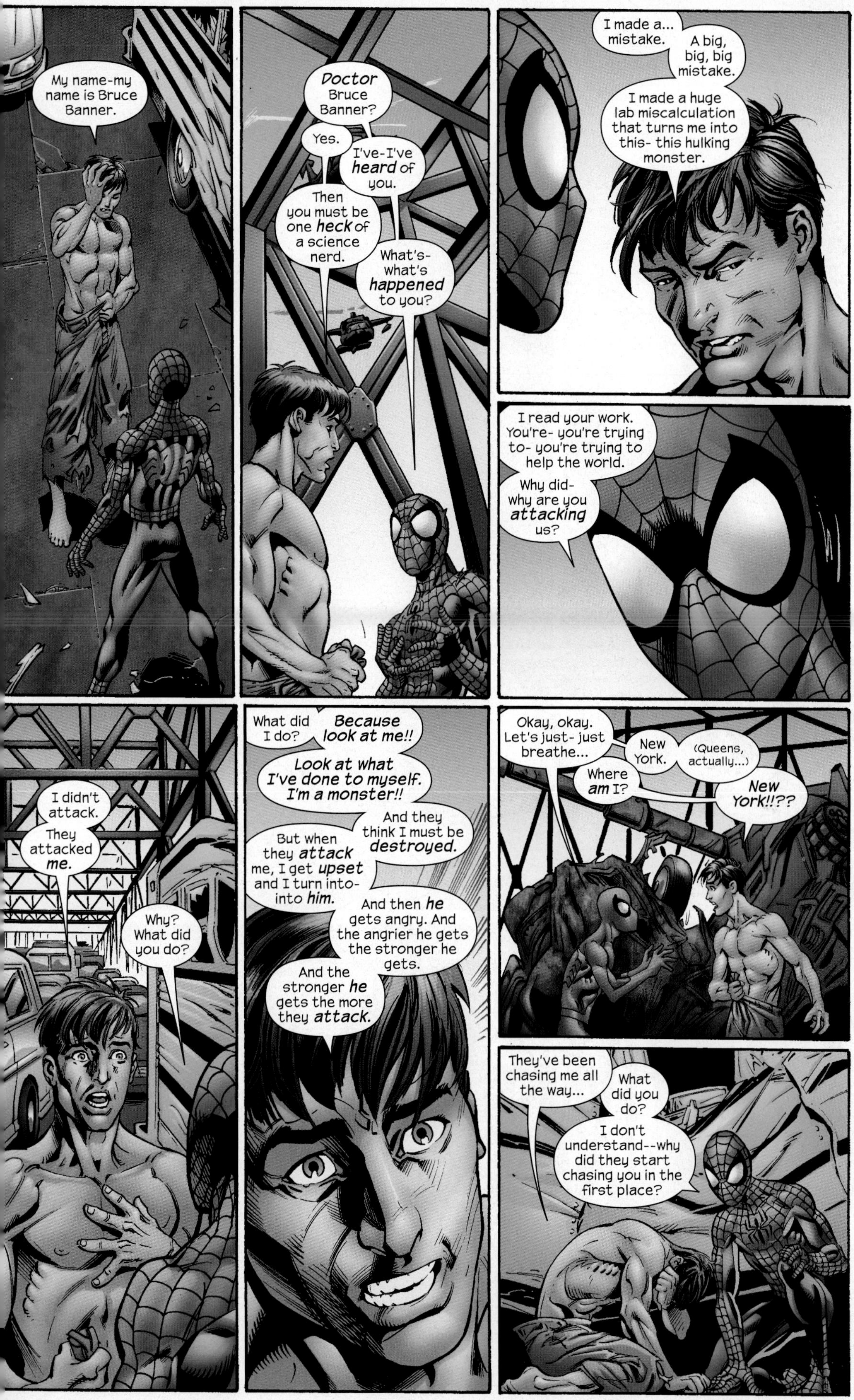

My name-my name is Bruce Banner.
Doctor Bruce Banner?
Yes.
I've-I've heard of you.
Then you must be one heck of a science nerd.
What's-what's happened to you?
I made a... mistake.
A big, big, big mistake.
I made a huge lab miscalculation that turns me into this- this hulking monster.
I read your work. You're- you're trying to- you're trying to help the world.
Why did- why are you attacking us?
I didn't attack.
They attacked me.
Why? What did you do?
What did I do?
Because look at me!!
Look at what I've done to myself. I'm a monster!!
And they think I must be destroyed.
But when they attack me, I get upset and I turn into- into him.
And then he gets angry. And the angrier he gets the stronger he gets.
And the stronger he gets the more they attack.
Okay, okay. Let's just- just breathe...
New York.
(Queens, actually...)
Where am I?
New York!!??
They've been chasing me all the way...
What did you do?
I don't understand--why did they start chasing you in the first place?

Because that's what we *do*. That's why the world is the way the world is.

We *attack* that which we don't understand.

We *attack* that which looks different.

Instead of trying to understand what makes someone different, we lash *out*.

I don't want to fight! I don't want to run!!

I don't want to *hurt* little children!!

I-I want to help *save* children!!

This isn't what my life was supposed to be...

Let's try and just talk to them...

I've tried. You can't.

And we're all so surprised the world's the way it is.

FREEZE!!

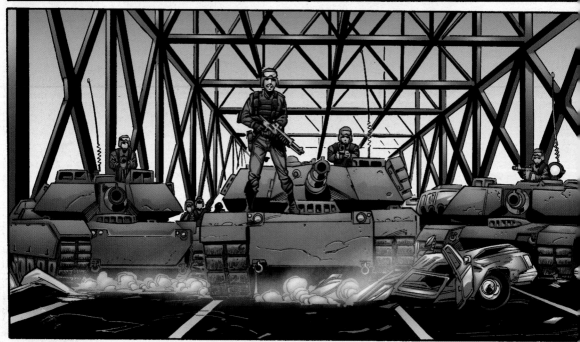

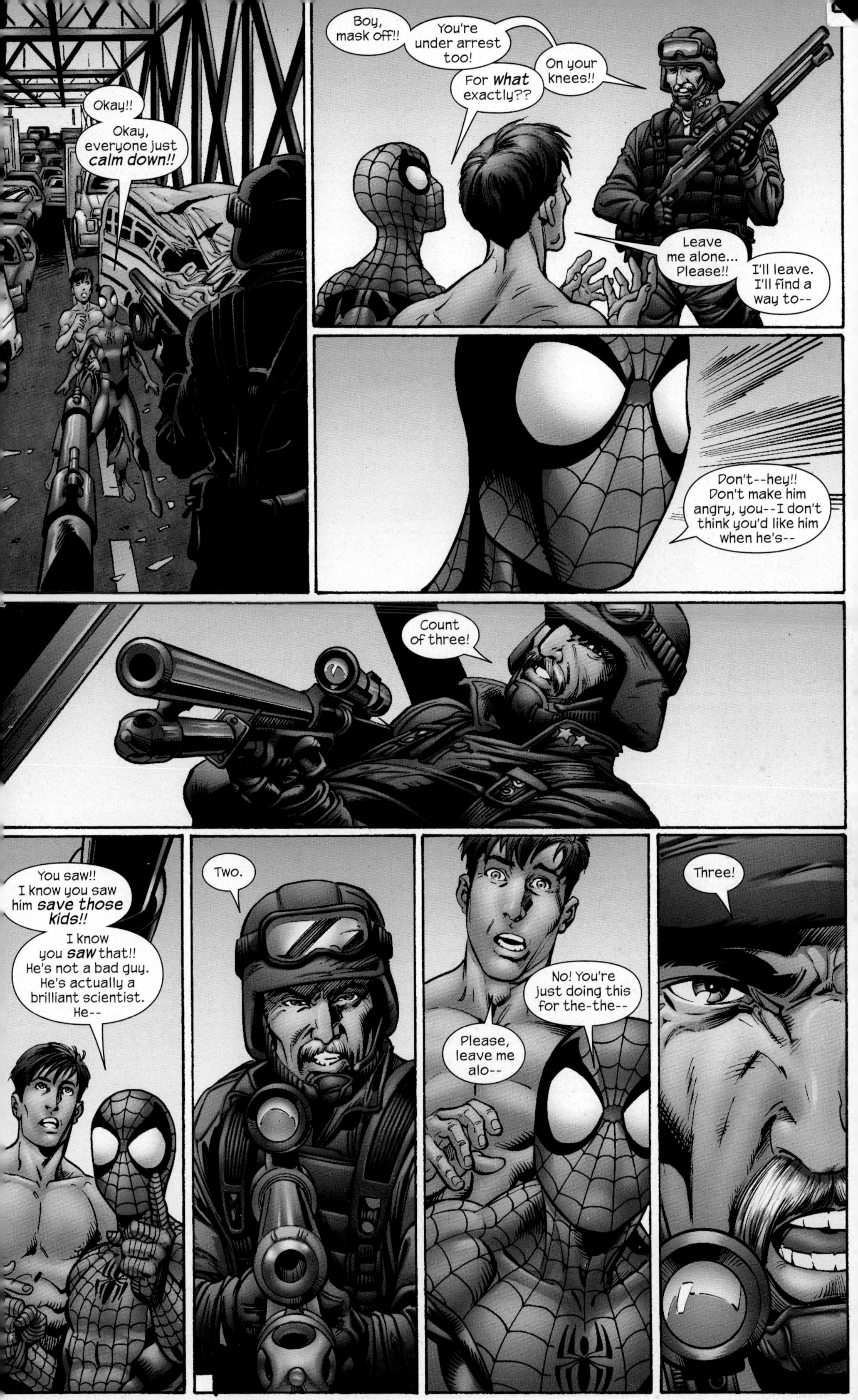
Okay!!
Okay, everyone just calm down!!
Boy, mask off!!
You're under arrest too!
On your knees!!
For what exactly??
Leave me alone... Please!!
I'll leave. I'll find a way to--
Don't--hey!! Don't make him angry, you--I don't think you'd like him when he's--
Count of three!
You saw!! I know you saw him save those kids!!
I know you saw that!! He's not a bad guy. He's actually a brilliant scientist. He--
Two.
No! You're just doing this for the-the--
Please, leave me alo--
Three!

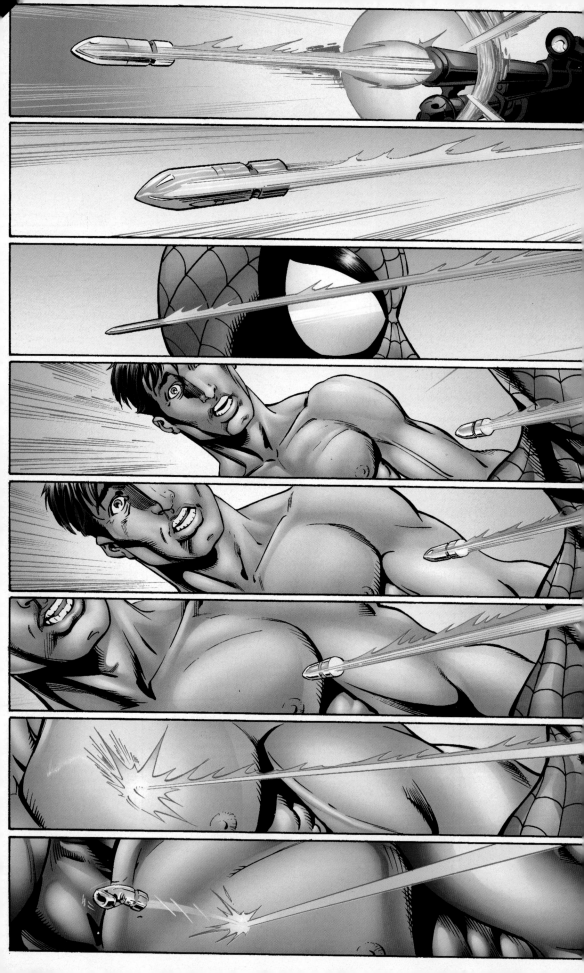

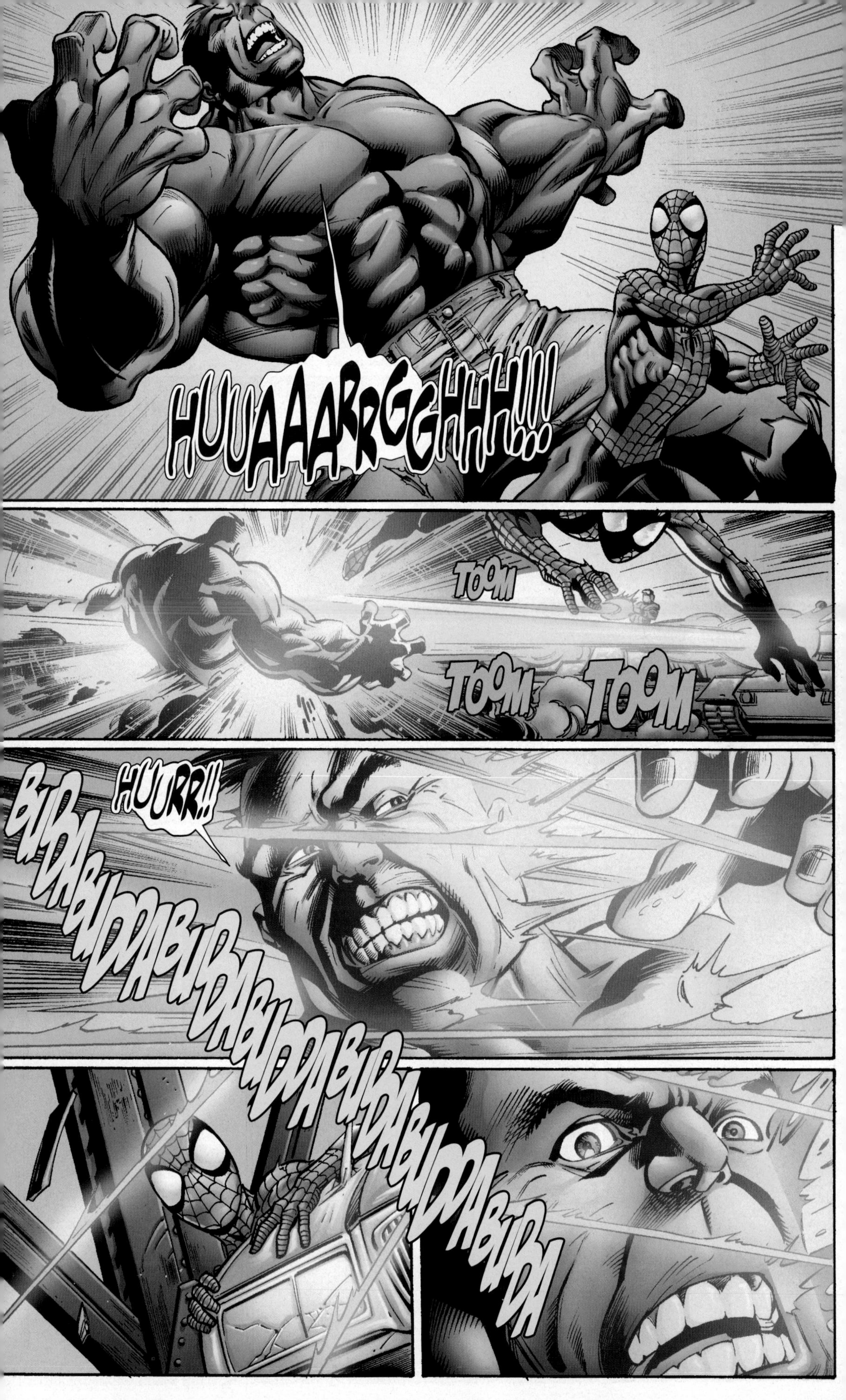
HUUAAARRGGHHH!!!
TOOM
TOOM TOOM
HUURR!!
BUDABUDDABUDABUDDABUDABUDDABUDA

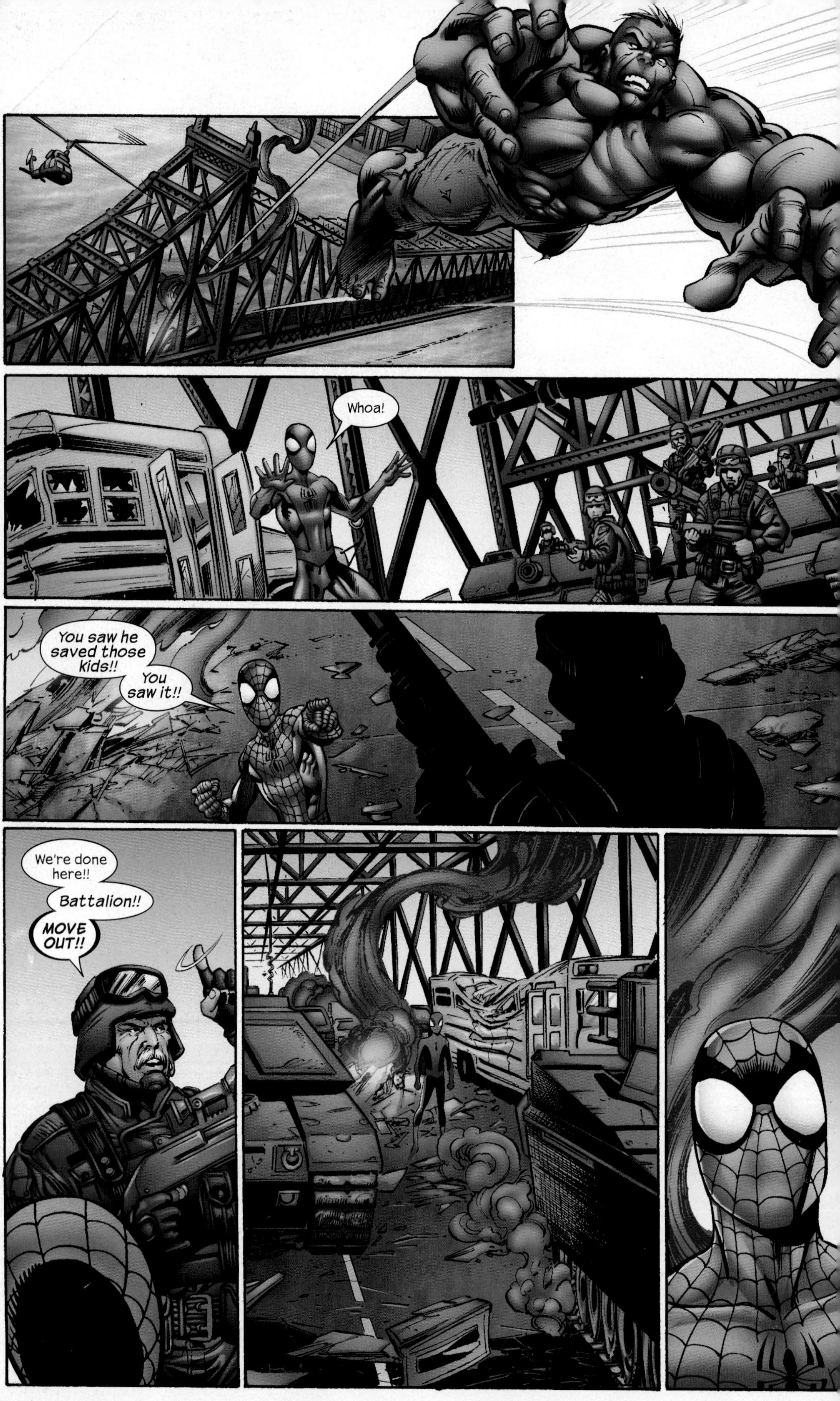

Whoa!
You saw he saved those kids!!
You saw it!!
We're done here!!
Battalion!!
MOVE OUT!!

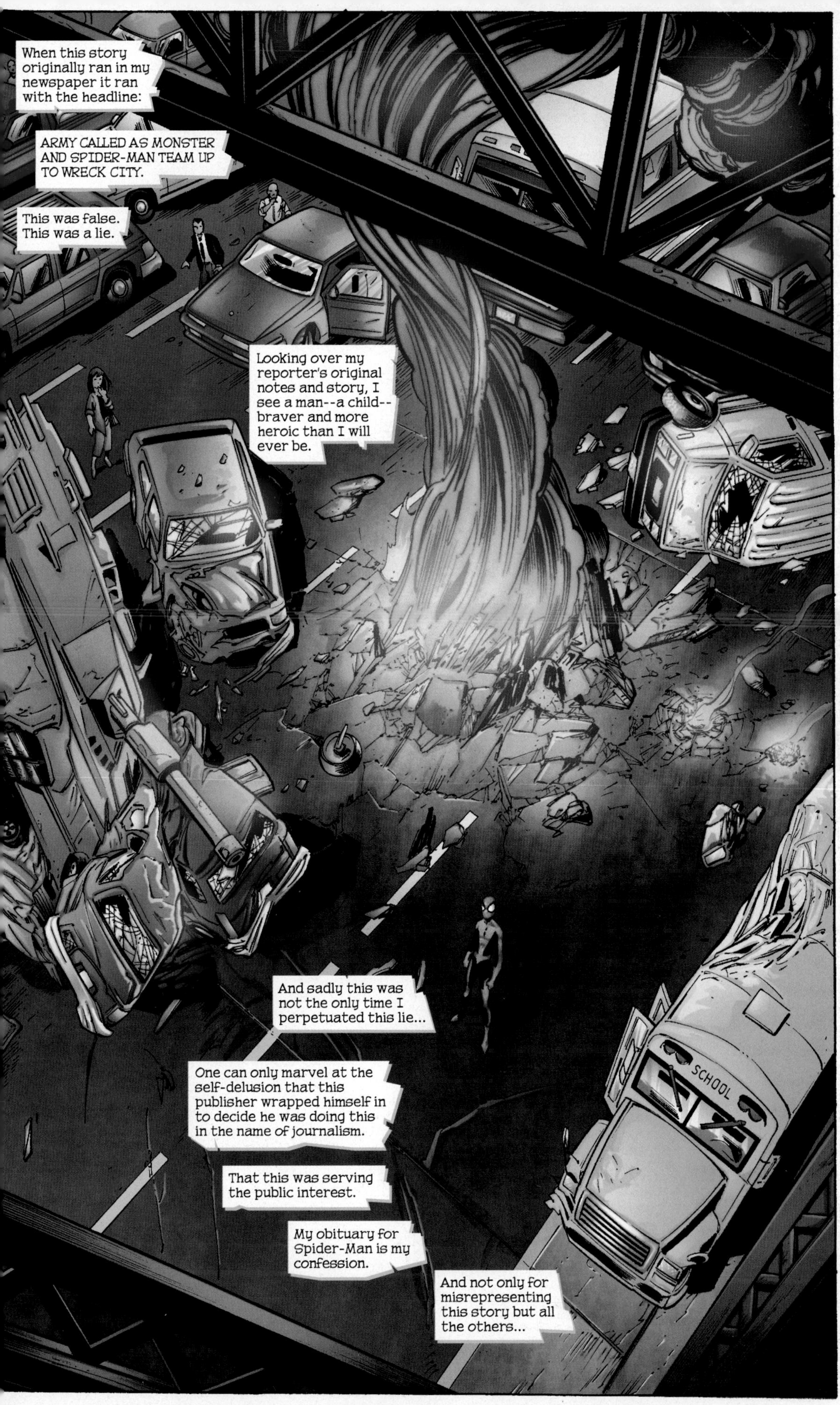
When this story originally ran in my newspaper it ran with the headline:
ARMY CALLED AS MONSTER AND SPIDER-MAN TEAM UP TO WRECK CITY.
This was false. This was a lie.
Looking over my reporter's original notes and story, I see a man--a child--braver and more heroic than I will ever be.
And sadly this was not the only time I perpetuated this lie...
One can only marvel at the self-delusion that this publisher wrapped himself in to decide he was doing this in the name of journalism.
That this was serving the public interest.
My obituary for Spider-Man is my confession.
And not only for misrepresenting this story but all the others...
SCHOOL

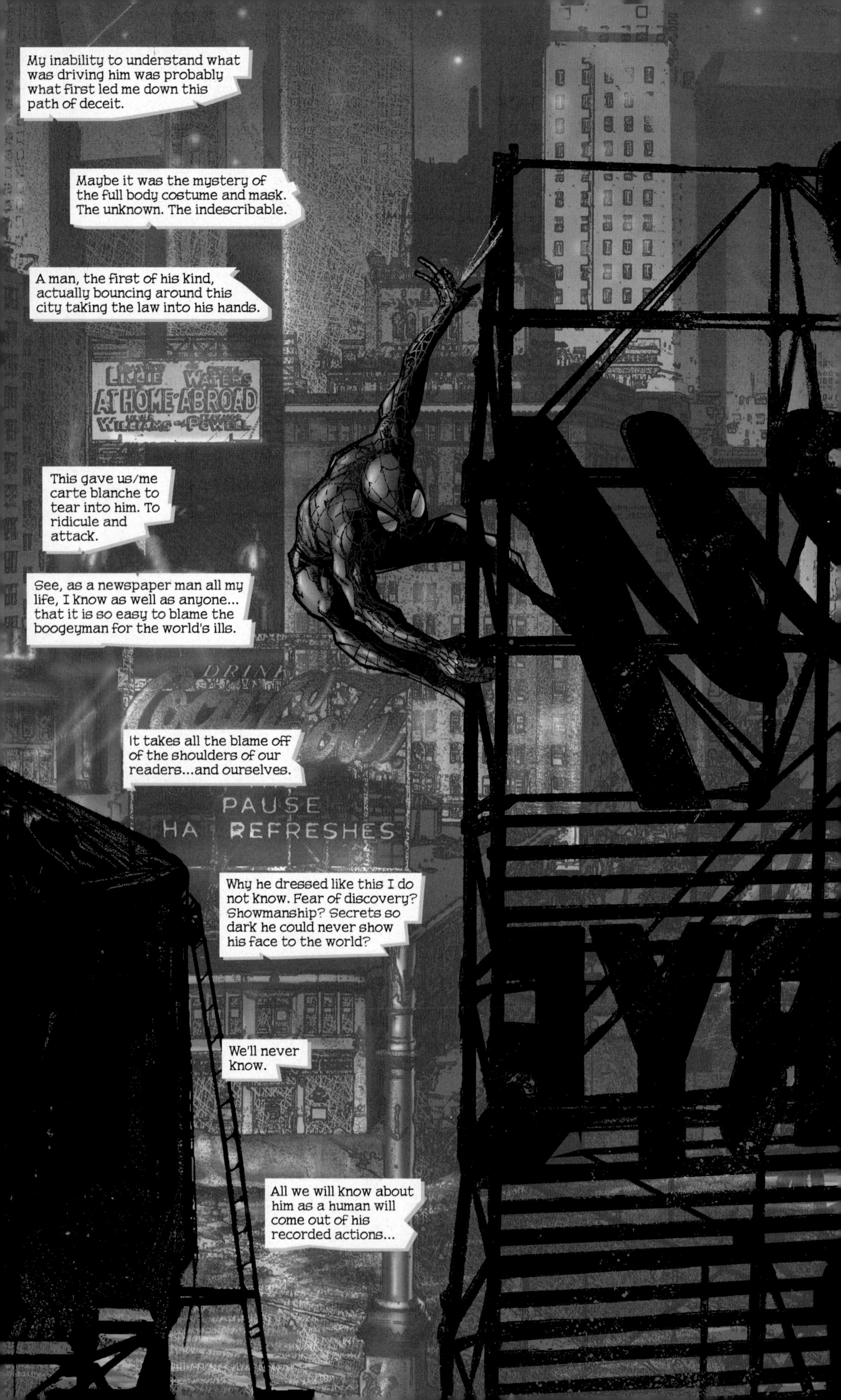

My inability to understand what was driving him was probably what first led me down this path of deceit.
Maybe it was the mystery of the full body costume and mask. The unknown. The indescribable.
A man, the first of his kind, actually bouncing around this city taking the law into his hands.
LILLIE WATERS
AT HOME ABROAD
WILLIAMS POWELL
This gave us/me carte blanche to tear into him. To ridicule and attack.
See, as a newspaper man all my life, I know as well as anyone... that it is so easy to blame the boogeyman for the world's ills.
DRINK
It takes all the blame off of the shoulders of our readers...and ourselves.
PAUSE
HA REFRESHES
Why he dressed like this I do not know. Fear of discovery? Showmanship? Secrets so dark he could never show his face to the world?
We'll never know.
All we will know about him as a human will come out of his recorded actions...

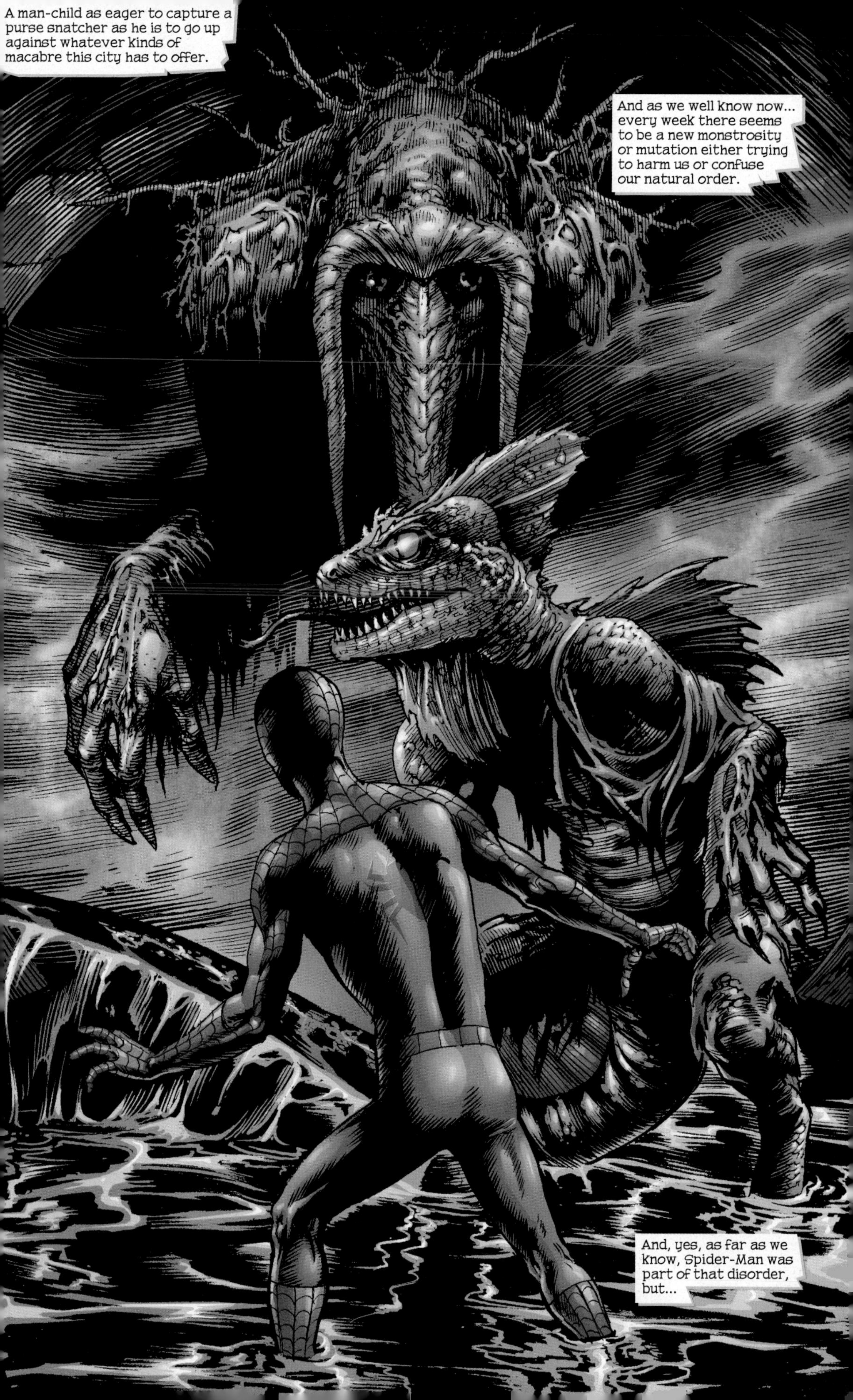
A man-child as eager to capture a purse snatcher as he is to go up against whatever kinds of macabre this city has to offer.
And as we well know now... every week there seems to be a new monstrosity or mutation either trying to harm us or confuse our natural order.
And, yes, as far as we know, Spider-Man was part of that disorder, but...

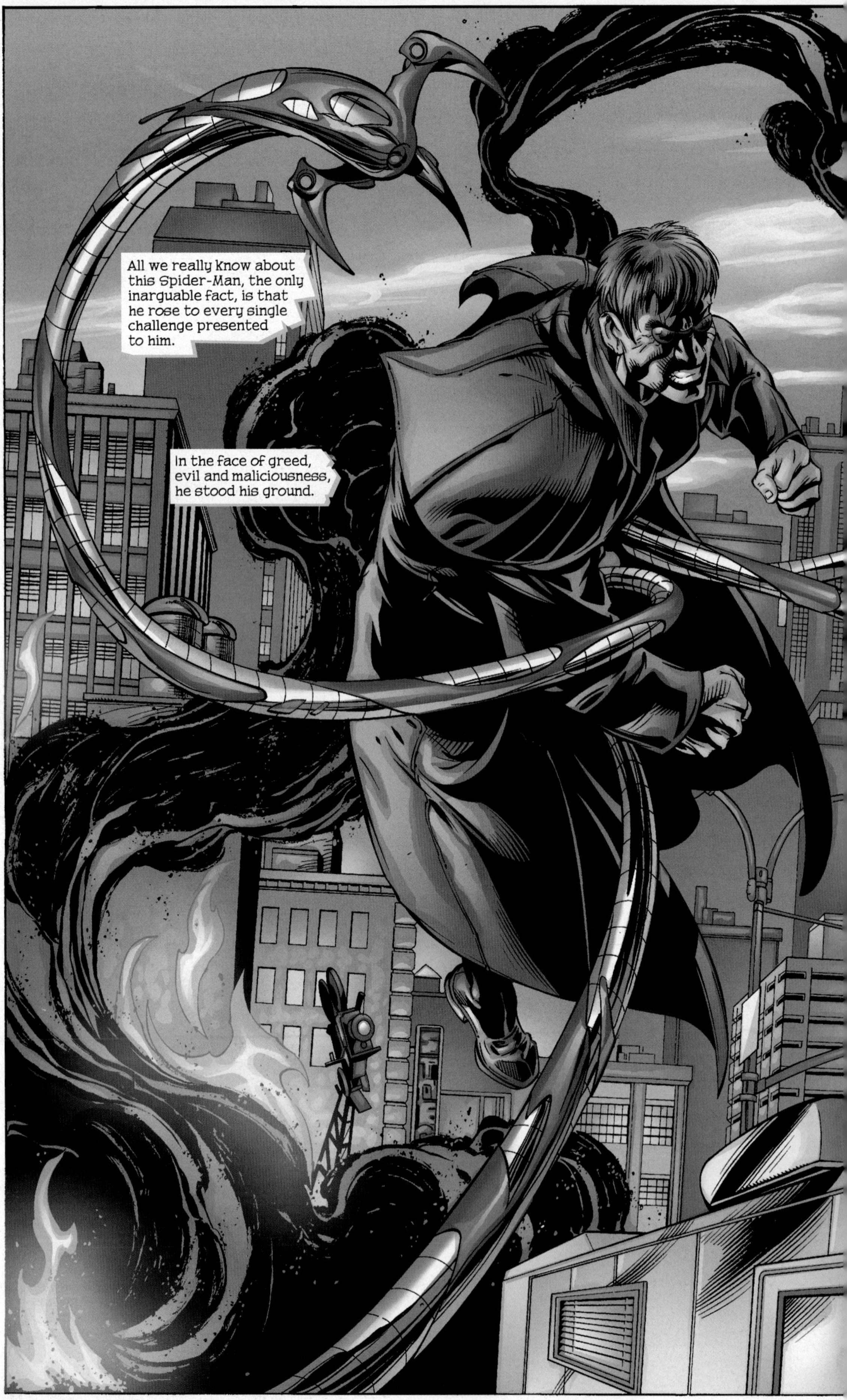
All we really know about this Spider-Man, the only inarguable fact, is that he rose to every single challenge presented to him.
In the face of greed, evil and maliciousness, he stood his ground.

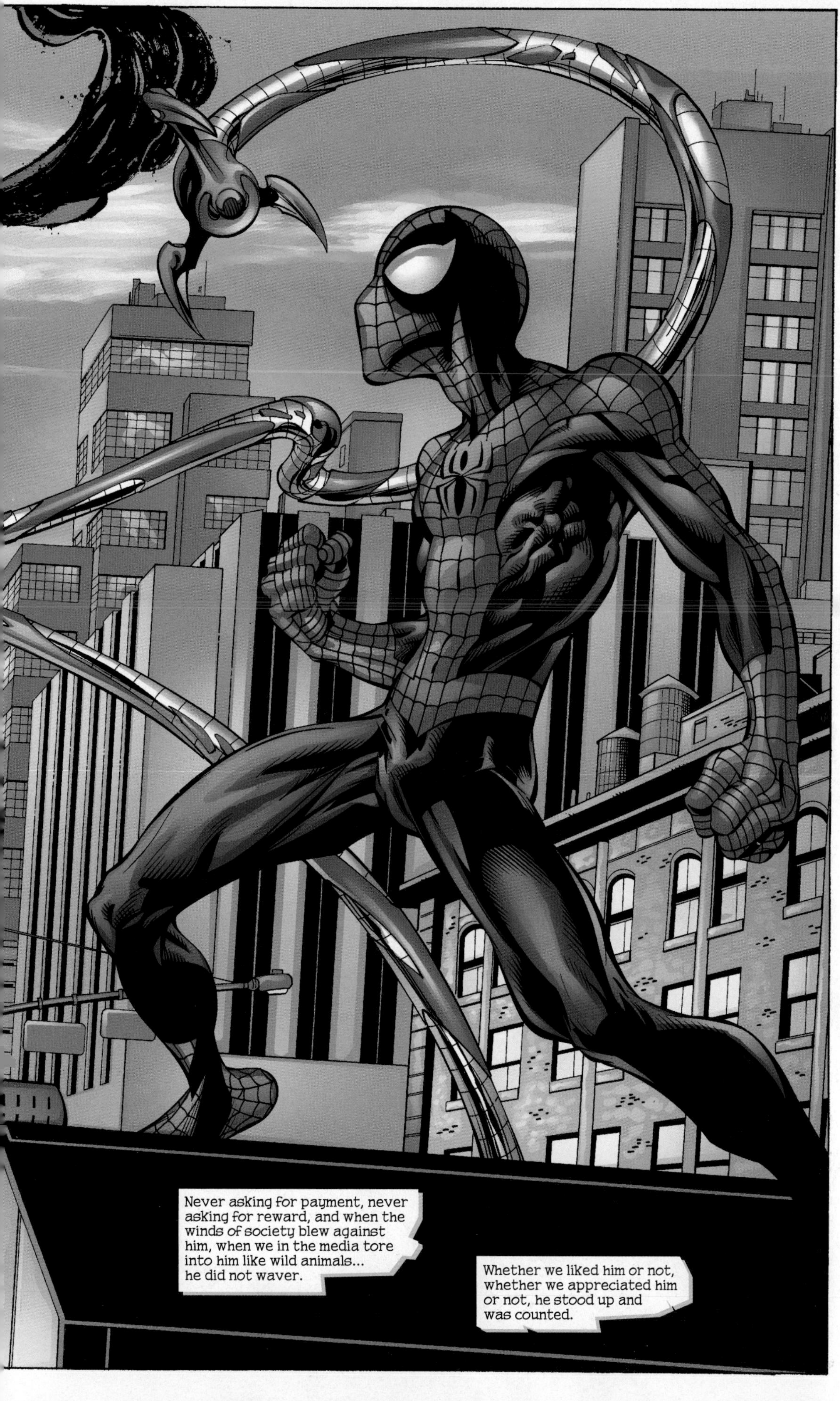
Never asking for payment, never asking for reward, and when the winds of society blew against him, when we in the media tore into him like wild animals... he did not waver.
Whether we liked him or not, whether we appreciated him or not, he stood up and was counted.

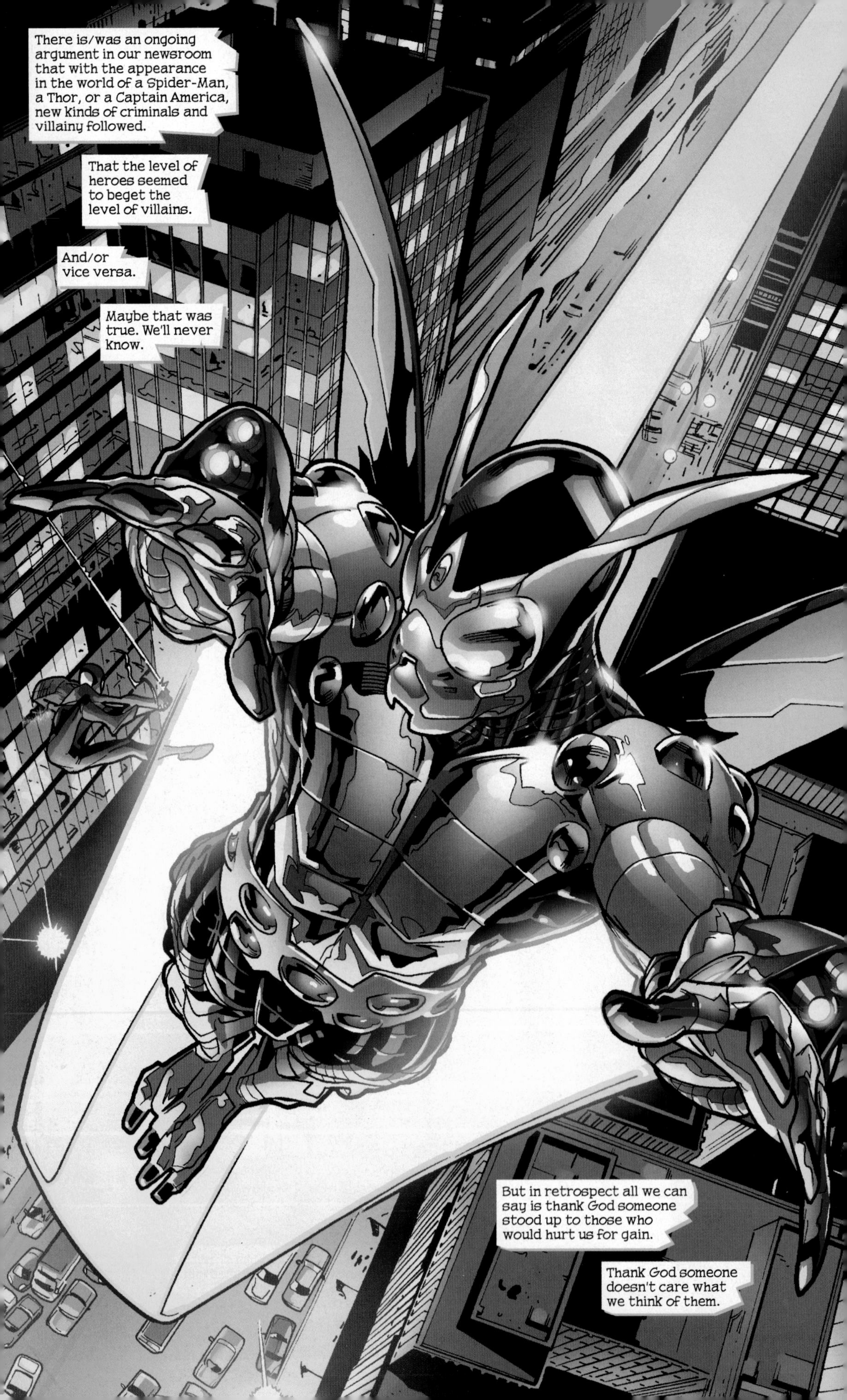
There is/was an ongoing argument in our newsroom that with the appearance in the world of a Spider-Man, a Thor, or a Captain America, new kinds of criminals and villainy followed.
That the level of heroes seemed to beget the level of villains.
And/or vice versa.
Maybe that was true. We'll never know.
But in retrospect all we can say is thank God someone stood up to those who would hurt us for gain.
Thank God someone doesn't care what we think of them.

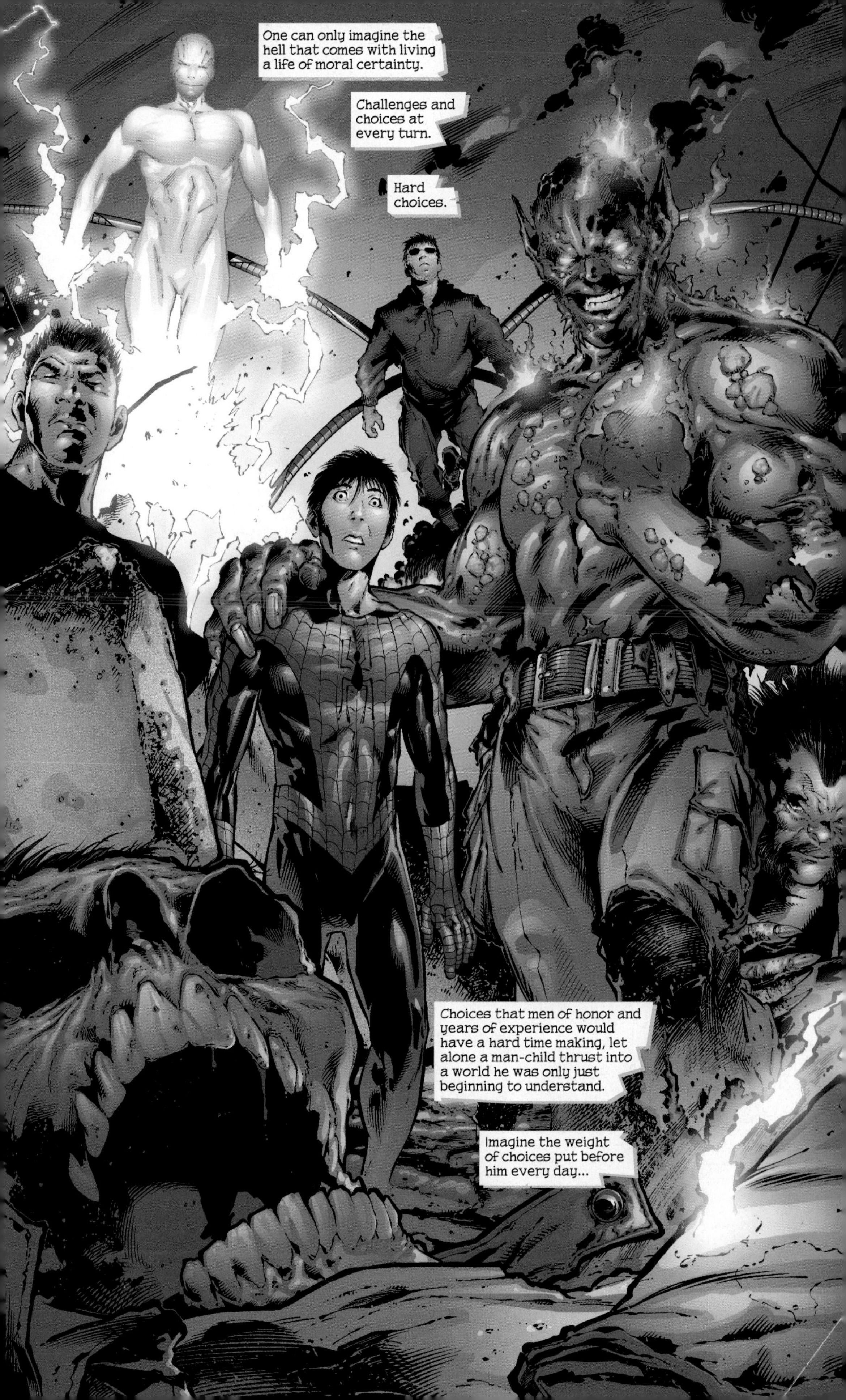
One can only imagine the hell that comes with living a life of moral certainty.
Challenges and choices at every turn.
Hard choices.
Choices that men of honor and years of experience would have a hard time making, let alone a man-child thrust into a world he was only just beginning to understand.
Imagine the weight of choices put before him every day...

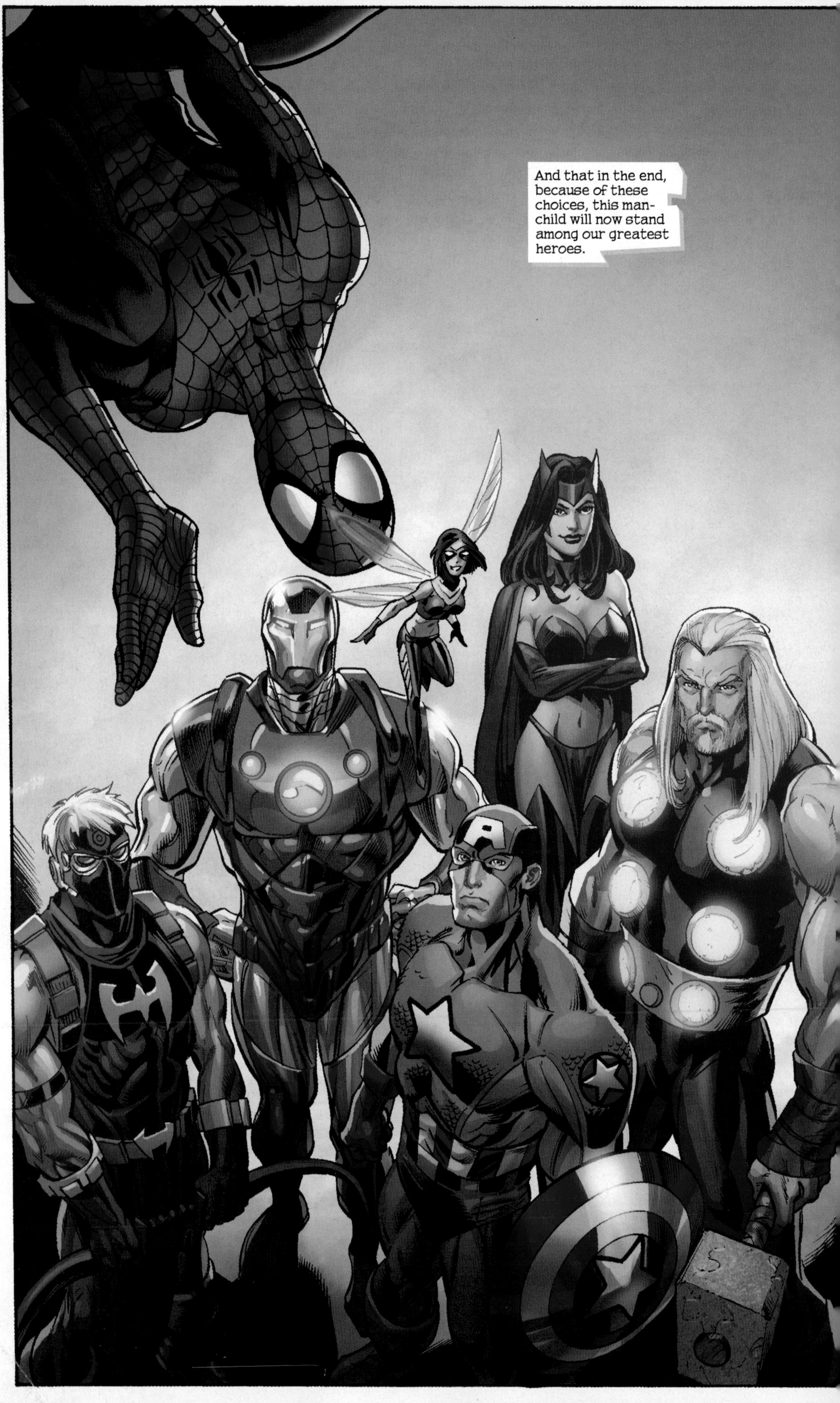
And that in the end, because of these choices, this man-child will now stand among our greatest heroes.

As the days and weeks roll ahead, we will hear many heart-wrenching stories of bravery and selflessness.

This I know.

When this city falls, it rises to even greater glories.

TapTapTapTapTapTapTapTapTapTapTapTapTapTap

For most of us, today, that idea is the only thing keeping us sane.

But what I hope against all hope is that no word I have written against this hero has turned any of you against the idea of helping your fellow man.

TapTapTapTapTapTapTapTapTapTapTapTapTapTap

Let the actions of our fallen hero guide you to do the right thing here in this our most desperate hour.

Do not let one word I have written in the past dissuade you from being the person you need to be today.

TapTapTapTapTapTapTapTapTapTapTapTapTapTap

I may never know who Spider-Man was or why he did what he did.

All I will know is that he would have wanted you to be your best today, New York.

DAILY BUGLE

Do not falter. Do not weaken in the face of challenge.

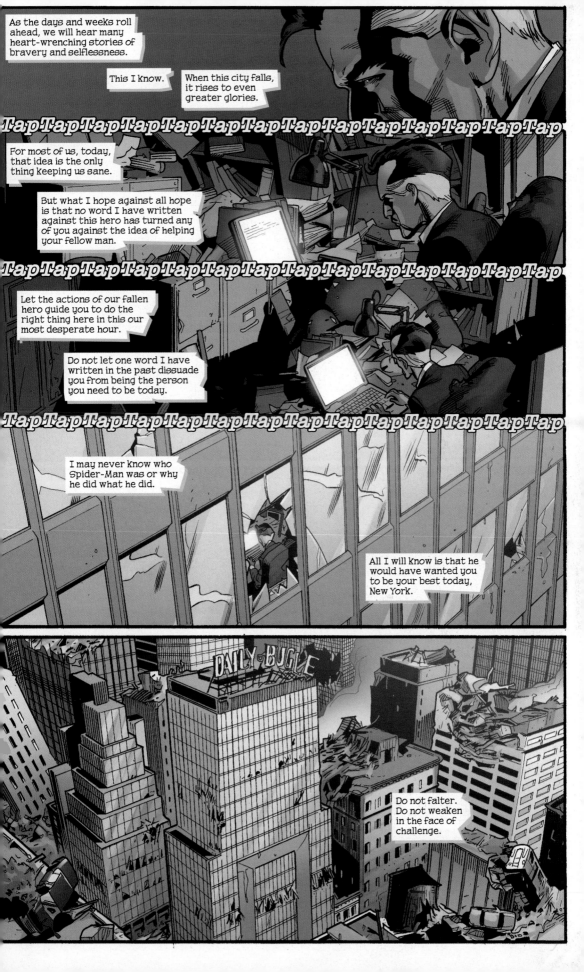

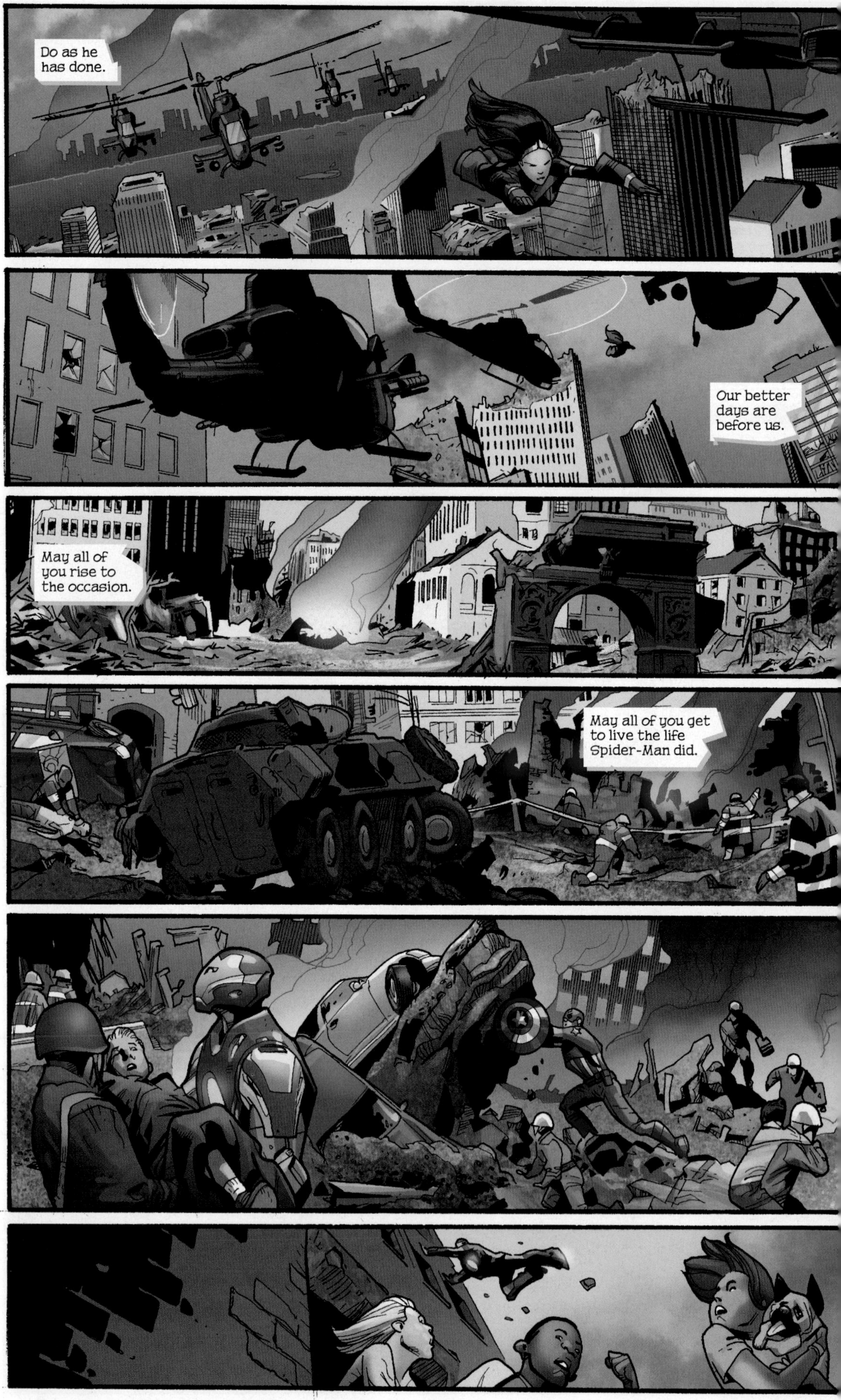
Do as he has done.
Our better days are before us.
May all of you rise to the occasion.
May all of you get to live the life Spider-Man did.

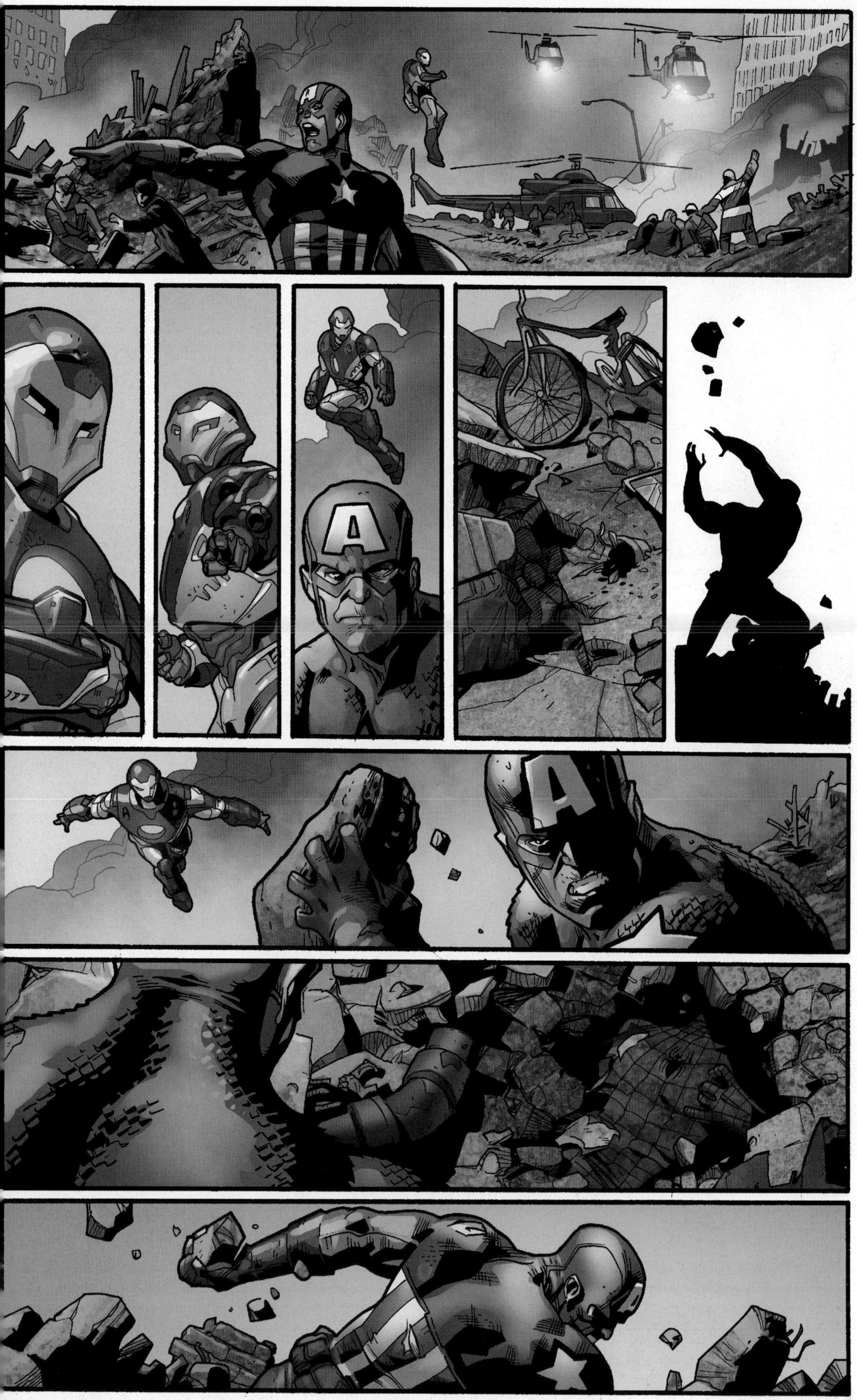

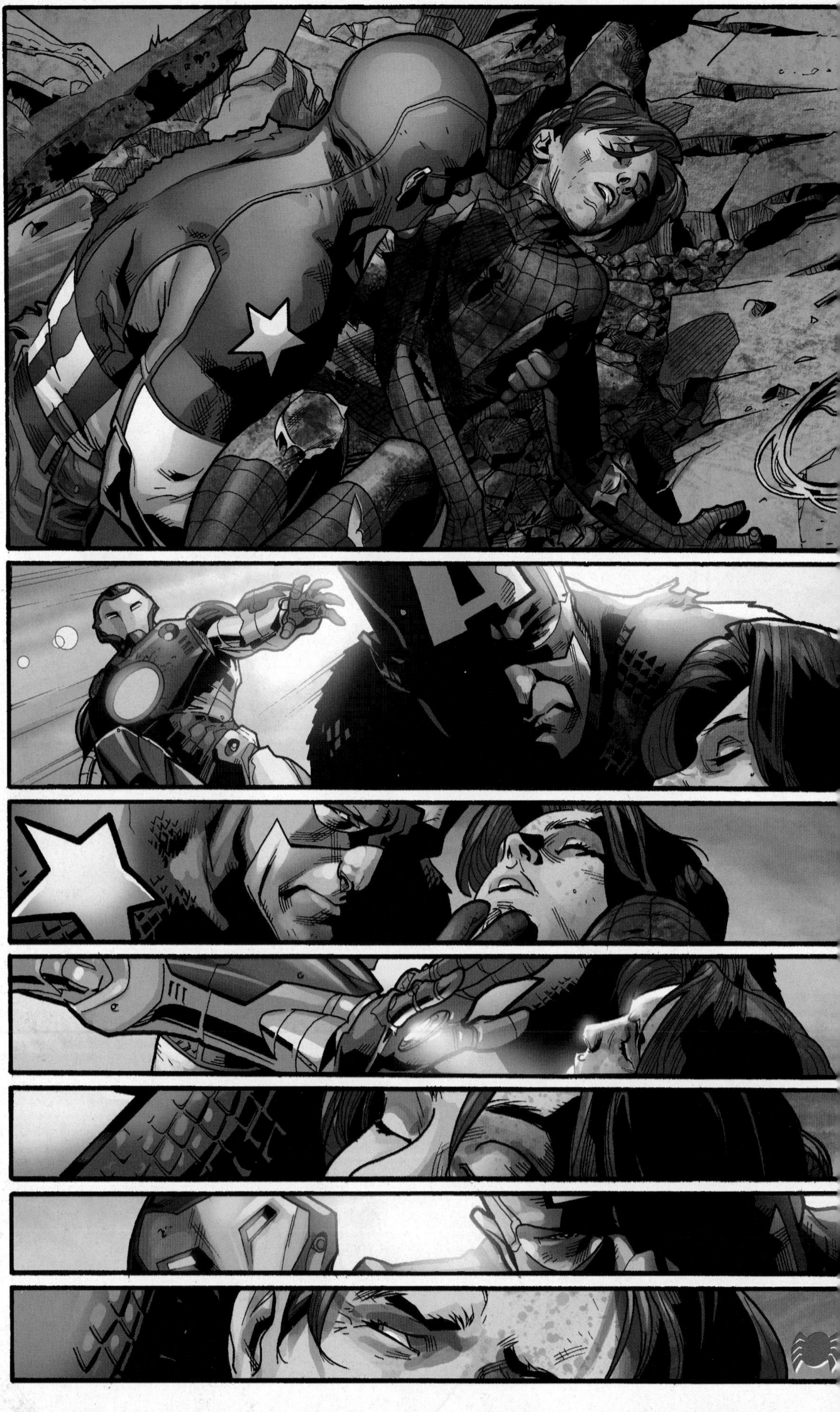

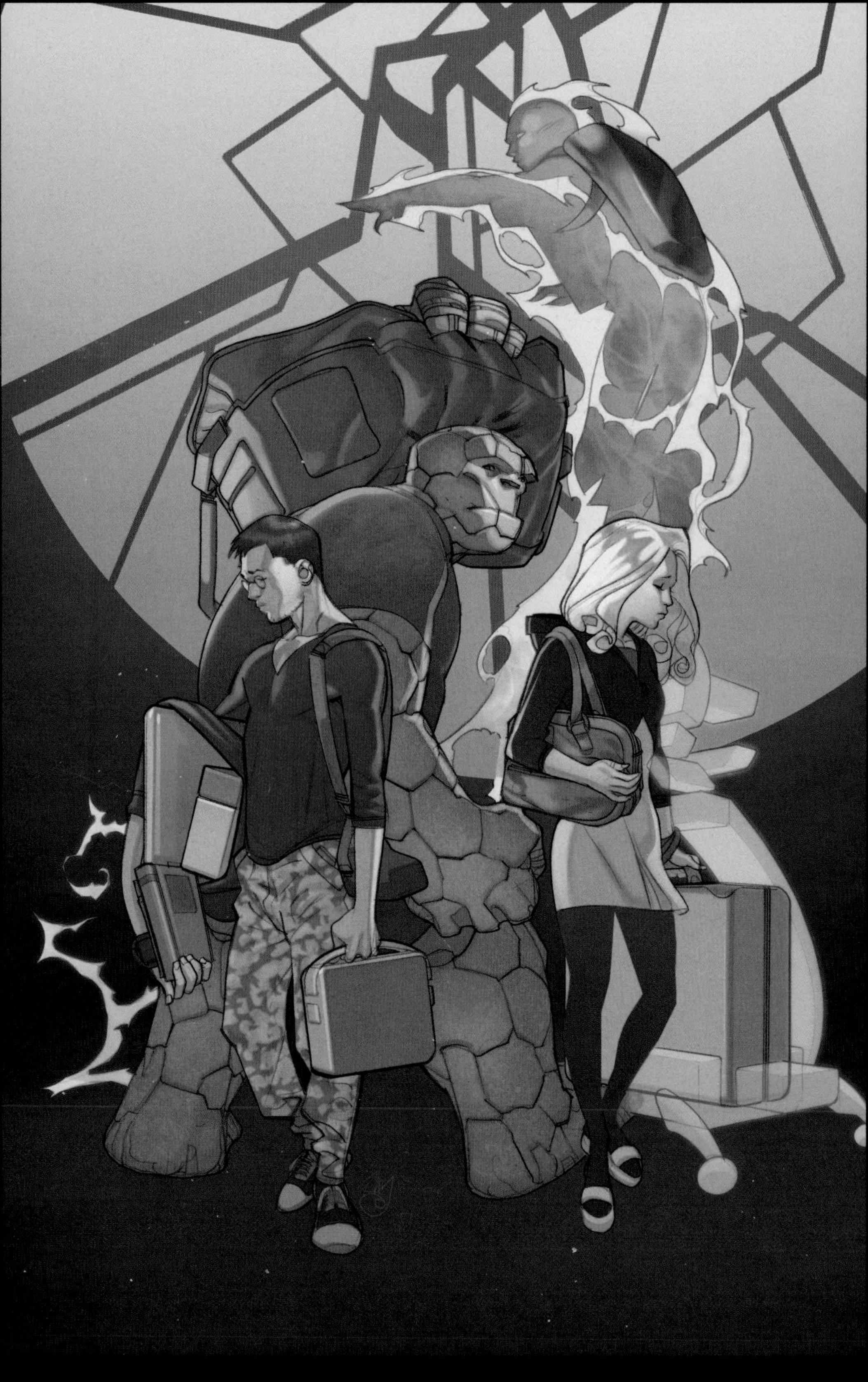

Ultimatum: Fantastic Four Requiem #1

PREVIOUSLY IN ULTIMATE FANTASTIC FOUR:

Doom. Nihil. Namor. Psycho Man. Thanos. The Seven.

Reed thought the Fantastic Four had faced the worst the universe could offer · and after surviving some rocky times with Sue – he finally worked up the nerve to take their relationship to the next level and propose to her. But then the Ultimatum Wave hit New York – leaving behind untold destruction and countless casualties. With Johnny missing and Sue lying near death, a vengeful Reed felt he had no choice but to track down the man he believed responsible for the devastation...

...which left Ben Grimm behind to pick up the pieces. As Sue's condition deteriorated, Ben sought out the help of former Baxter Building professor and FF foe, Dr. Arthur Molekevic, aka the Mole Man. With his help, they brought Sue back from the brink of death – only to discover that the nanobots in her system had been placed there by Reed. Seeking a way to amplify the nanobots' signal in order to track down Johnny and Reed, they descend to the ruins of Atlantis in search of the Equinox Antenna – only to be ambushed by the vengeful denizens of the sunken city. But nothing can stop Sue's quest to find her brother – not even the discovery that he's been trapped in a dark demon dimension...

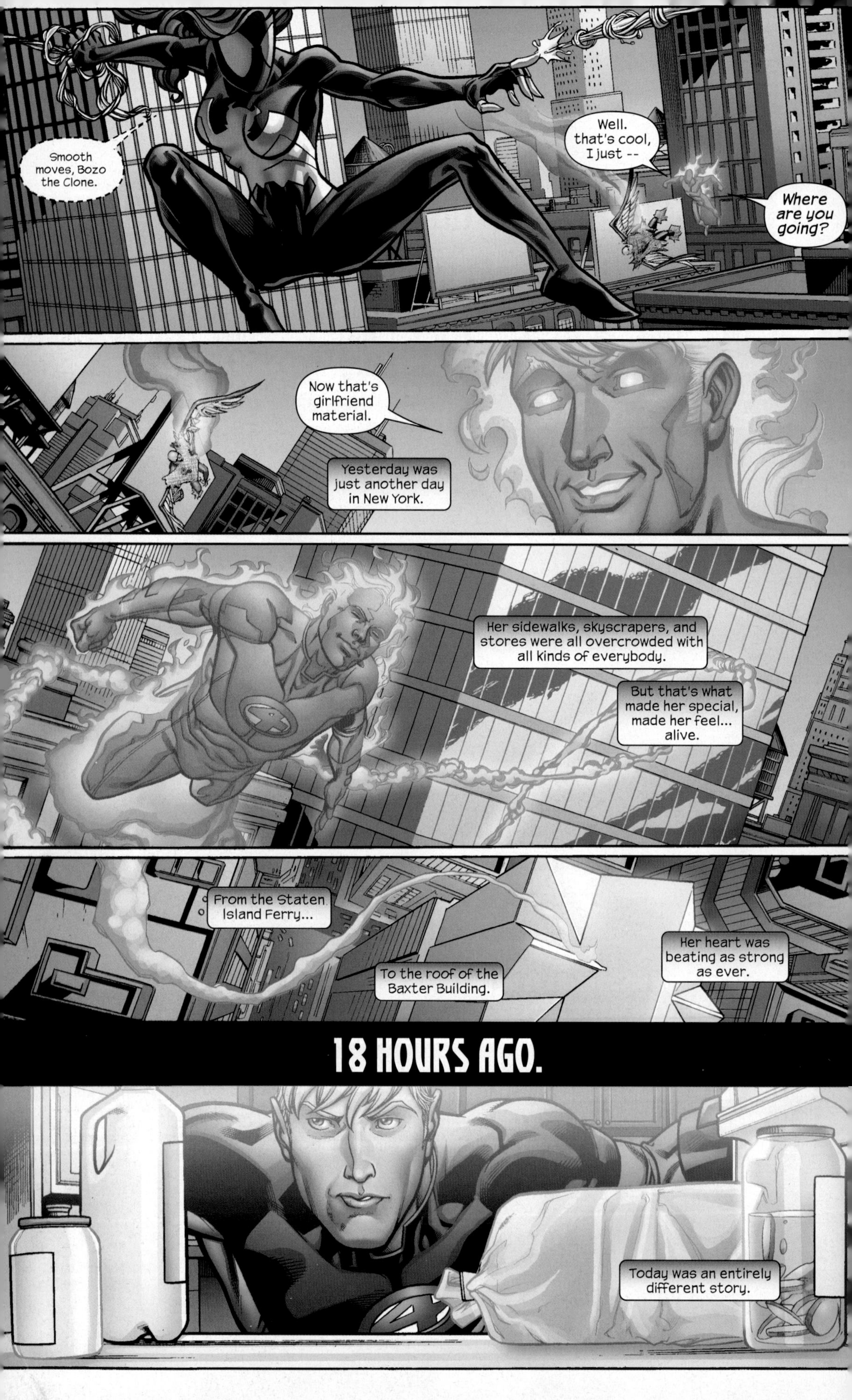
Smooth moves, Bozo the Clone.
Well. that's cool, I just --
Where are you going?
Now that's girlfriend material.
Yesterday was just another day in New York.
Her sidewalks, skyscrapers, and stores were all overcrowded with all kinds of everybody.
But that's what made her special, made her feel... alive.
From the Staten Island Ferry...
To the roof of the Baxter Building.
Her heart was beating as strong as ever.
18 HOURS AGO.
Today was an entirely different story.

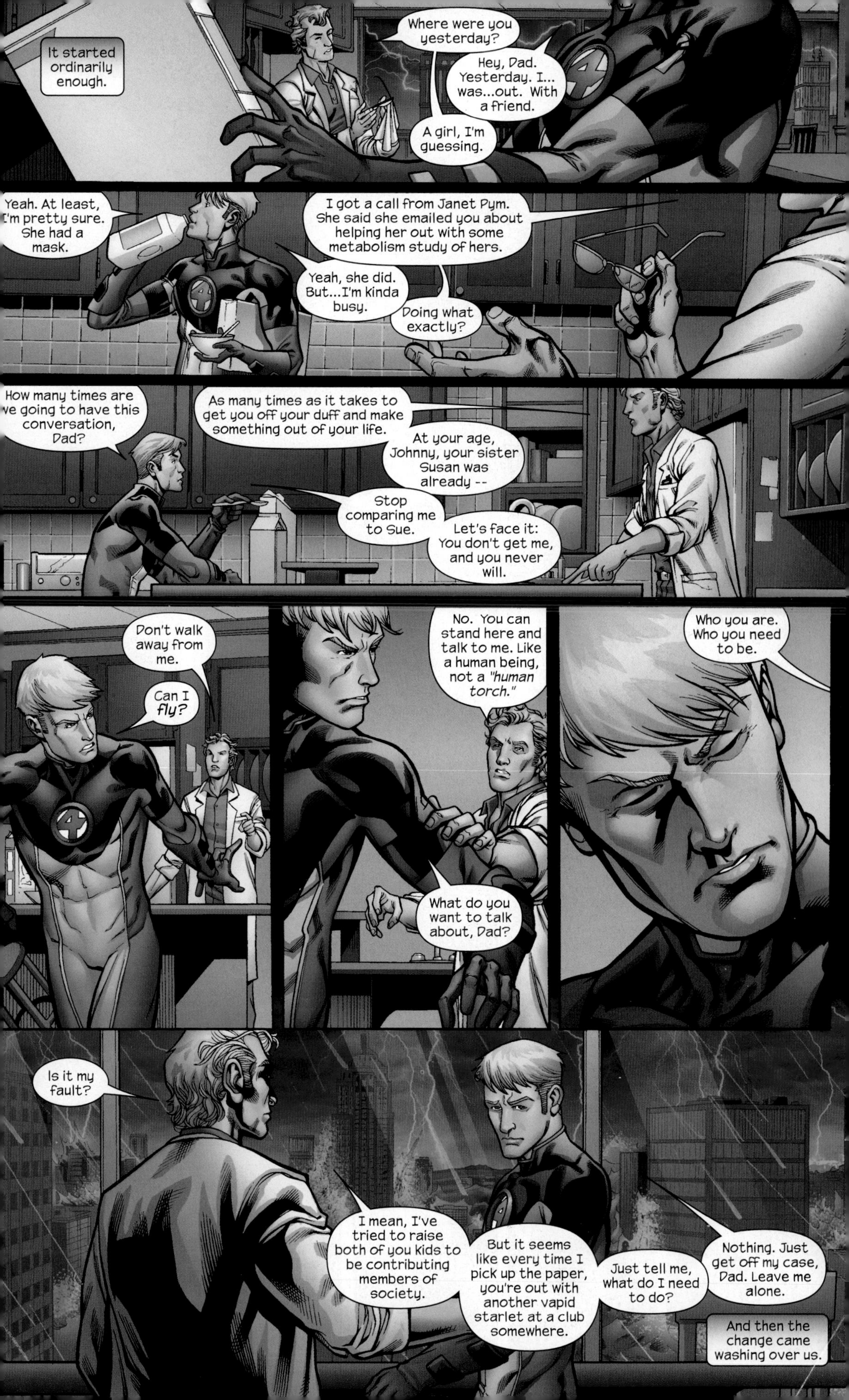

It started ordinarily enough.
Where were you yesterday?
Hey, Dad. Yesterday. I... was...out. With a friend.
A girl, I'm guessing.
Yeah. At least, I'm pretty sure. She had a mask.
I got a call from Janet Pym. She said she emailed you about helping her out with some metabolism study of hers.
Yeah, she did. But...I'm kinda busy.
Doing what exactly?
How many times are we going to have this conversation, Dad?
As many times as it takes to get you off your duff and make something out of your life.
At your age, Johnny, your sister Susan was already --
Stop comparing me to Sue.
Let's face it: You don't get me, and you never will.
Don't walk away from me.
Can I *fly?*
No. You can stand here and talk to me. Like a human being, not a *"human torch."*
What do you want to talk about, Dad?
Who you are. Who you need to be.
Is it my fault?
I mean, I've tried to raise both of you kids to be contributing members of society.
But it seems like every time I pick up the paper, you're out with another vapid starlet at a club somewhere.
Just tell me, what do I need to do?
Nothing. Just get off my case, Dad. Leave me alone.
And then the change came washing over us.

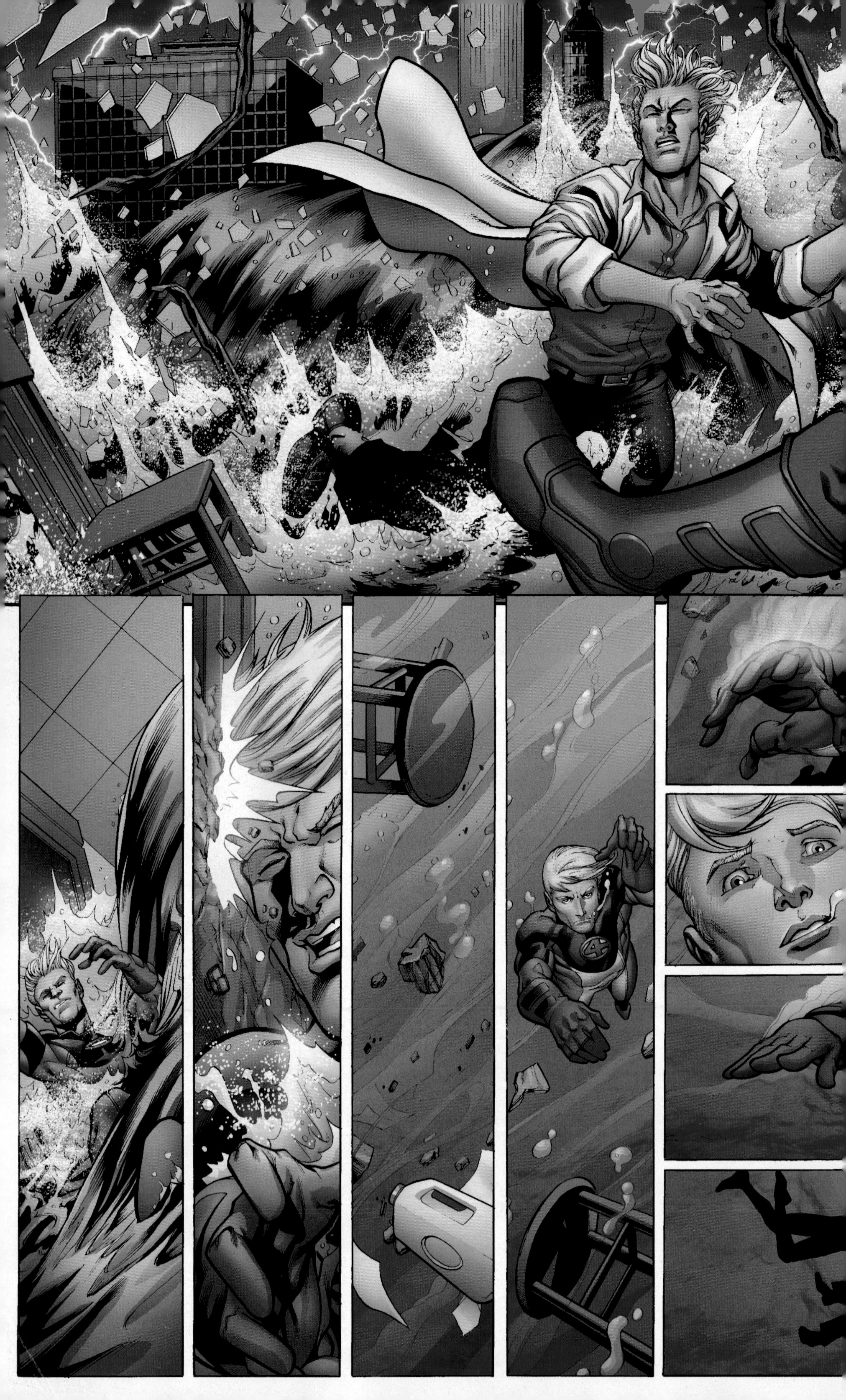

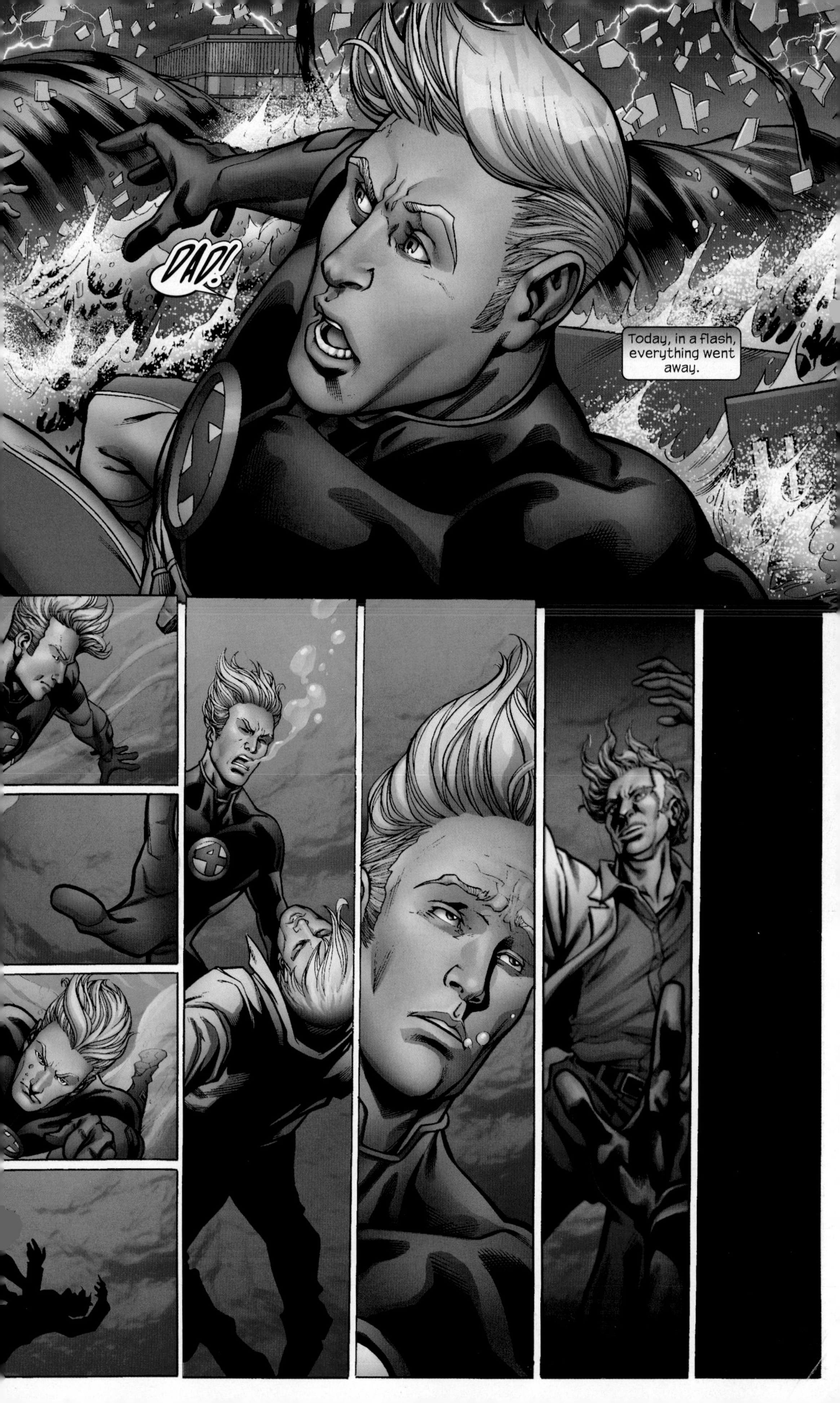
DAD!
Today, in a flash, everything went away.

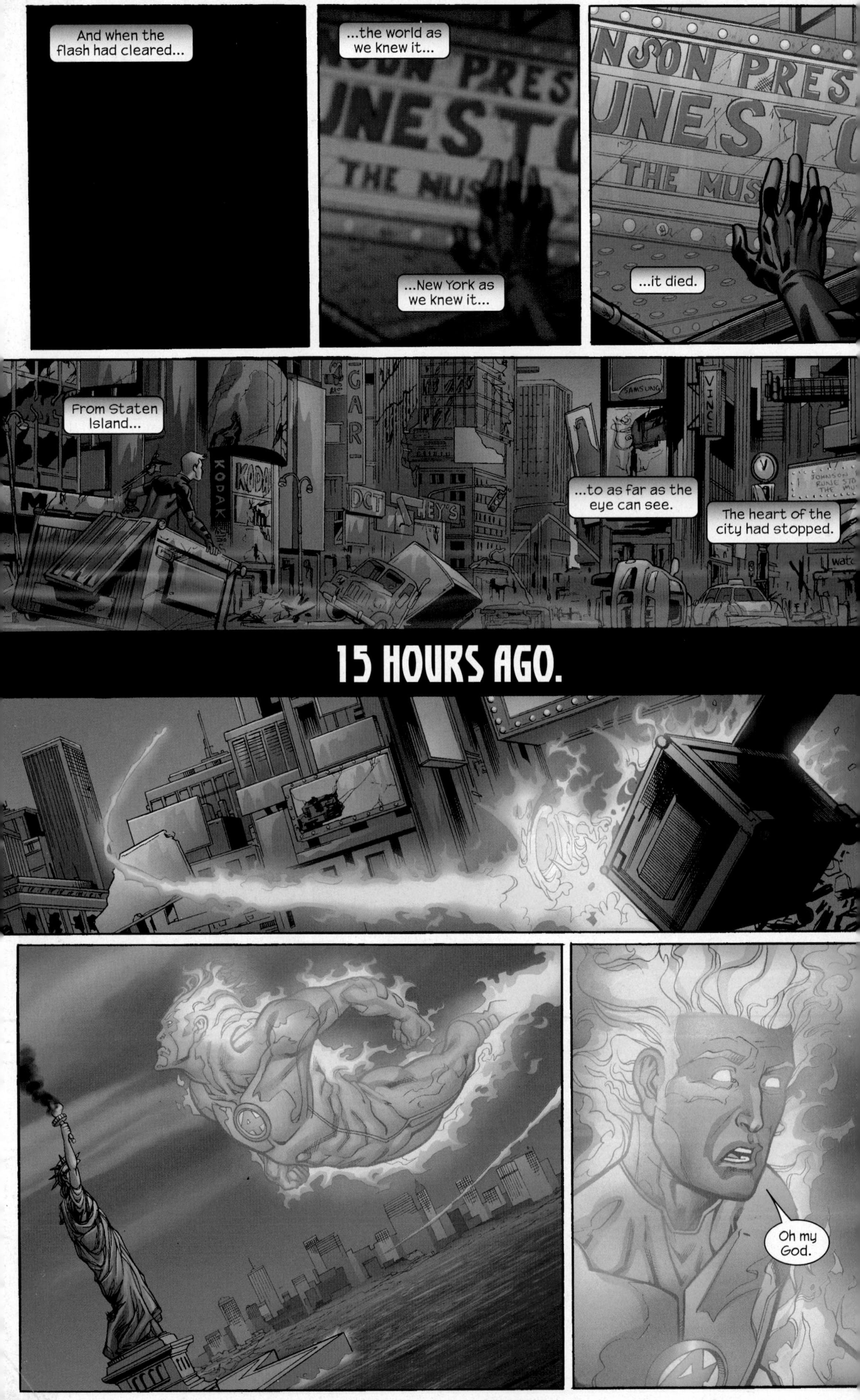
And when the flash had cleared...
...the world as we knew it...
...New York as we knew it...
...it died.
From Staten Island...
...to as far as the eye can see.
The heart of the city had stopped.
15 HOURS AGO.
Oh my God.

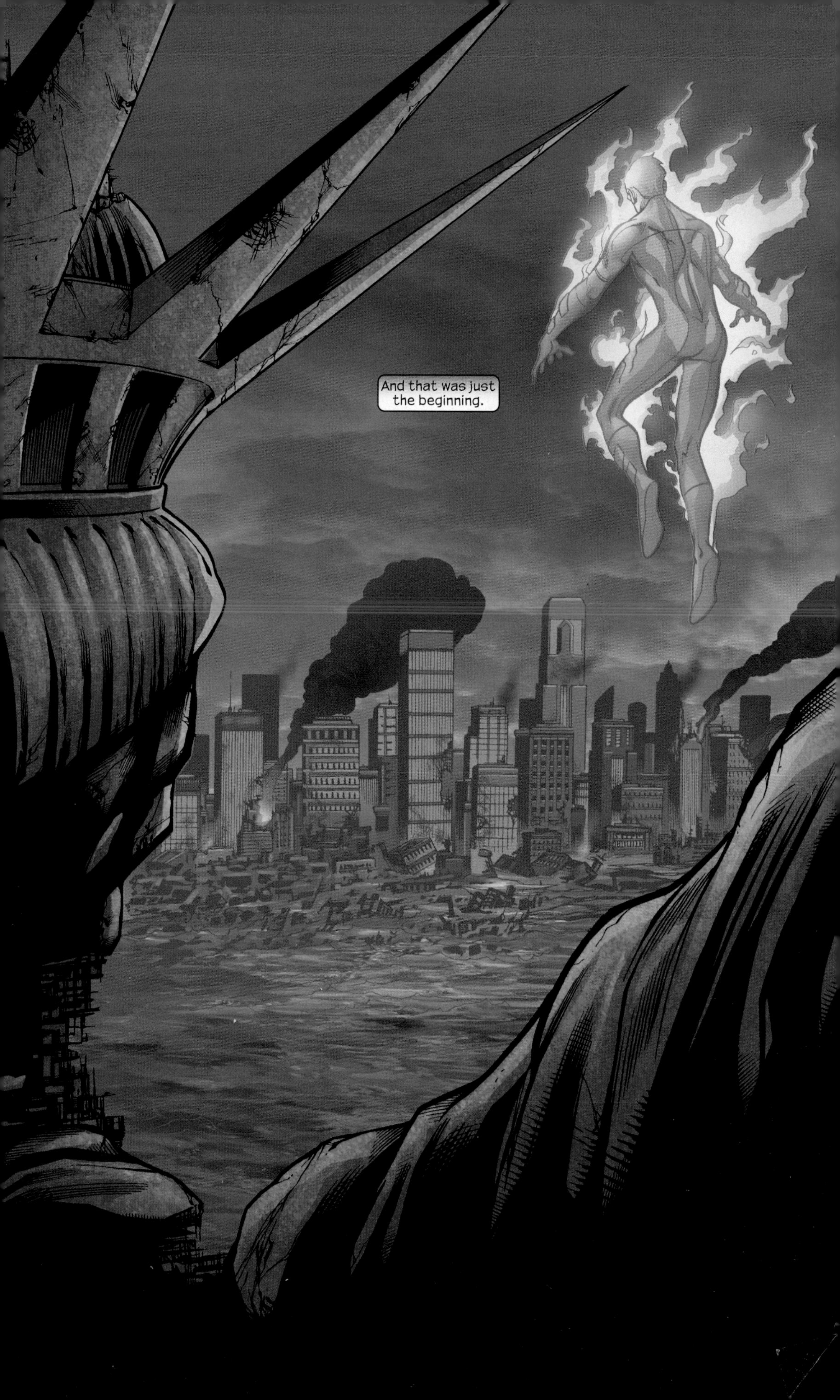
And that was just the beginning.

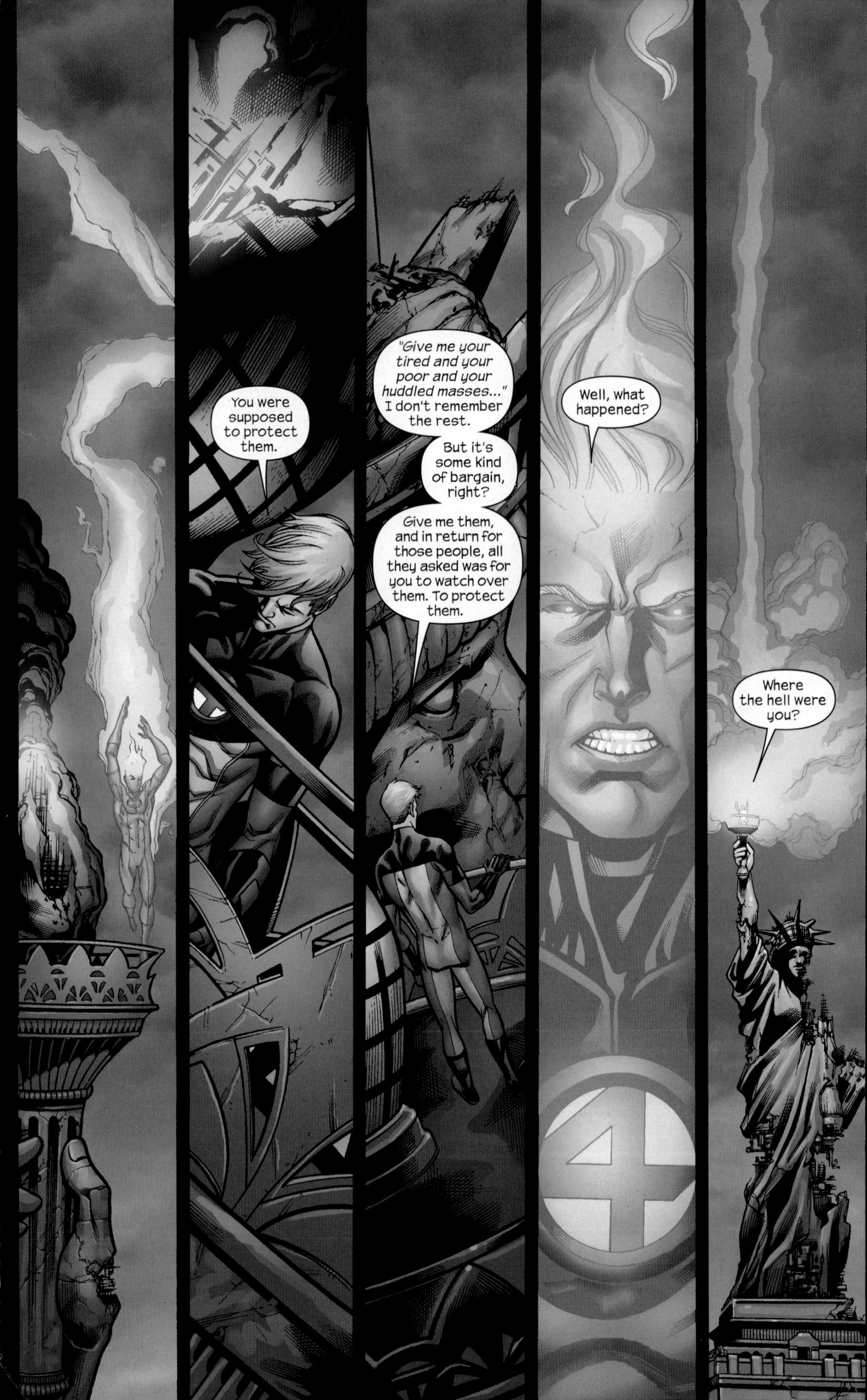
You were supposed to protect them.
"Give me your tired and your poor and your huddled masses..." I don't remember the rest.
But it's some kind of bargain, right?
Give me them, and in return for those people, all they asked was for you to watch over them. To protect them.
Well, what happened?
Where the hell were you?

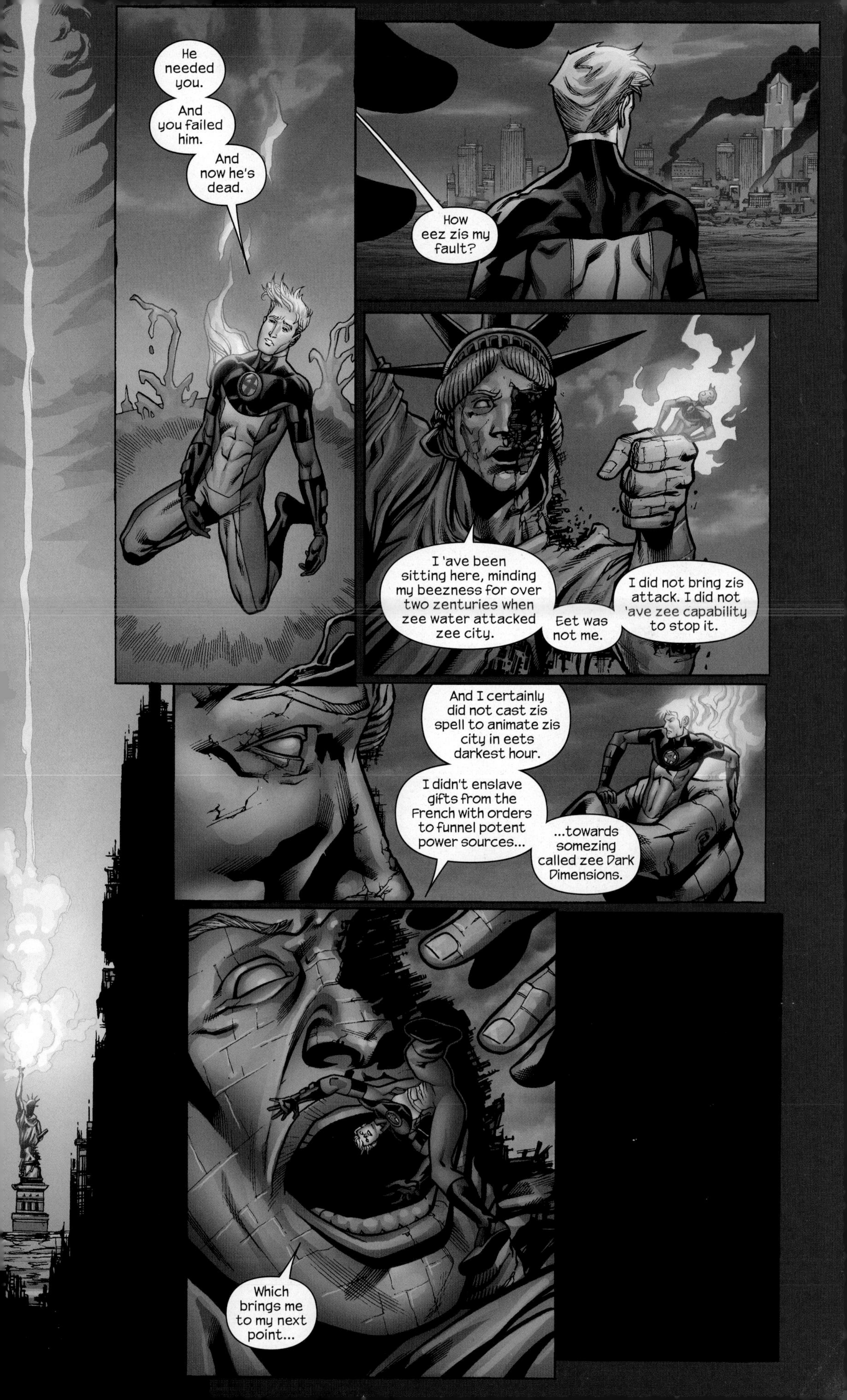
He needed you.
And you failed him.
And now he's dead.
How eez zis my fault?
I 'ave been sitting here, minding my beezness for over two zenturies when zee water attacked zee city.
Eet was not me.
I did not bring zis attack. I did not 'ave zee capability to stop it.
And I certainly did not cast zis spell to animate zis city in eets darkest hour.
I didn't enslave gifts from the French with orders to funnel potent power sources...
...towards somezing called zee Dark Dimensions.
Which brings me to my next point...

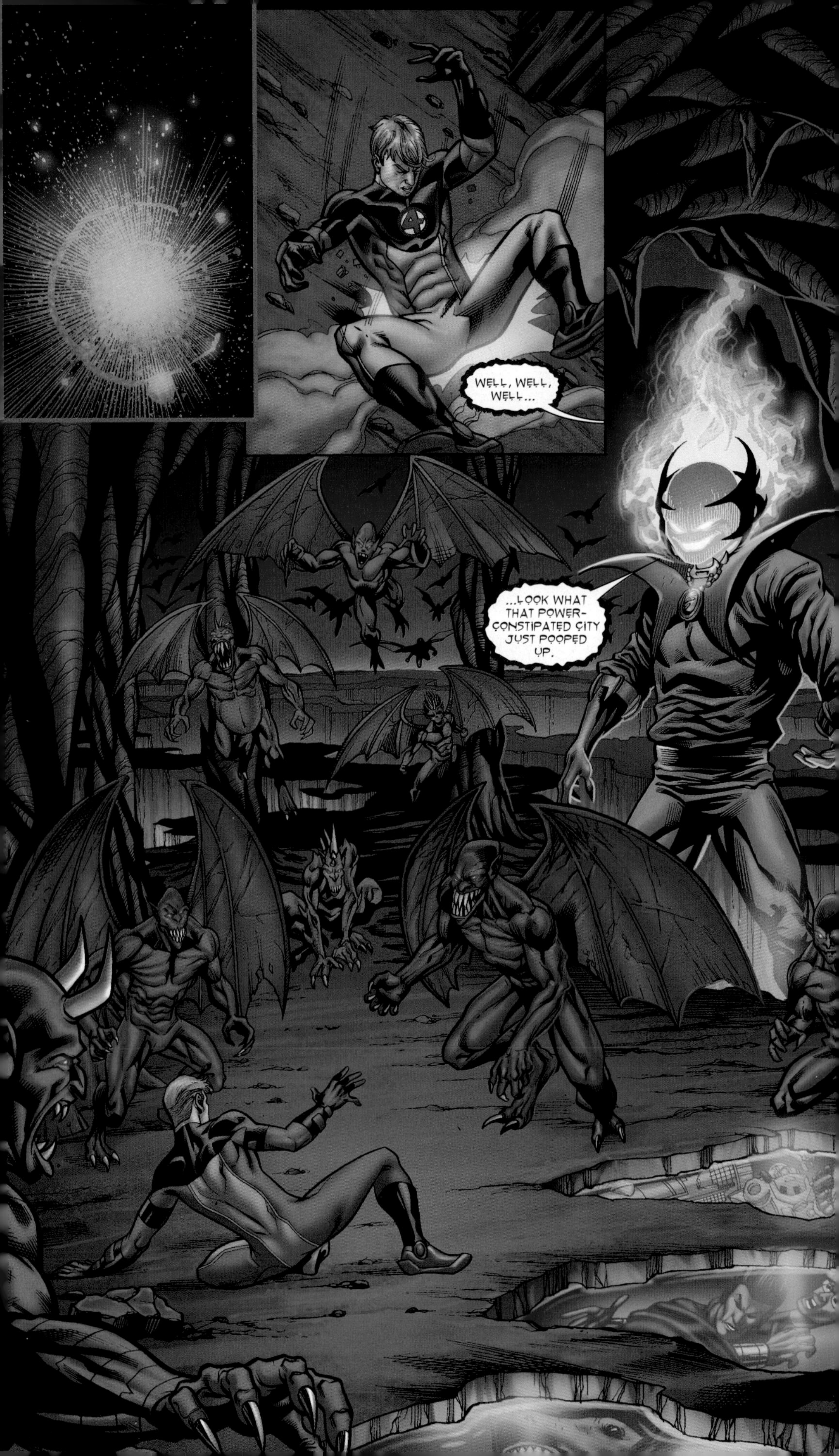
WELL, WELL, WELL...
...LOOK WHAT THAT POWER-CONSTIPATED CITY JUST POOPED UP.

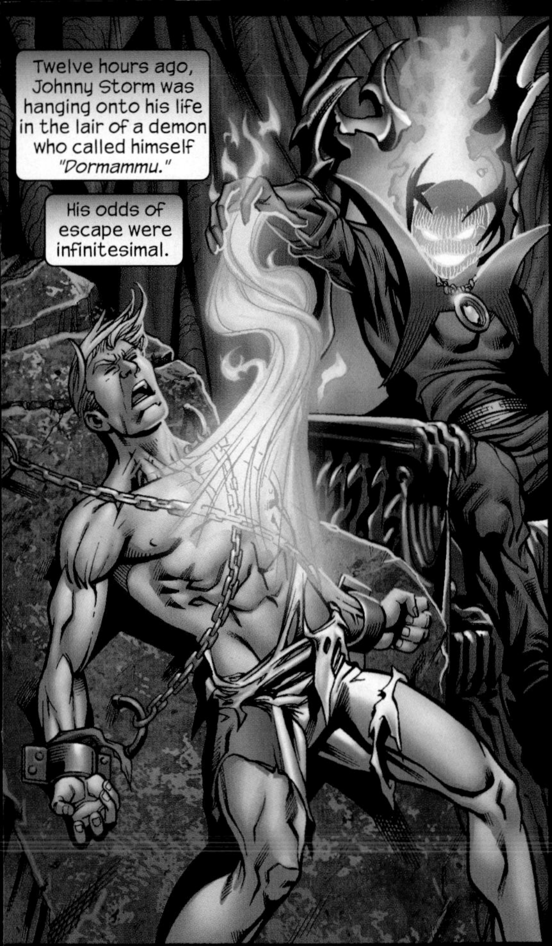
Twelve hours ago, Johnny Storm was hanging onto his life in the lair of a demon who called himself "Dormammu."
His odds of escape were infinitesimal.

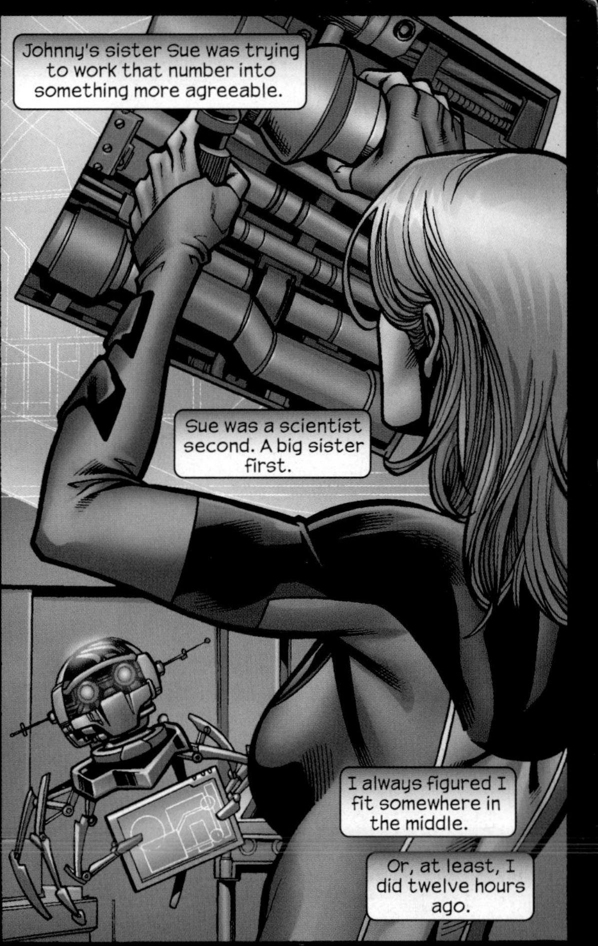
Johnny's sister Sue was trying to work that number into something more agreeable.
Sue was a scientist second. A big sister first.
I always figured I fit somewhere in the middle.
Or, at least, I did twelve hours ago.

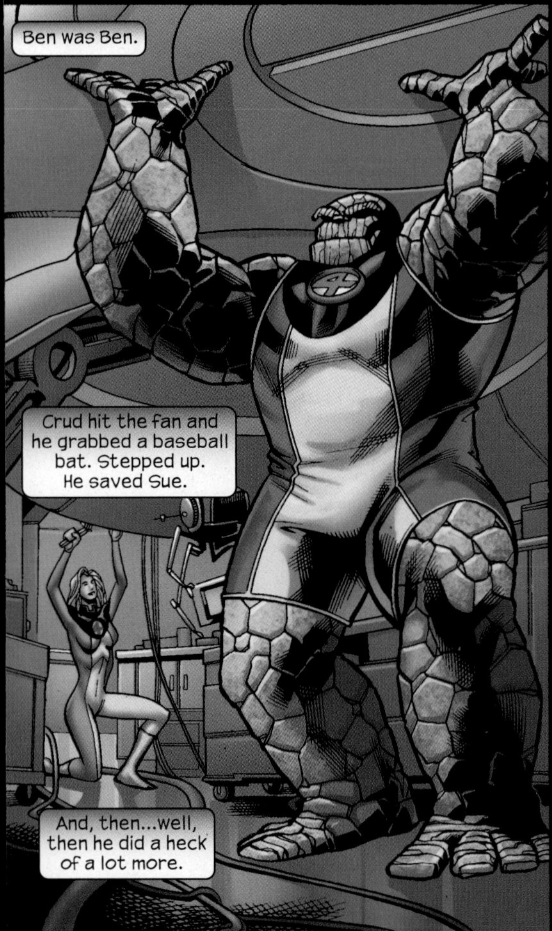
Ben was Ben.
Crud hit the fan and he grabbed a baseball bat. Stepped up. He saved Sue.
And, then...well, then he did a heck of a lot more.

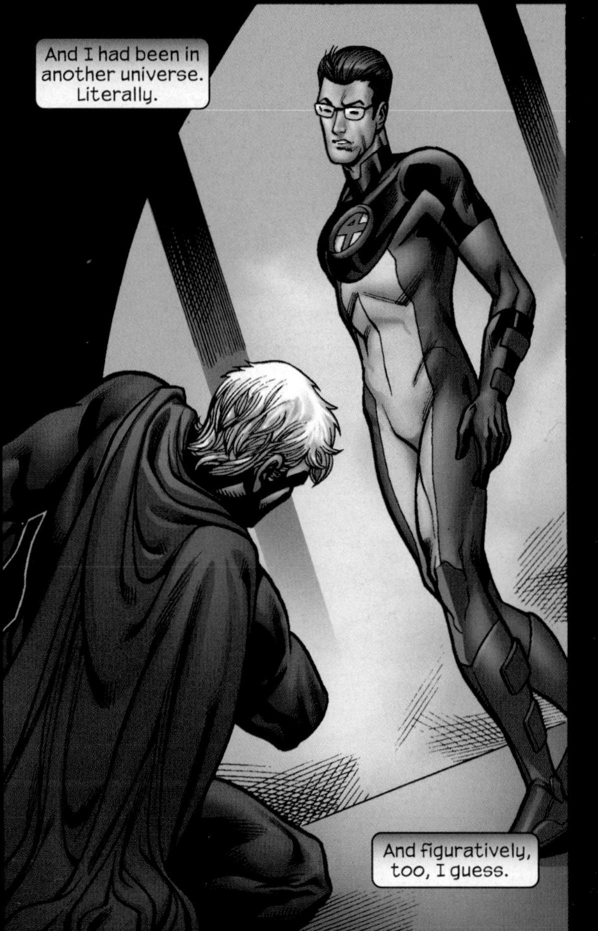
And I had been in another universe. Literally.
And figuratively, too, I guess.

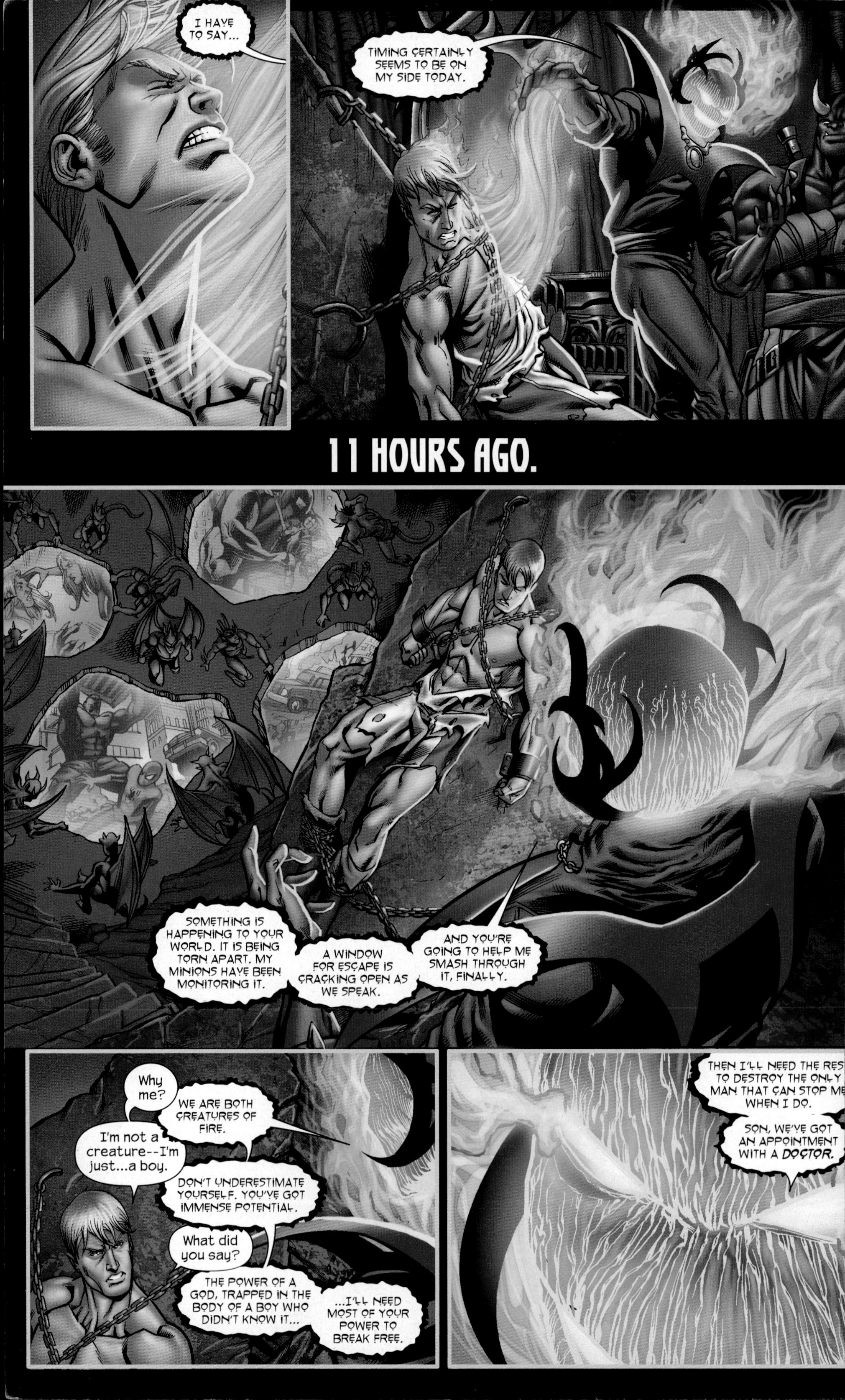

I HAVE TO SAY...
TIMING CERTAINLY SEEMS TO BE ON MY SIDE TODAY.
11 HOURS AGO.
SOMETHING IS HAPPENING TO YOUR WORLD. IT IS BEING TORN APART. MY MINIONS HAVE BEEN MONITORING IT.
A WINDOW FOR ESCAPE IS CRACKING OPEN AS WE SPEAK.
AND YOU'RE GOING TO HELP ME SMASH THROUGH IT, FINALLY.
Why me?
WE ARE BOTH CREATURES OF FIRE.
I'm not a creature--I'm just...a boy.
DON'T UNDERESTIMATE YOURSELF. YOU'VE GOT IMMENSE POTENTIAL.
What did you say?
THE POWER OF A GOD, TRAPPED IN THE BODY OF A BOY WHO DIDN'T KNOW IT...
...I'LL NEED MOST OF YOUR POWER TO BREAK FREE.
THEN I'LL NEED THE REST TO DESTROY THE ONLY MAN THAT CAN STOP ME WHEN I DO.
SON, WE'VE GOT AN APPOINTMENT WITH A *DOCTOR*.

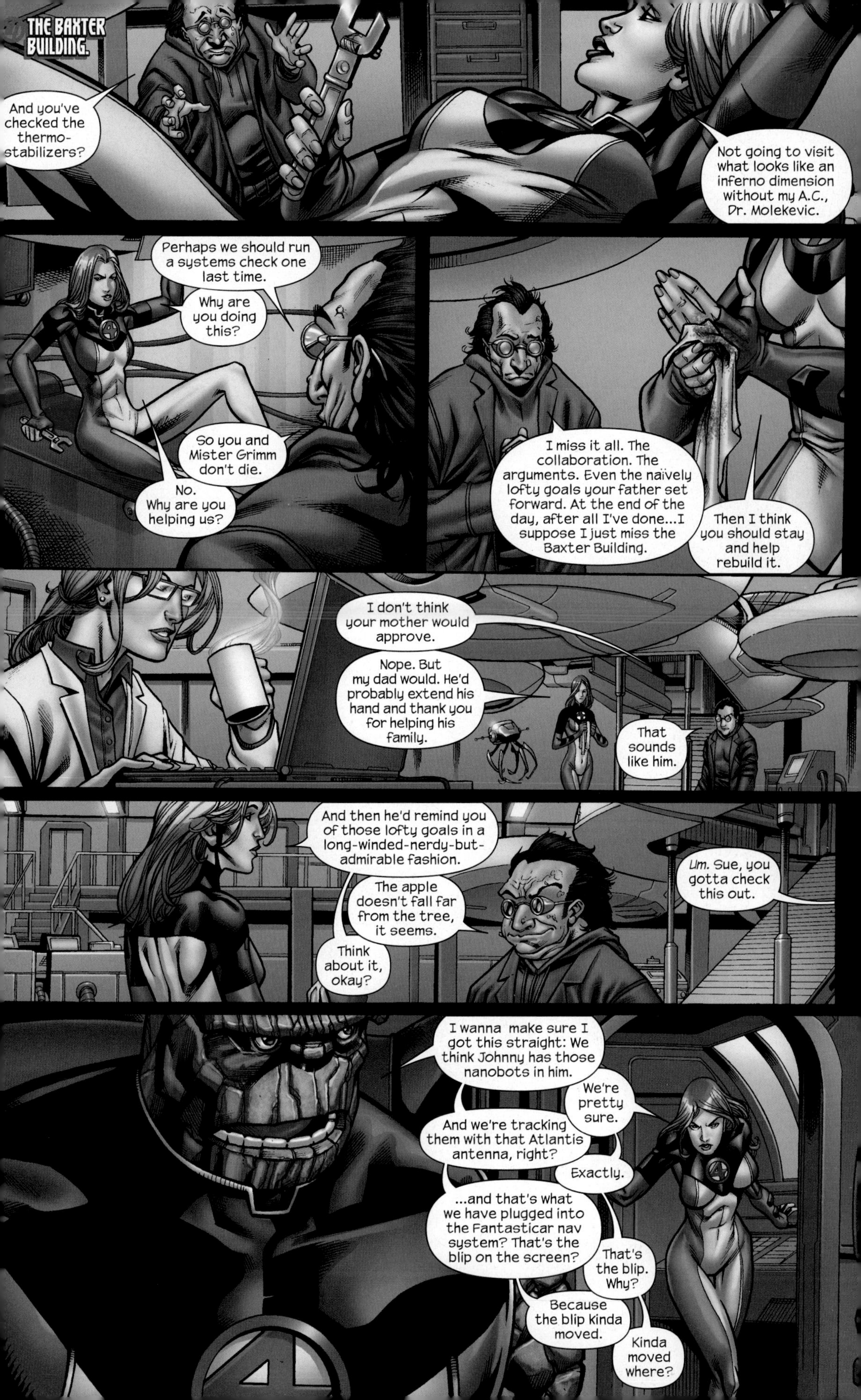
THE BAXTER BUILDING.
And you've checked the thermo-stabilizers?
Not going to visit what looks like an inferno dimension without my A.C., Dr. Molekevic.
Perhaps we should run a systems check one last time.
Why are you doing this?
So you and Mister Grimm don't die.
No. Why are you helping us?
I miss it all. The collaboration. The arguments. Even the naïvely lofty goals your father set forward. At the end of the day, after all I've done...I suppose I just miss the Baxter Building.
Then I think you should stay and help rebuild it.
I don't think your mother would approve.
Nope. But my dad would. He'd probably extend his hand and thank you for helping his family.
That sounds like him.
And then he'd remind you of those lofty goals in a long-winded-nerdy-but-admirable fashion.
The apple doesn't fall far from the tree, it seems.
Think about it, okay?
Um. Sue, you gotta check this out.
I wanna make sure I got this straight: We think Johnny has those nanobots in him.
We're pretty sure.
And we're tracking them with that Atlantis antenna, right?
Exactly.
...and that's what we have plugged into the Fantasticar nav system? That's the blip on the screen?
That's the blip. Why?
Because the blip kinda moved.
Kinda moved where?

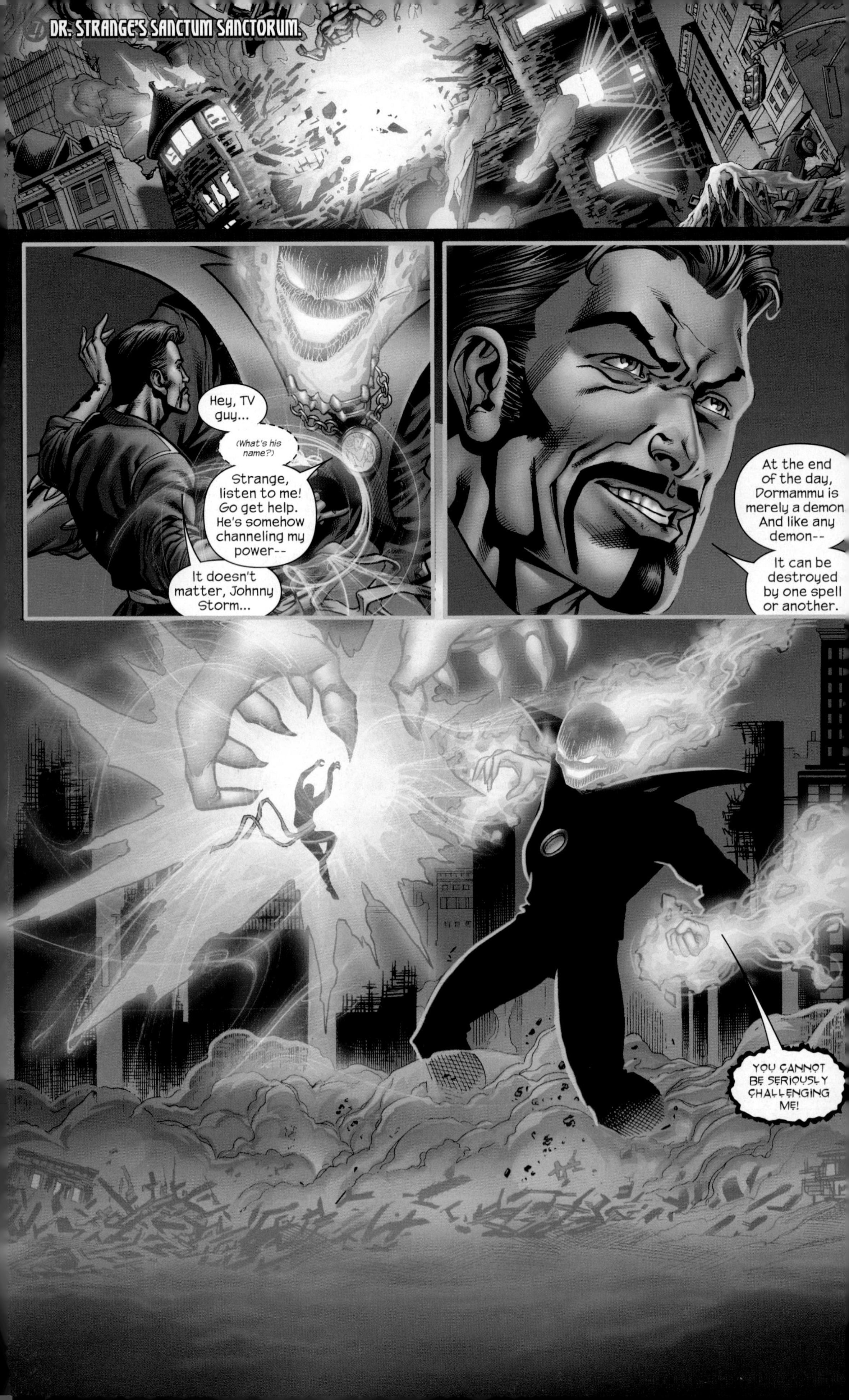
DR. STRANGE'S SANCTUM SANCTORUM.
Hey, TV guy...
(What's his name?)
Strange, listen to me! Go get help. He's somehow channeling my power--
It doesn't matter, Johnny Storm...
At the end of the day, Dormammu is merely a demon And like any demon--
It can be destroyed by one spell or another.
YOU CANNOT BE SERIOUSLY CHALLENGING ME!

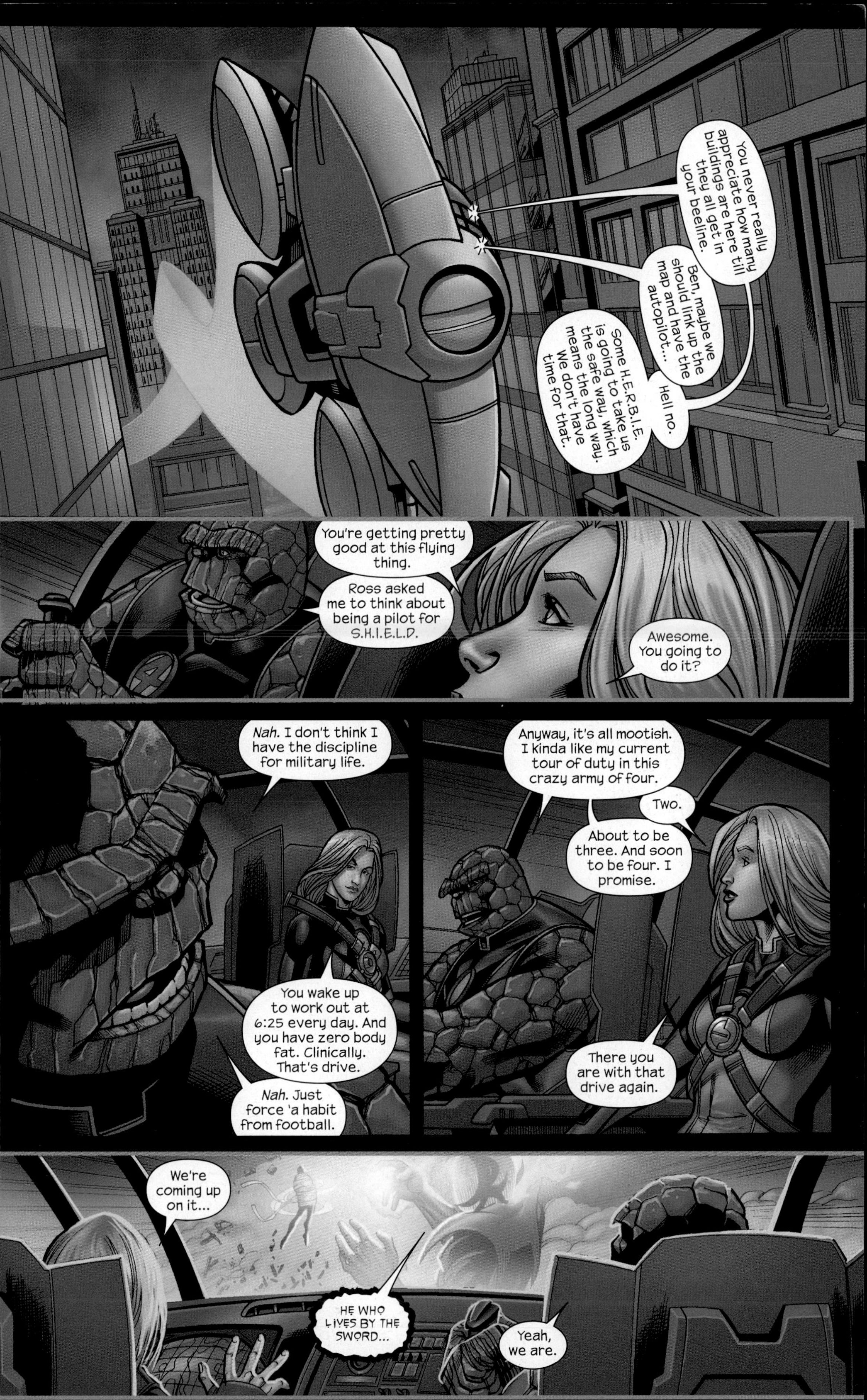

You never really appreciate how many buildings are here till they all get in your beeline.
Ben, maybe we should link up the map and have the autopilot...
Hell no.
Some H.E.R.B.I.E. is going to take us the safe way, which means the long way. We don't have time for that.
You're getting pretty good at this flying thing.
Ross asked me to think about being a pilot for S.H.I.E.L.D.
Awesome. You going to do it?
Nah. I don't think I have the discipline for military life.
You wake up to work out at 6:25 every day. And you have zero body fat. Clinically. That's drive.
Nah. Just force 'a habit from football.
Anyway, it's all mootish. I kinda like my current tour of duty in this crazy army of four.
Two.
About to be three. And soon to be four. I promise.
There you are with that drive again.
We're coming up on it...
HE WHO LIVES BY THE SWORD...
Yeah, we are.

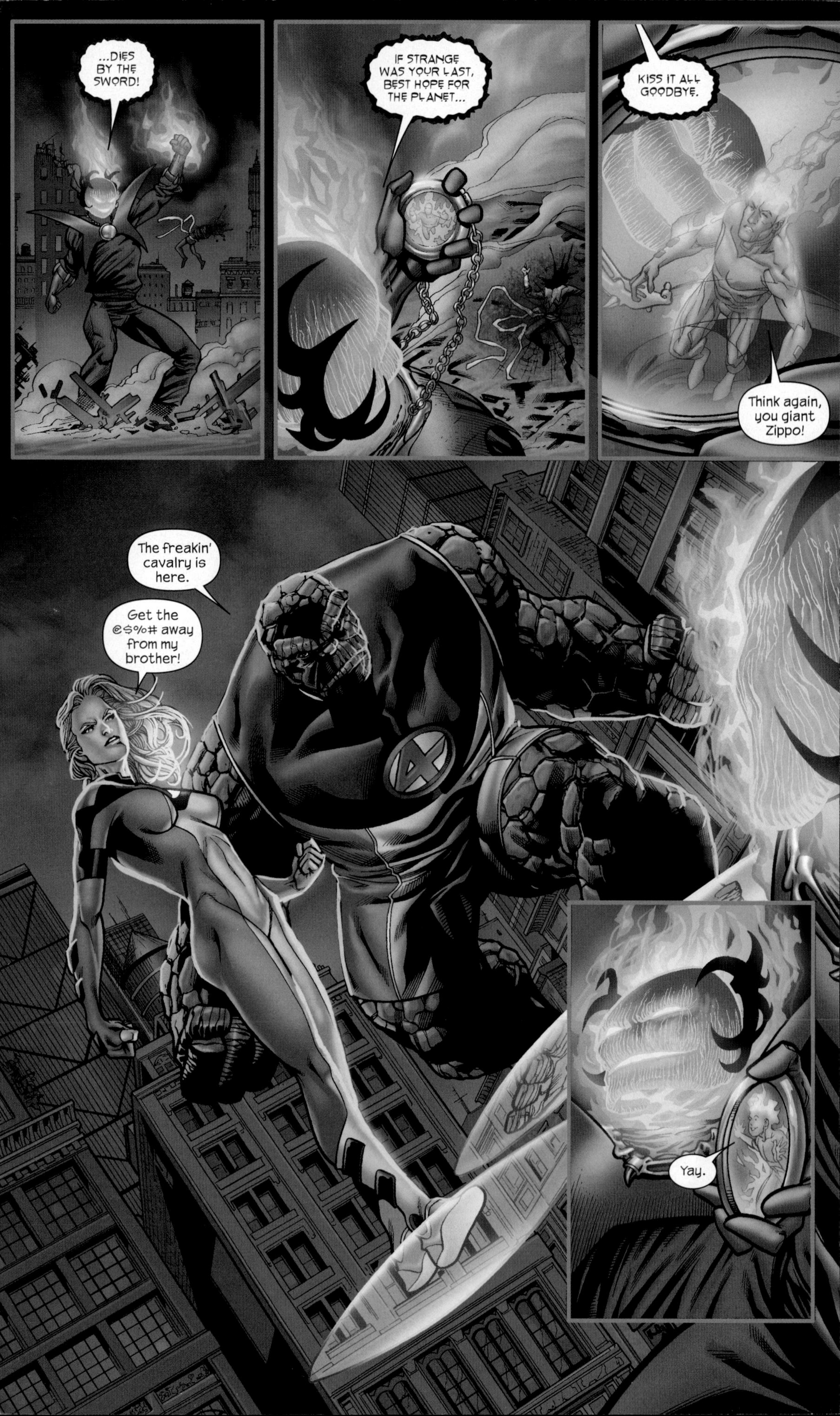
...DIES BY THE SWORD!
IF STRANGE WAS YOUR LAST, BEST HOPE FOR THE PLANET...
KISS IT ALL GOODBYE.
Think again, you giant Zippo!
The freakin' cavalry is here.
Get the @$%# away from my brother!
Yay.

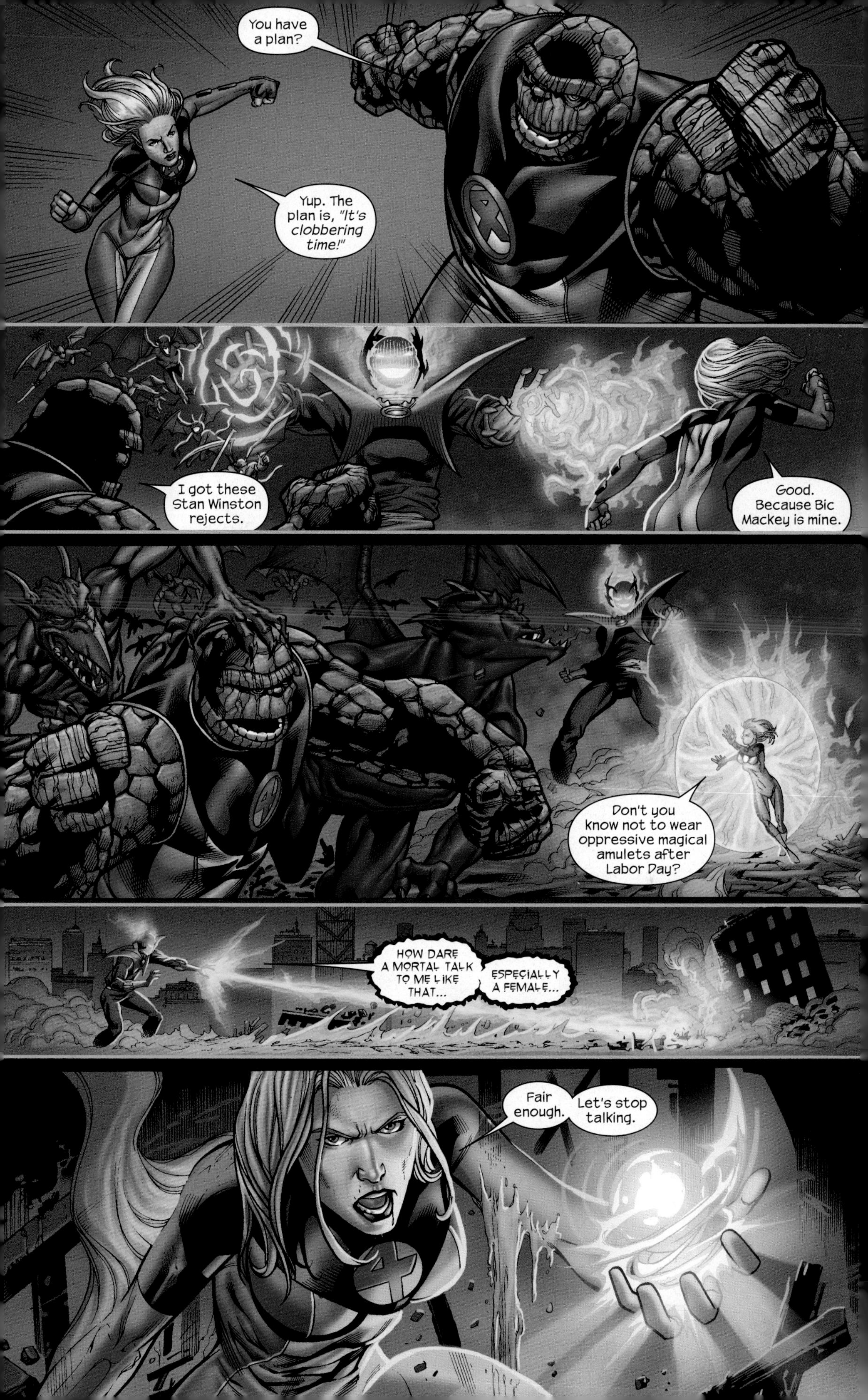
You have a plan?
Yup. The plan is, "It's clobbering time!"
I got these Stan Winston rejects.
Good. Because Bic Mackey is mine.
Don't you know not to wear oppressive magical amulets after Labor Day?
HOW DARE A MORTAL TALK TO ME LIKE THAT...
ESPECIALLY A FEMALE...
Fair enough.
Let's stop talking.

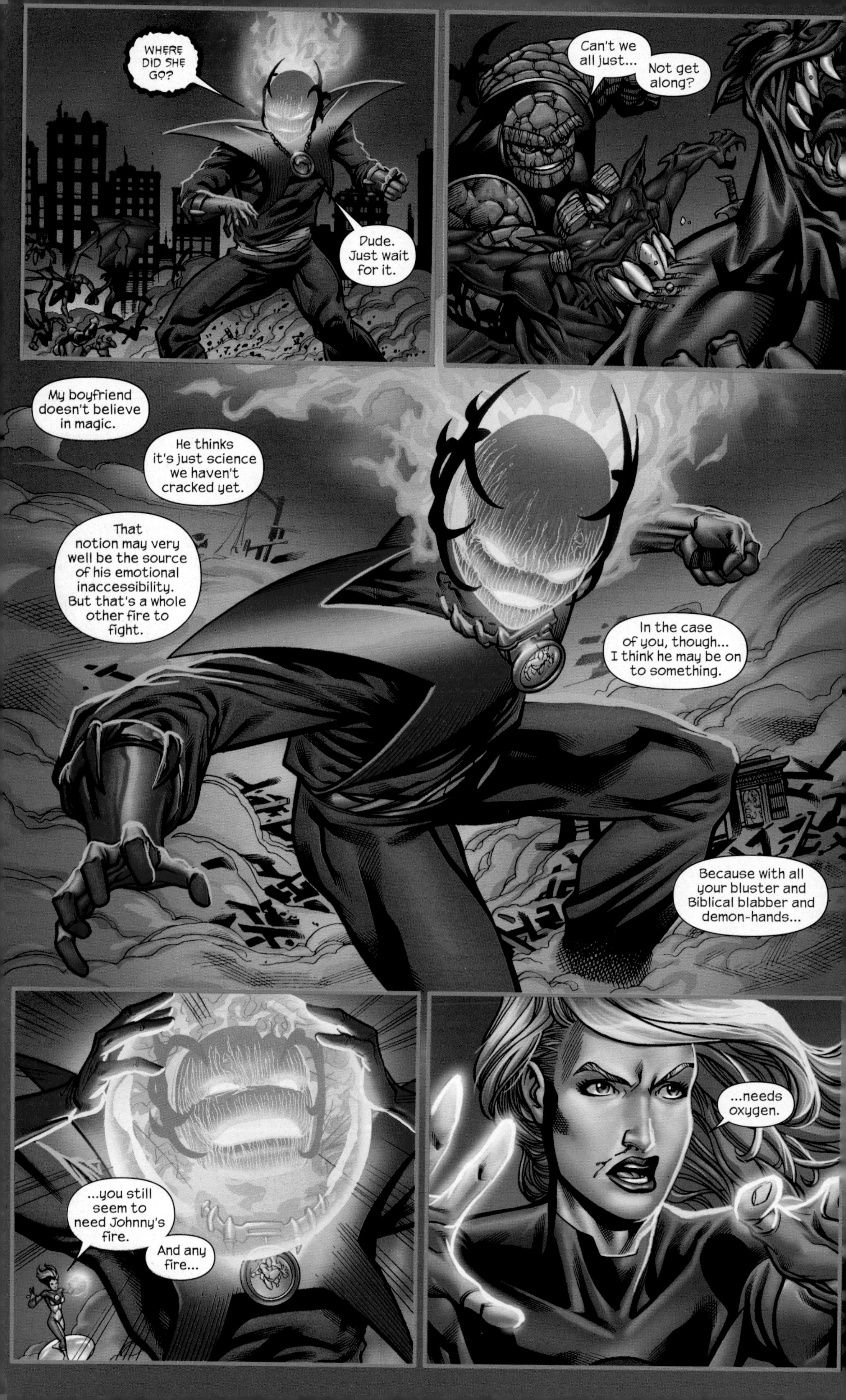
WHERE DID SHE GO?
Dude. Just wait for it.
Can't we all just...
Not get along?
My boyfriend doesn't believe in magic.
He thinks it's just science we haven't cracked yet.
That notion may very well be the source of his emotional inaccessibility. But that's a whole other fire to fight.
In the case of you, though... I think he may be on to something.
Because with all your bluster and Biblical blabber and demon-hands...
...you still seem to need Johnny's fire.
And any fire...
...needs oxygen.

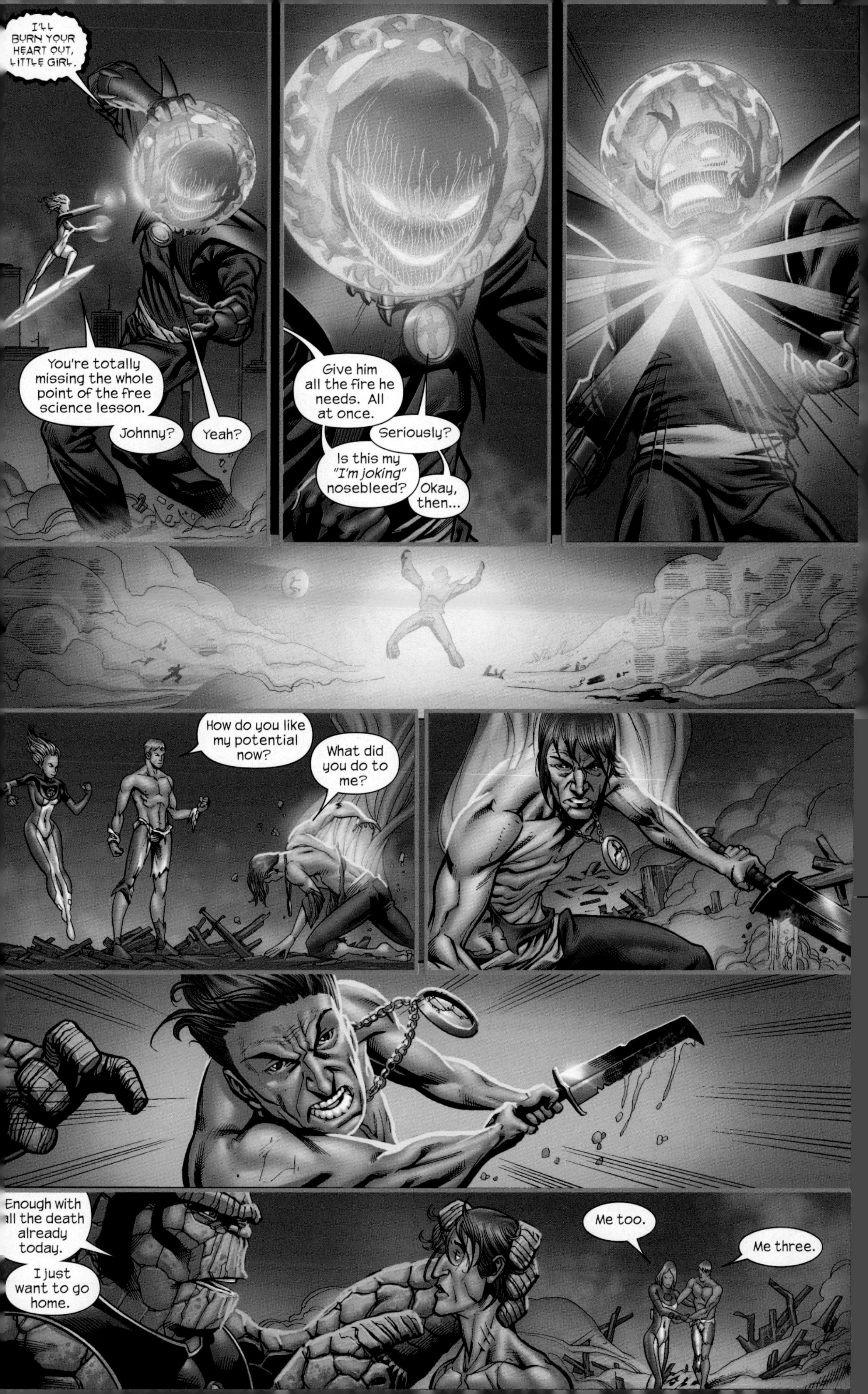
I'LL BURN YOUR HEART OUT, LITTLE GIRL.
You're totally missing the whole point of the free science lesson.
Johnny?
Yeah?
Give him all the fire he needs. All at once.
Seriously?
Is this my "I'm joking" nosebleed?
Okay, then...
How do you like my potential now?
What did you do to me?
Enough with all the death already today.
I just want to go home.
Me too.
Me three.

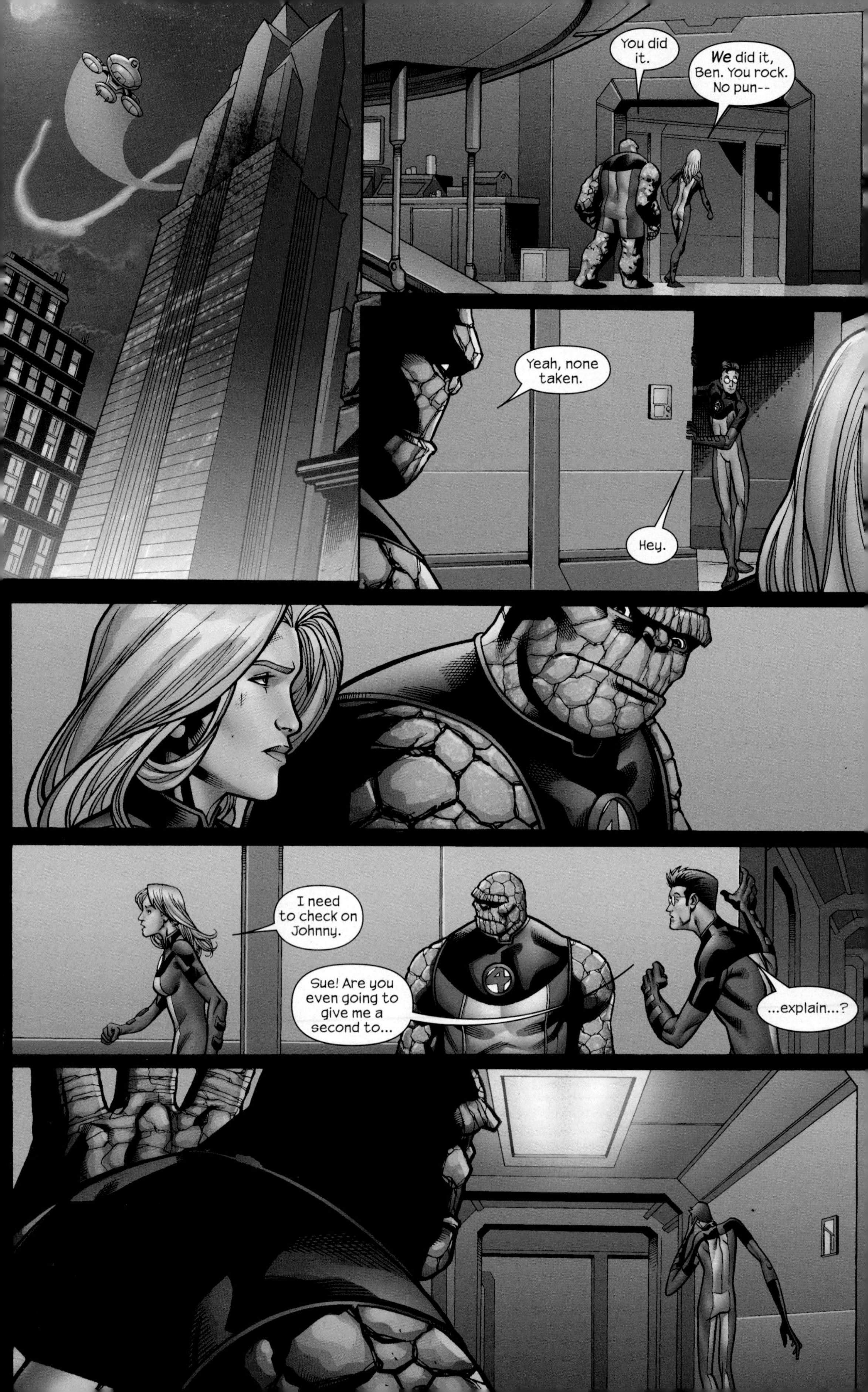
You did it.
We did it, Ben. You rock. No pun--
Yeah, none taken.
Hey.
I need to check on Johnny.
Sue! Are you even going to give me a second to...
...explain...?

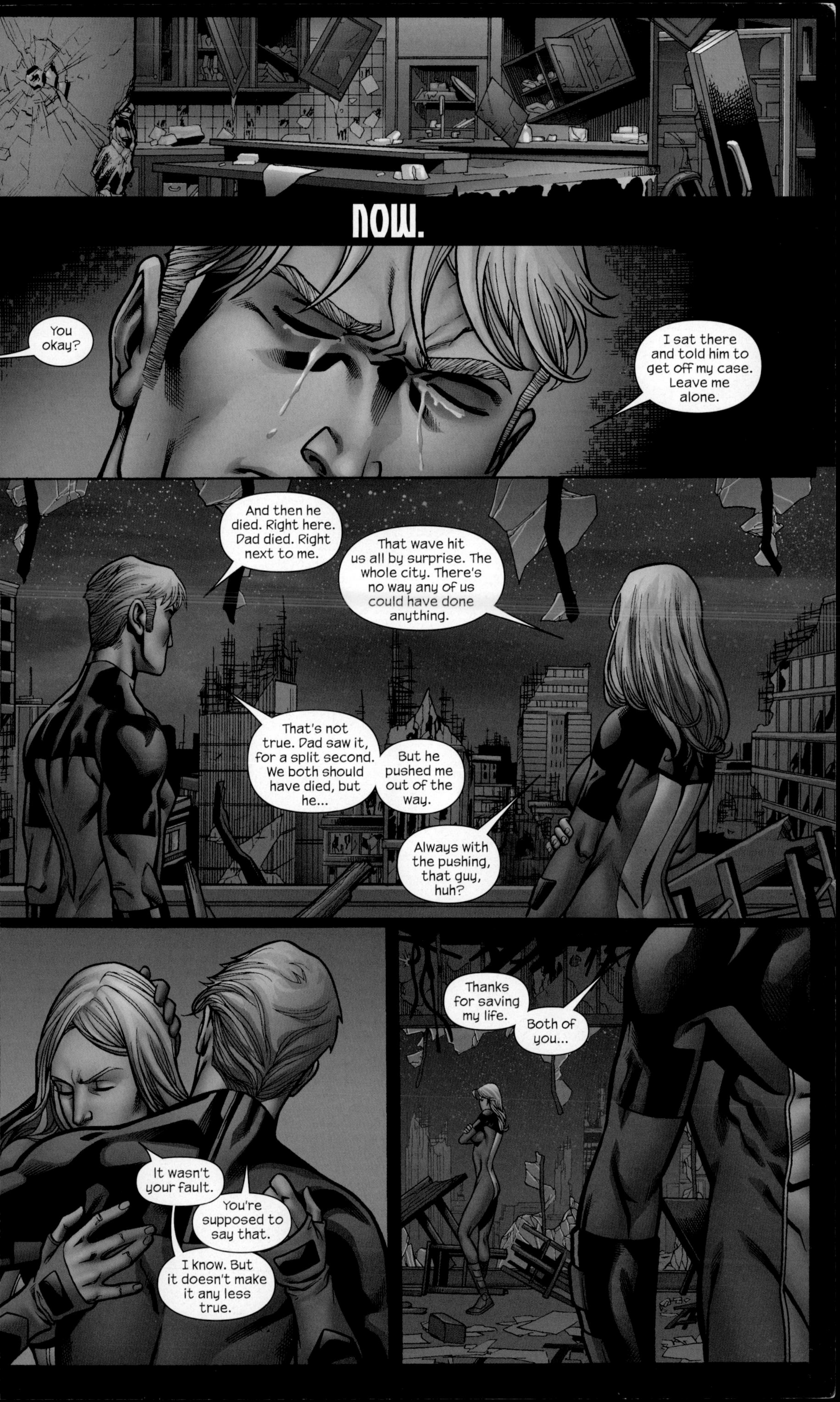
NOW.
You okay?
I sat there and told him to get off my case. Leave me alone.
And then he died. Right here. Dad died. Right next to me.
That wave hit us all by surprise. The whole city. There's no way any of us could have done anything.
That's not true. Dad saw it, for a split second. We both should have died, but he...
But he pushed me out of the way.
Always with the pushing, that guy, huh?
It wasn't your fault.
You're supposed to say that.
I know. But it doesn't make it any less true.
Thanks for saving my life.
Both of you...

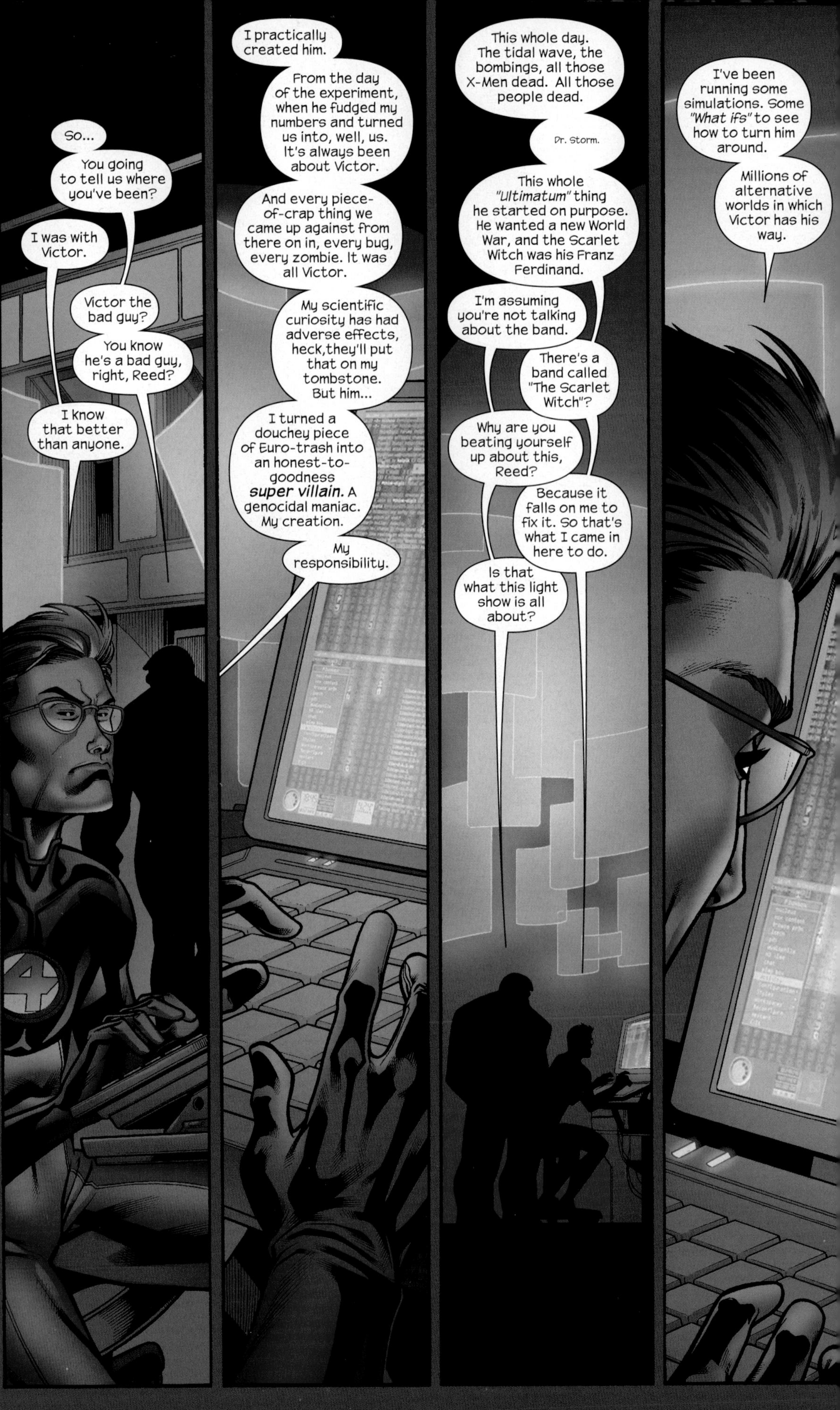
So...
You going to tell us where you've been?
I was with Victor.
Victor the bad guy?
You know he's a bad guy, right, Reed?
I know that better than anyone.
I practically created him.
From the day of the experiment, when he fudged my numbers and turned us into, well, us. It's always been about Victor.
And every piece-of-crap thing we came up against from there on in, every bug, every zombie. It was all Victor.
My scientific curiosity has had adverse effects, heck, they'll put that on my tombstone. But him...
I turned a douchey piece of Euro-trash into an honest-to-goodness super villain. A genocidal maniac. My creation.
My responsibility.
This whole day. The tidal wave, the bombings, all those X-Men dead. All those people dead.
Dr. Storm.
This whole "Ultimatum" thing he started on purpose. He wanted a new World War, and the Scarlet Witch was his Franz Ferdinand.
I'm assuming you're not talking about the band.
There's a band called "The Scarlet Witch"?
Why are you beating yourself up about this, Reed?
Because it falls on me to fix it. So that's what I came in here to do.
Is that what this light show is all about?
I've been running some simulations. Some "What ifs" to see how to turn him around.
Millions of alternative worlds in which Victor has his way.

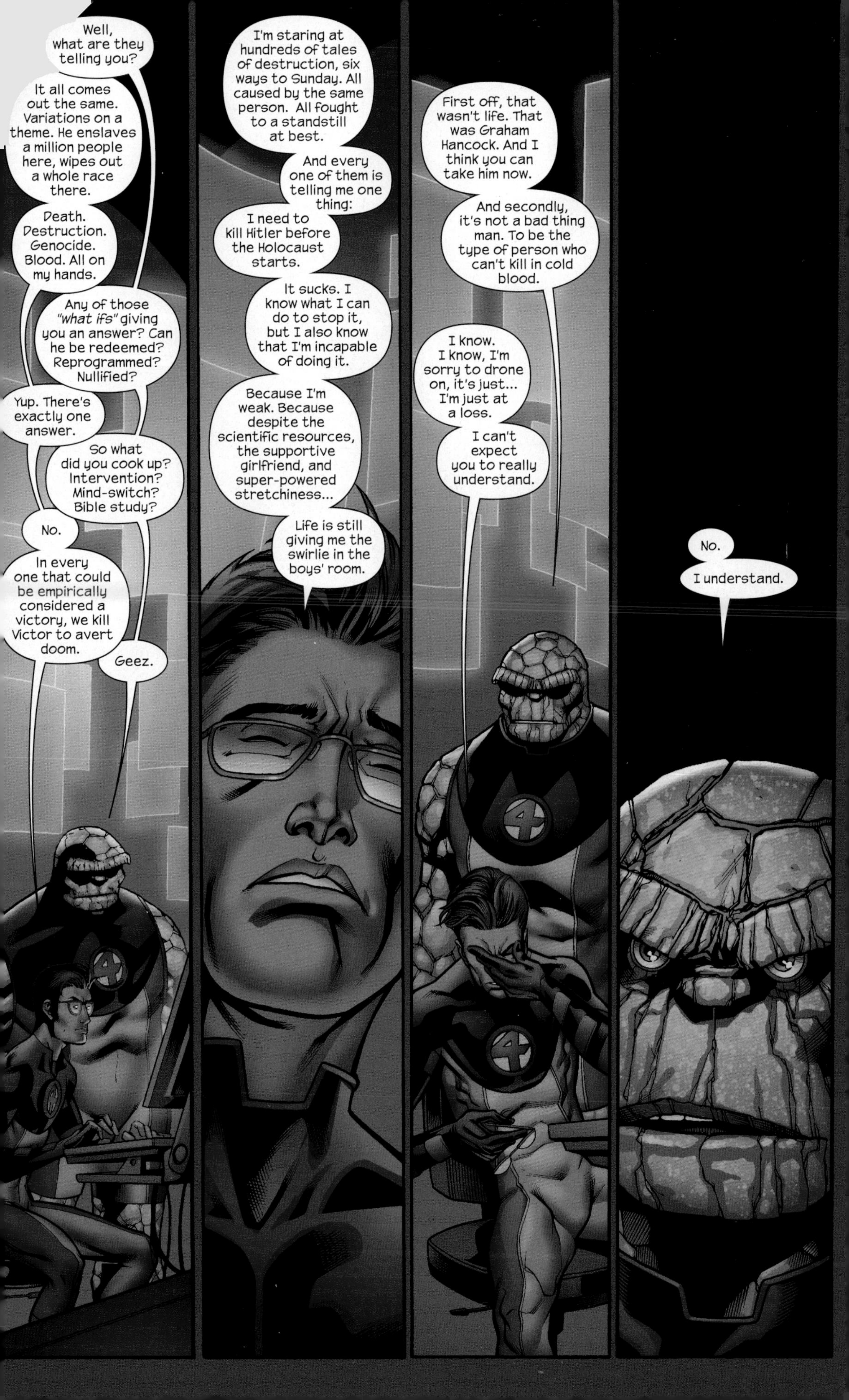
Well, what are they telling you?
It all comes out the same. Variations on a theme. He enslaves a million people here, wipes out a whole race there.
Death. Destruction. Genocide. Blood. All on my hands.
Any of those "what ifs" giving you an answer? Can he be redeemed? Reprogrammed? Nullified?
Yup. There's exactly one answer.
So what did you cook up? Intervention? Mind-switch? Bible study?
No.
In every one that could be empirically considered a victory, we kill Victor to avert doom.
Geez.
I'm staring at hundreds of tales of destruction, six ways to Sunday. All caused by the same person. All fought to a standstill at best.
And every one of them is telling me one thing:
I need to kill Hitler before the Holocaust starts.
It sucks. I know what I can do to stop it, but I also know that I'm incapable of doing it.
Because I'm weak. Because despite the scientific resources, the supportive girlfriend, and super-powered stretchiness...
Life is still giving me the swirlie in the boys' room.
First off, that wasn't life. That was Graham Hancock. And I think you can take him now.
And secondly, it's not a bad thing man. To be the type of person who can't kill in cold blood.
I know. I know, I'm sorry to drone on, it's just... I'm just at a loss.
I can't expect you to really understand.
No.
I understand.

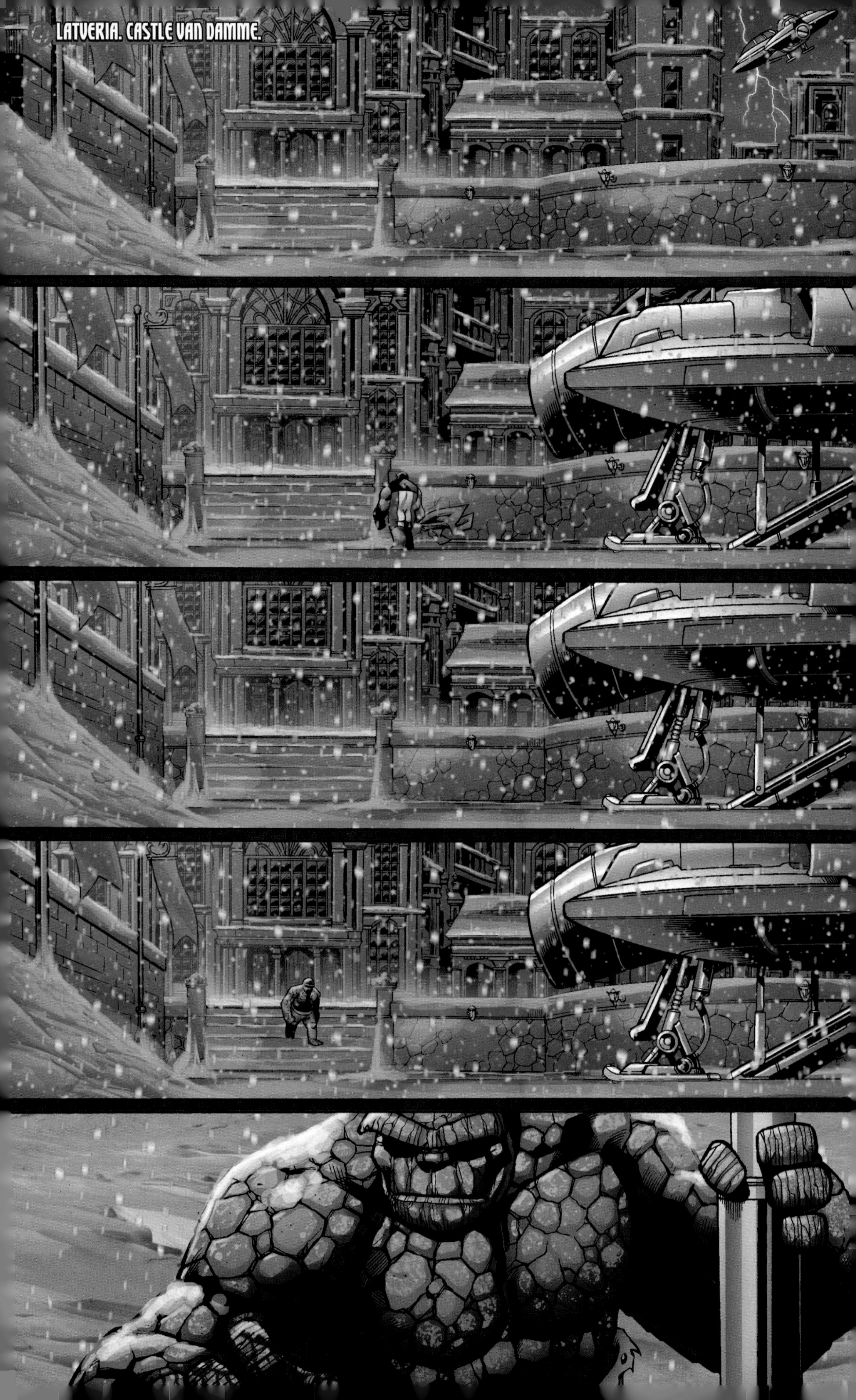
LATVERIA. CASTLE VAN DAMME.

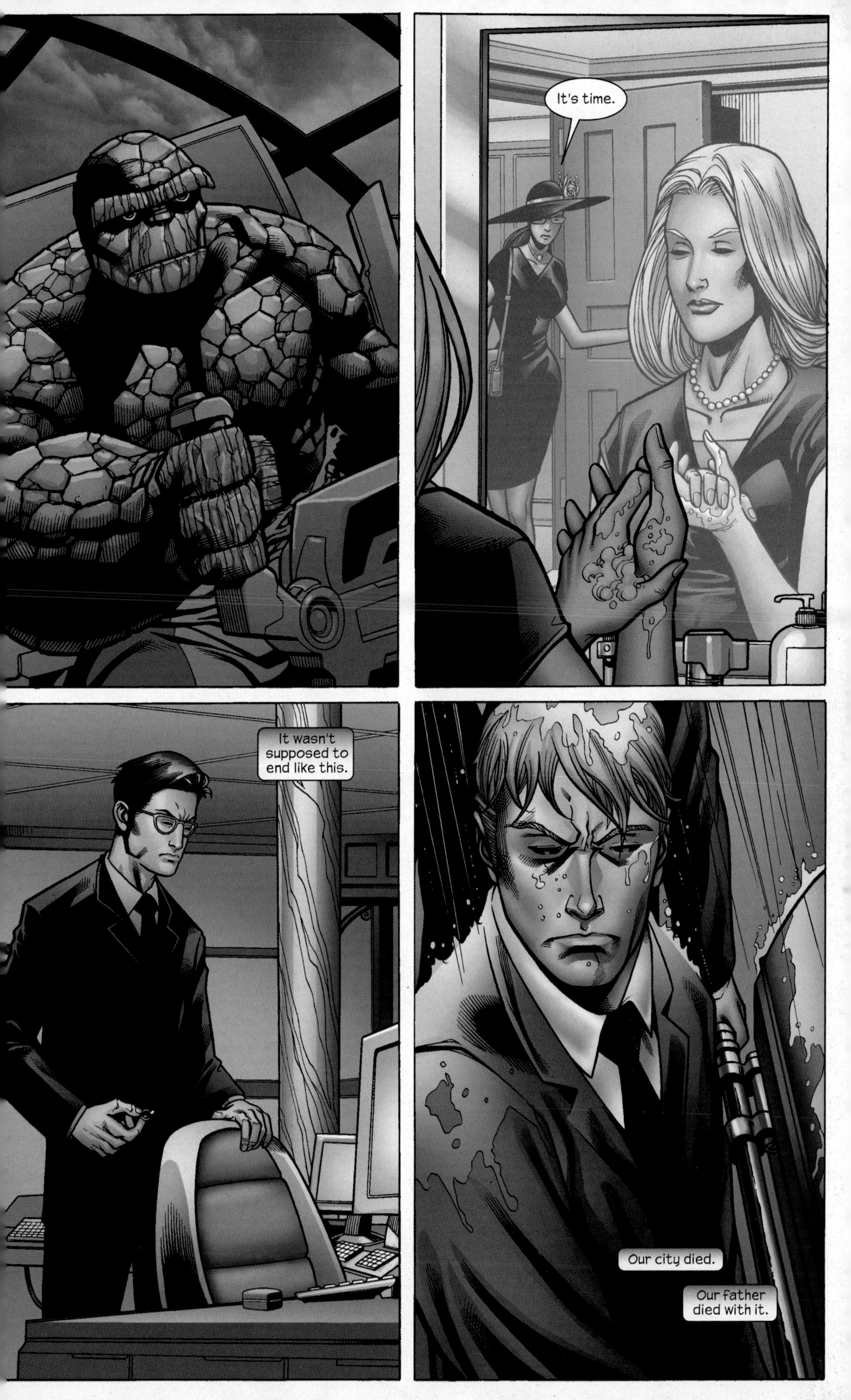
It's time.
It wasn't supposed to end like this.
Our city died.
Our father died with it.

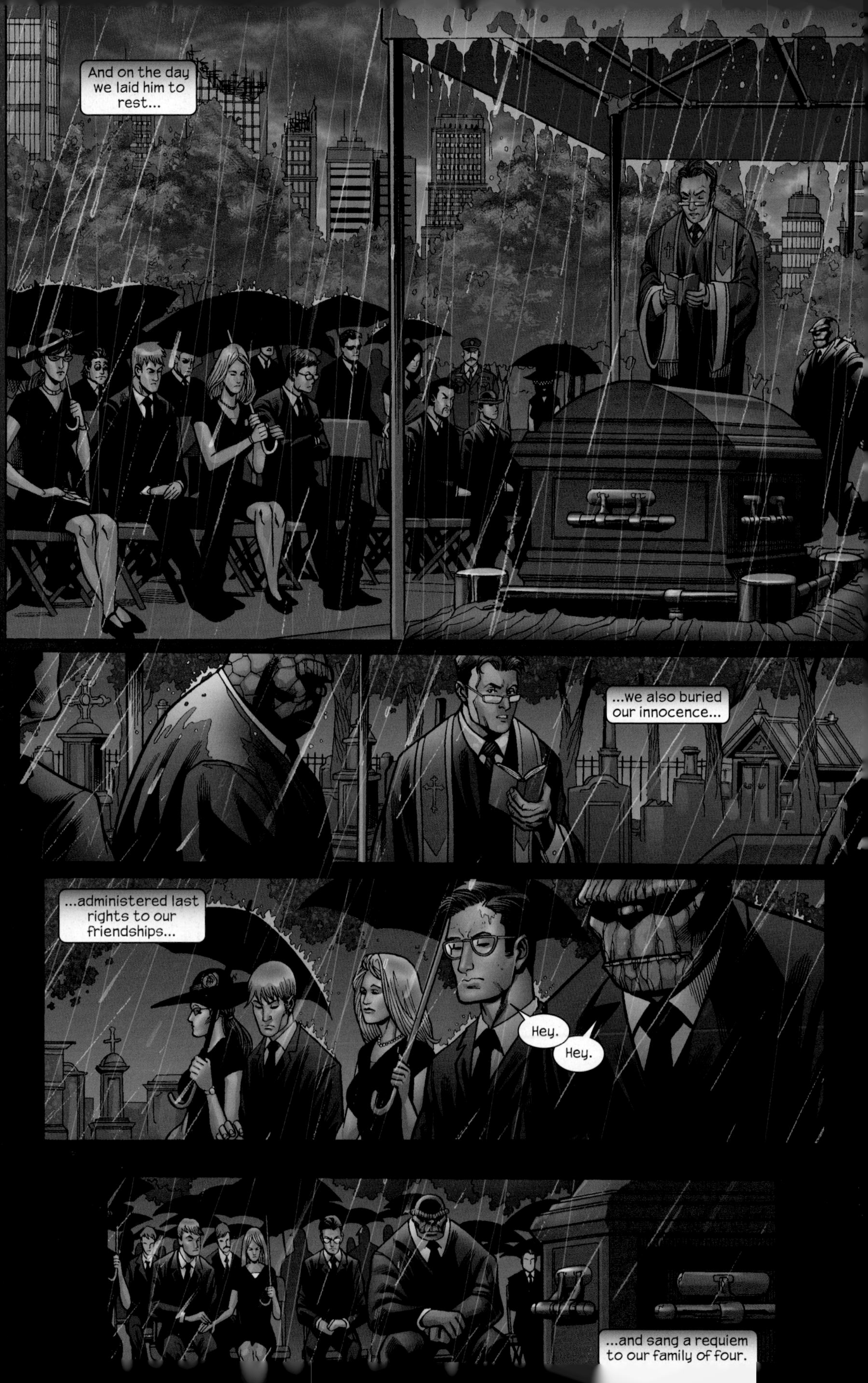
And on the day we laid him to rest...
...we also buried our innocence...
...administered last rights to our friendships...
Hey.
Hey.
...and sang a requiem to our family of four.

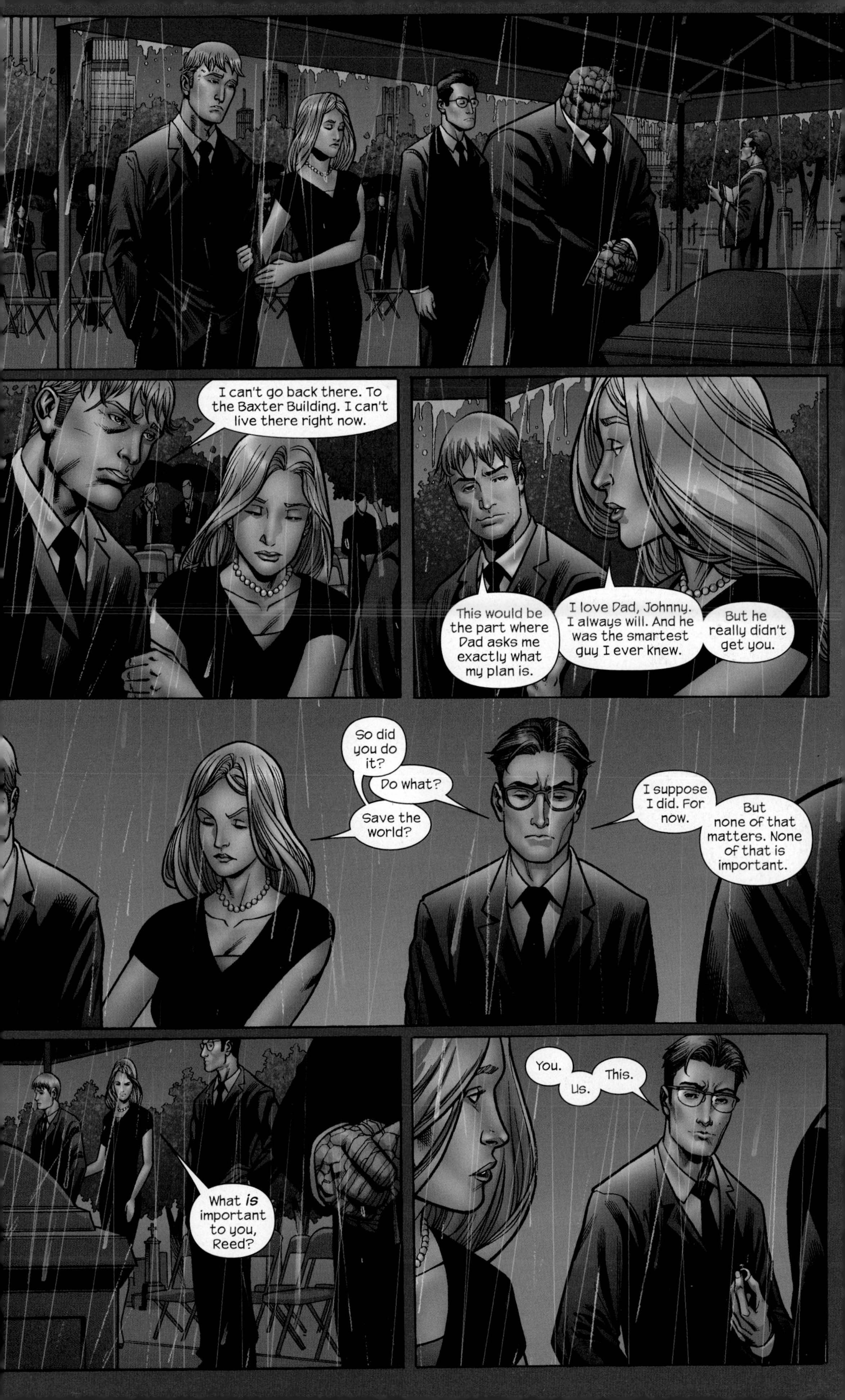

I can't go back there. To the Baxter Building. I can't live there right now.
This would be the part where Dad asks me exactly what my plan is.
I love Dad, Johnny. I always will. And he was the smartest guy I ever knew.
But he really didn't get you.
So did you do it?
Do what?
Save the world?
I suppose I did. For now.
But none of that matters. None of that is important.
What *is* important to you, Reed?
You.
Us.
This.

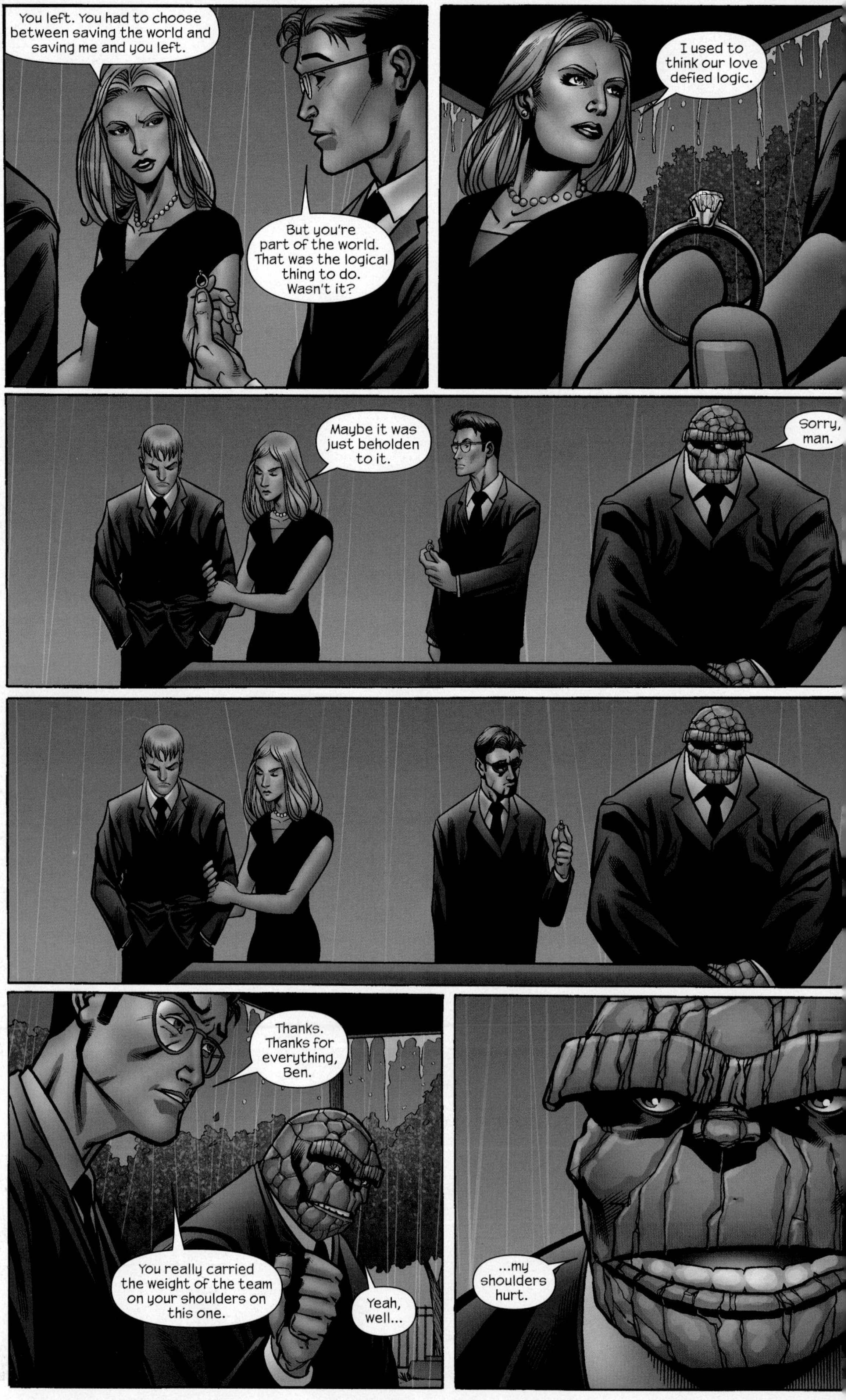
You left. You had to choose between saving the world and saving me and you left.
But you're part of the world. That was the logical thing to do. Wasn't it?
I used to think our love defied logic.
Maybe it was just beholden to it.
Sorry, man.
Thanks. Thanks for everything, Ben.
You really carried the weight of the team on your shoulders on this one.
Yeah, well...
...my shoulders hurt.

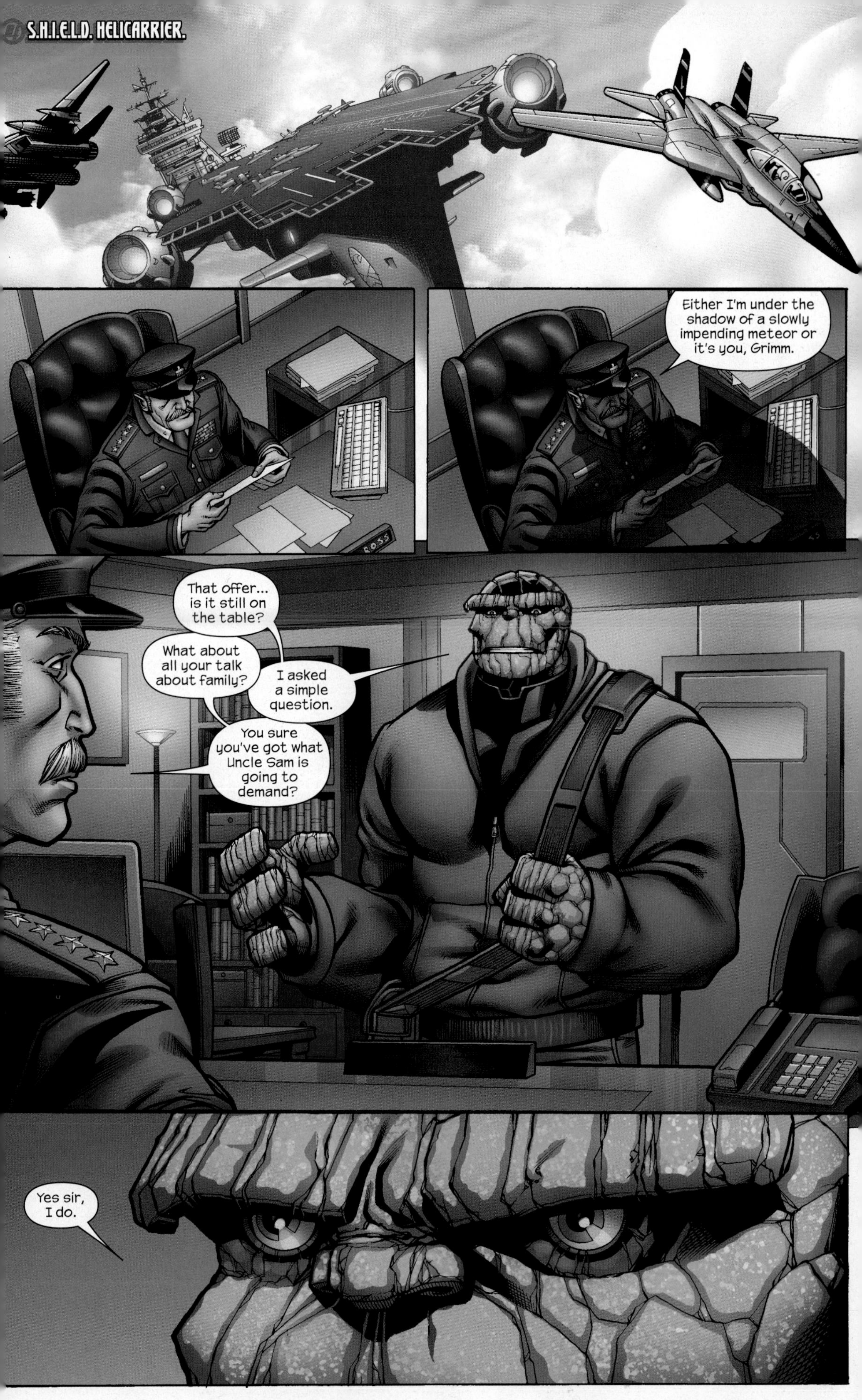
S.H.I.E.L.D. HELICARRIER.
Either I'm under the shadow of a slowly impending meteor or it's you, Grimm.
ROSS
That offer... is it still on the table?
What about all your talk about family?
I asked a simple question.
You sure you've got what Uncle Sam is going to demand?
Yes sir, I do.

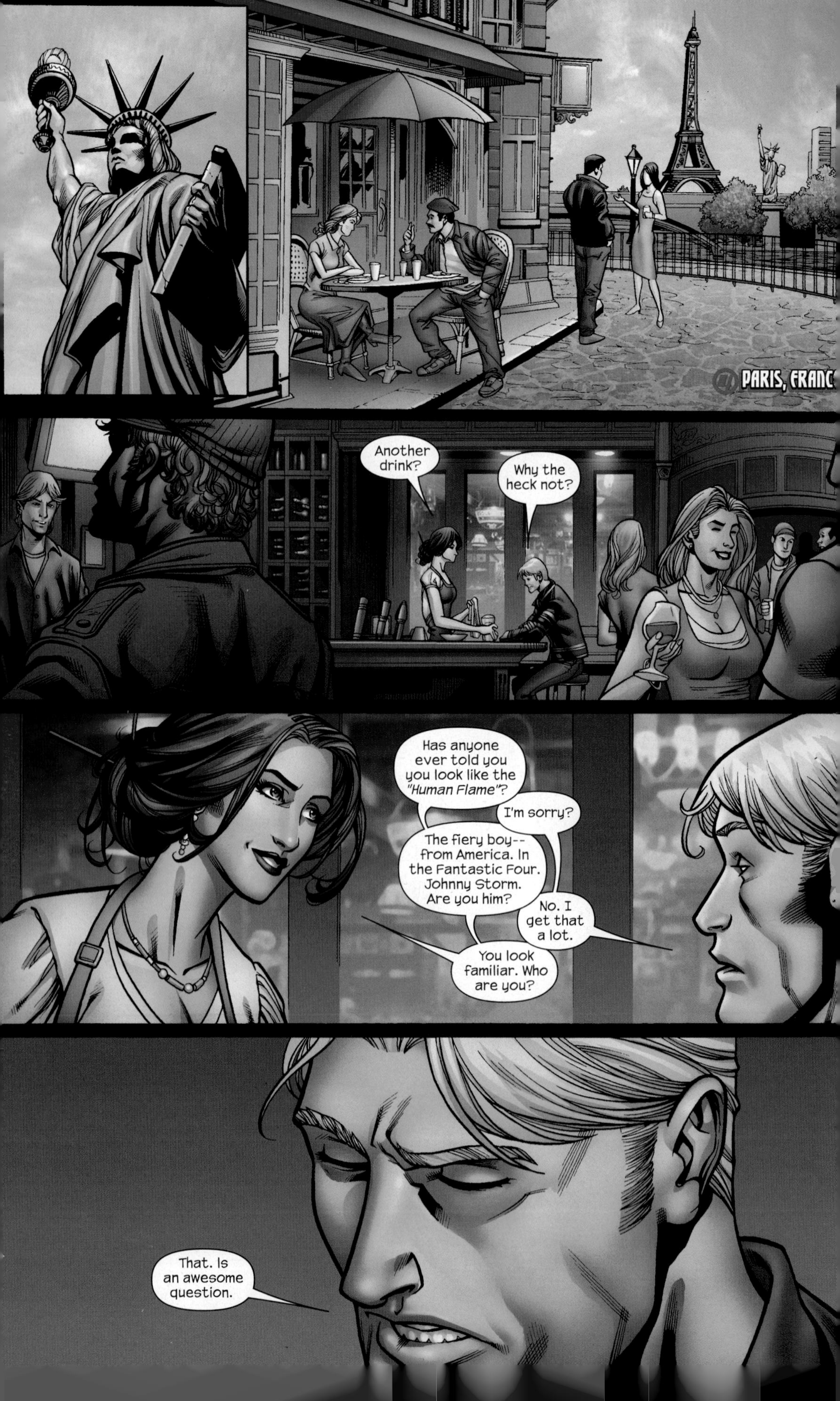
PARIS, FRANC
Another drink?
Why the heck not?
Has anyone ever told you you look like the "Human Flame"?
I'm sorry?
The fiery boy-- from America. In the Fantastic Four. Johnny Storm. Are you him?
No. I get that a lot.
You look familiar. Who are you?
That. Is an awesome question.

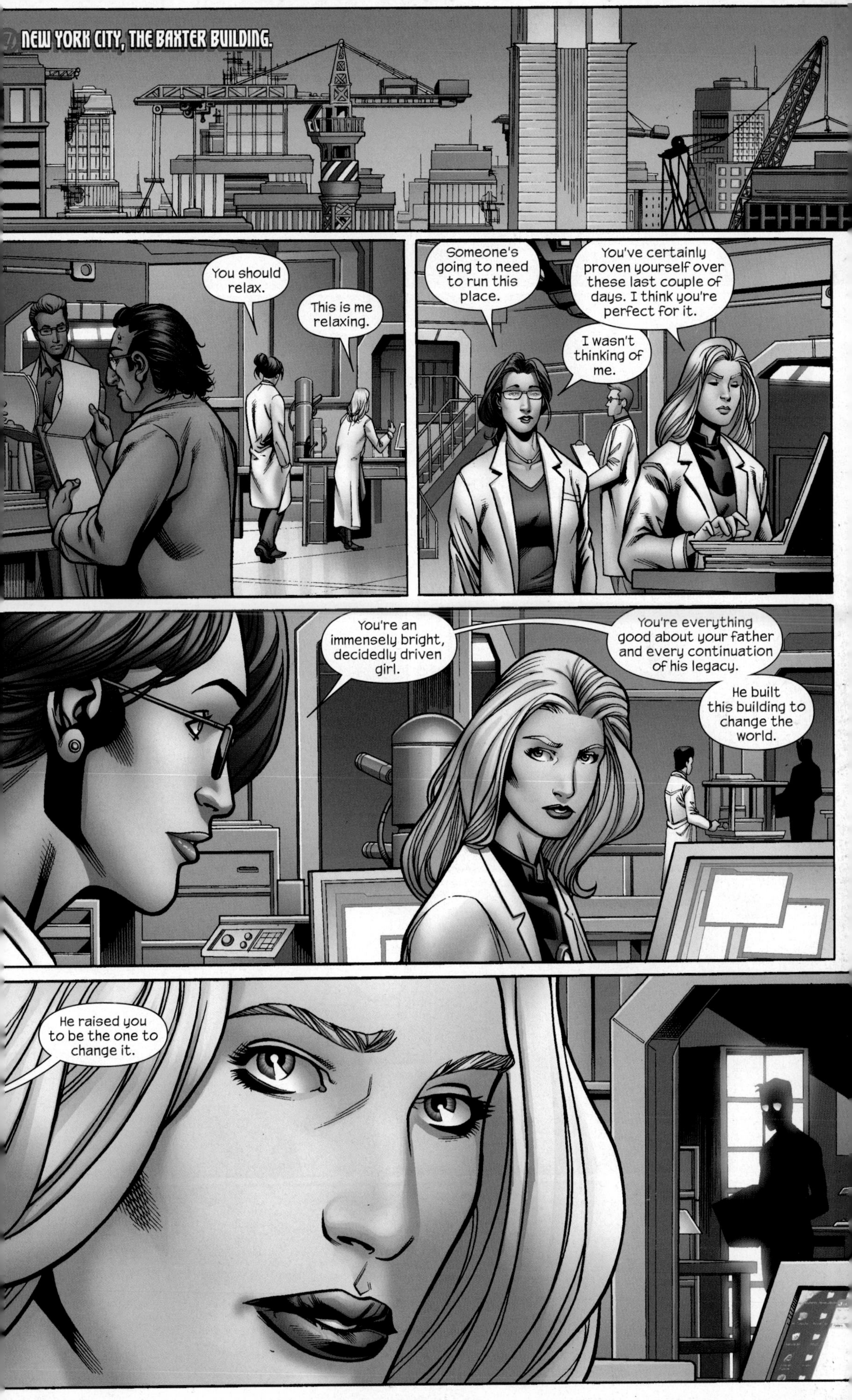
NEW YORK CITY, THE BAXTER BUILDING.
You should relax.
This is me relaxing.
Someone's going to need to run this place.
You've certainly proven yourself over these last couple of days. I think you're perfect for it.
I wasn't thinking of me.
You're an immensely bright, decidedly driven girl.
You're everything good about your father and every continuation of his legacy.
He built this building to change the world.
He raised you to be the one to change it.

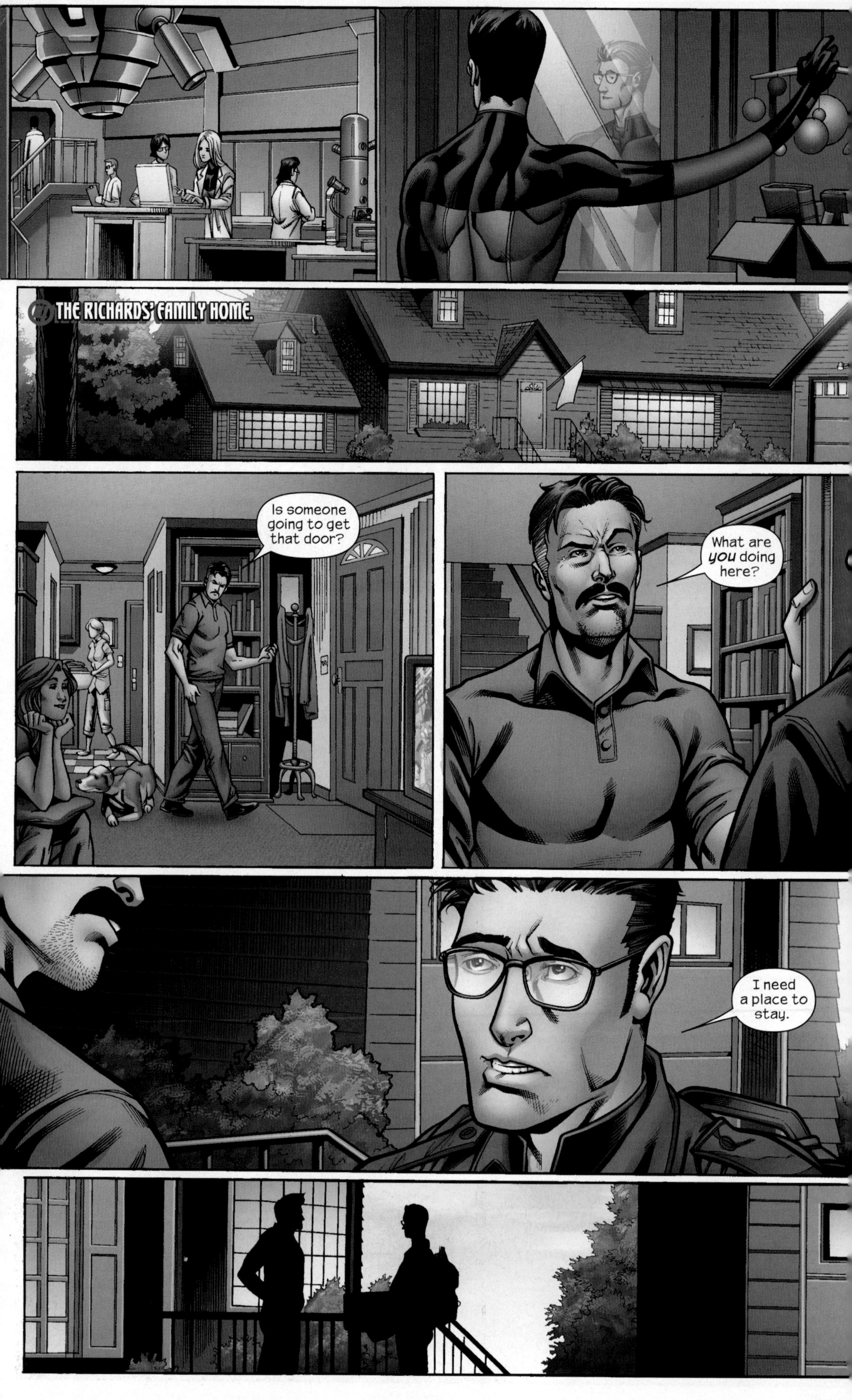
THE RICHARDS' FAMILY HOME.
Is someone going to get that door?
What are YOU doing here?
I need a place to stay.

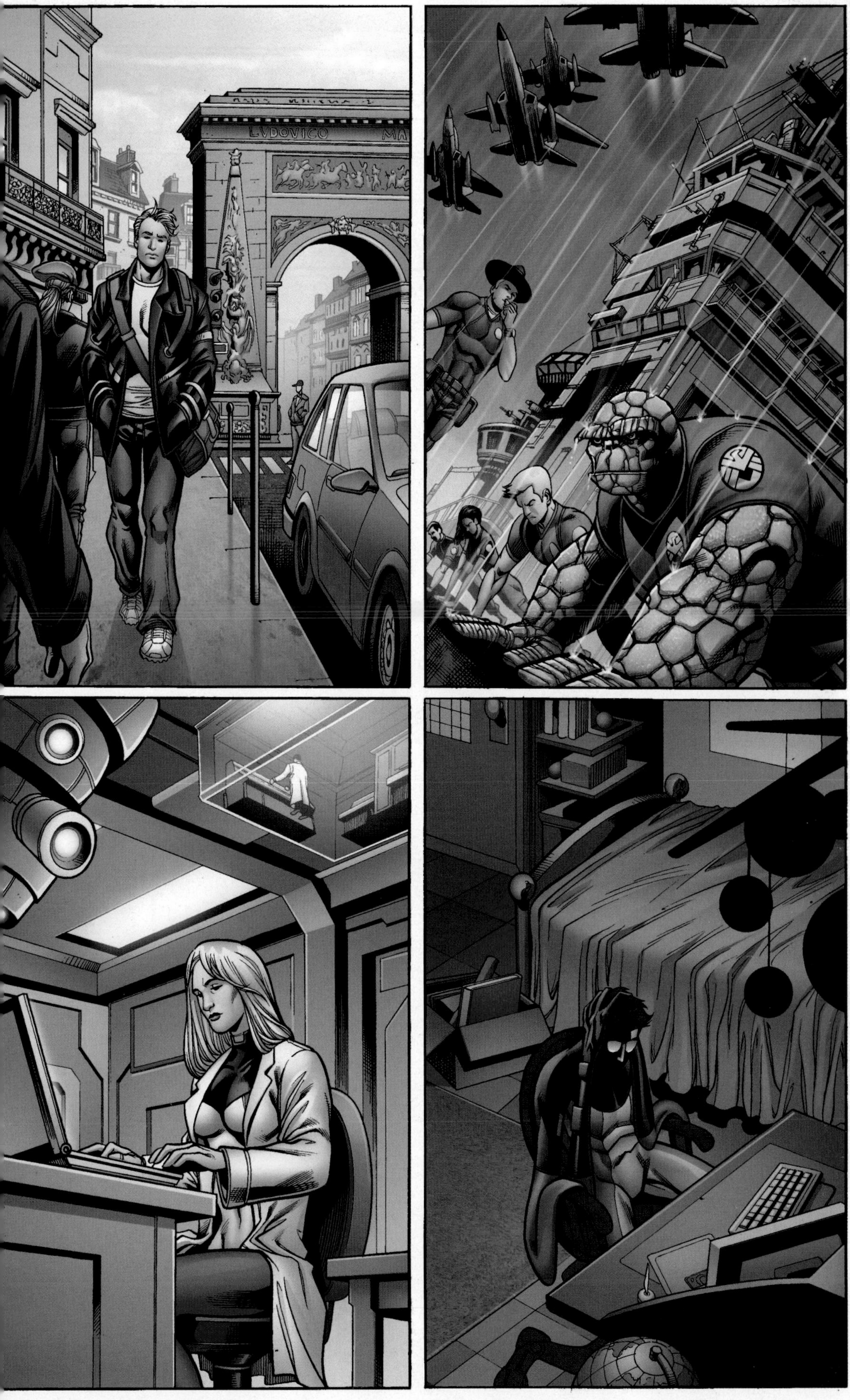
LVDOVICO

DAILY BUGLE

NEW YORK'S FINEST DAILY NEWSPAPER

OBITUARIES

p.

DR. FRANKLIN STORM

The scientific community lost one of its finest luminaries today. Dr. Franklin Richards dedicated his life to the establishment of America's foremost scientific think-tank – The Baxter Building – but perhaps his greatest contribution to humanity were his two children, Susan and Jonathan "Johnny" Storm of the Fantastic Four.

Along with renowned fellow scientist Reed Richards and Benjamin Grimm (commonly known as super-hero the Thing), the Storm children mourn the loss of their father along with the thousands of innocent civilians killed in the recent catastrophic meteorological phenomena sources have dubbed the "Ultimatum Wave."

In addition to the countless technological discoveries that marked a lifetime of scientific discovery, Dr. Storm fostered the young geniuses of the Baxter Building and helped discover the mysterious N-Zone, uncovered the lost city of Atlantis and helped save the world from alien threats. His life cut short by the mutant terrorist Magneto, Dr. Storm left a legacy of scientific curiosity that will be avenged by his family, the Fantastic Four, and will not be forgotten. ∎

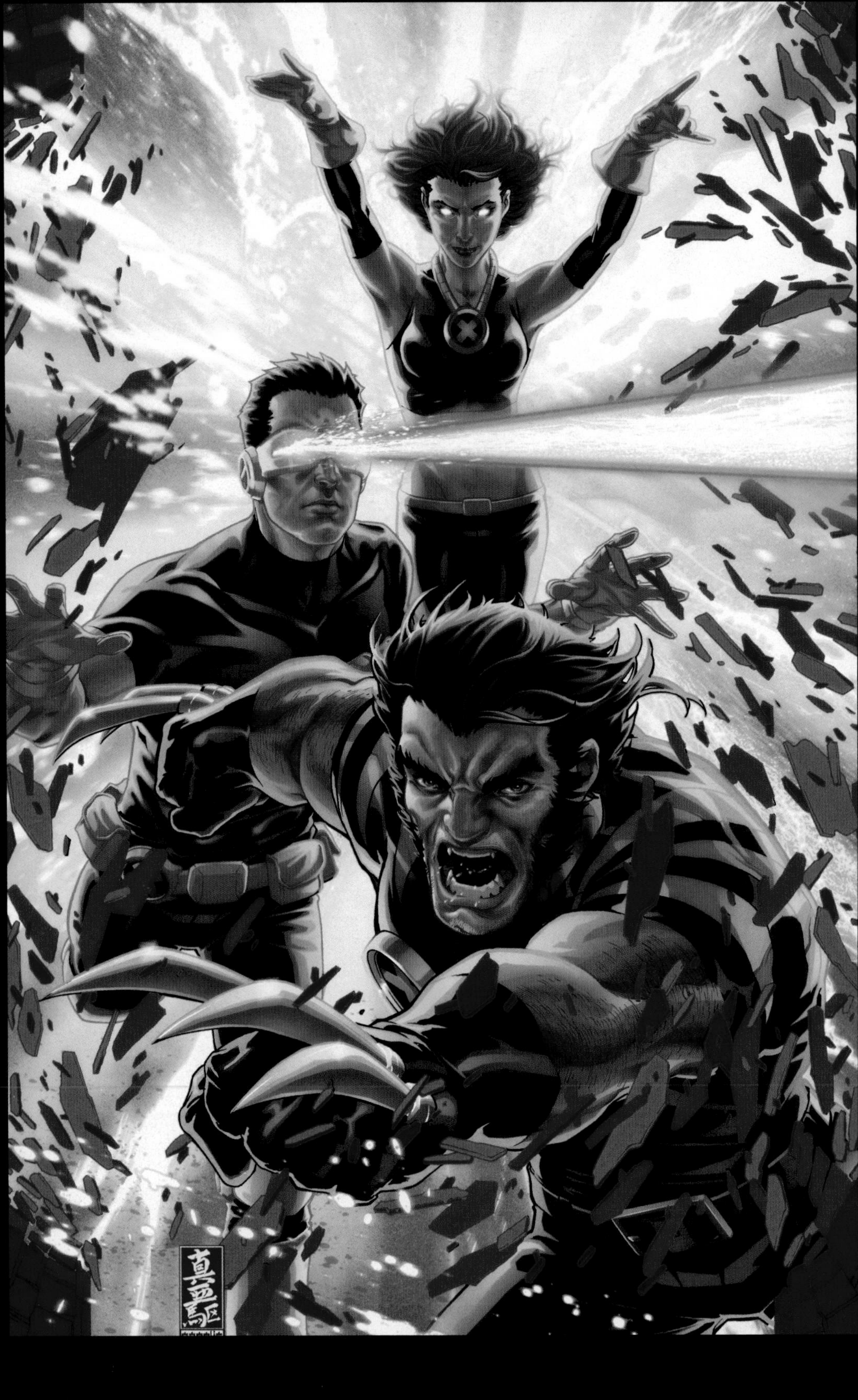

Ultimatum: X-Men Requiem #1

Born with strange powers and amazing abilities, the X-Men are young mutant heroes, sworn to protect a world that fears and hates them.

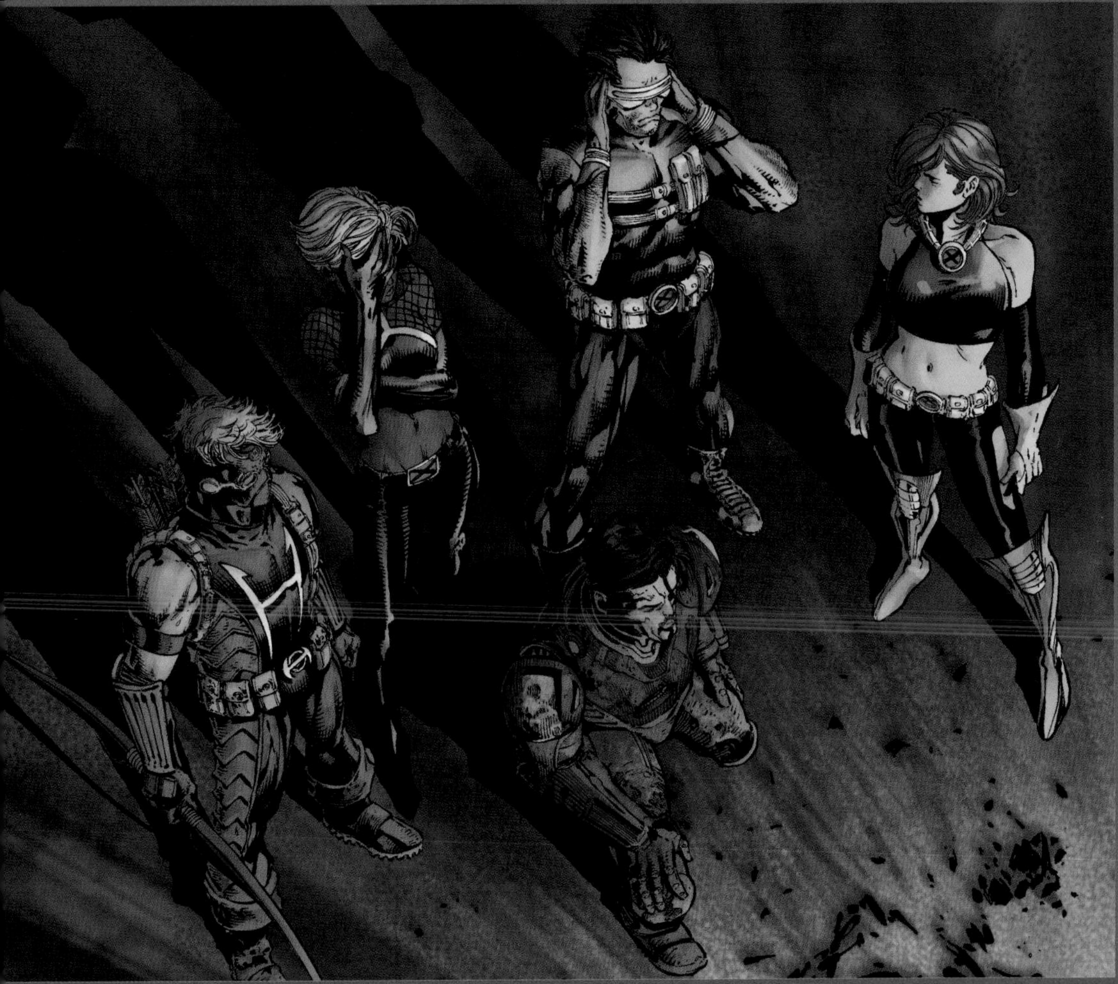

In the aftermath of Magneto's devastating attack on the planet, the surviving X-Men struggle to pick up the pieces. In the blink of an eye, the Ultimatum Wave swept away many of their closest friends and allies, while Jamie Madrox aka the Multiple Man, Magneto's replicating terrorist, unleashed a never-ending onslaught that killed thousands of innocents and dozens of heroes.

With the fate of the world hanging in the balance and the endless hordes of Multiple Men continuing to wreak havoc across the globe, Wolverine tracked down the original Madrox Prime and eliminated the threat.

In the wake of the Madrox attacks, the X-Men went after the source of the destruction: Magneto. During the ensuing battle, the unthinkable happened — Wolverine was killed.

Now, reeling from their unfathomable losses, the X-Men have returned home to honor the fallen and somehow gather strength for what lies ahead.

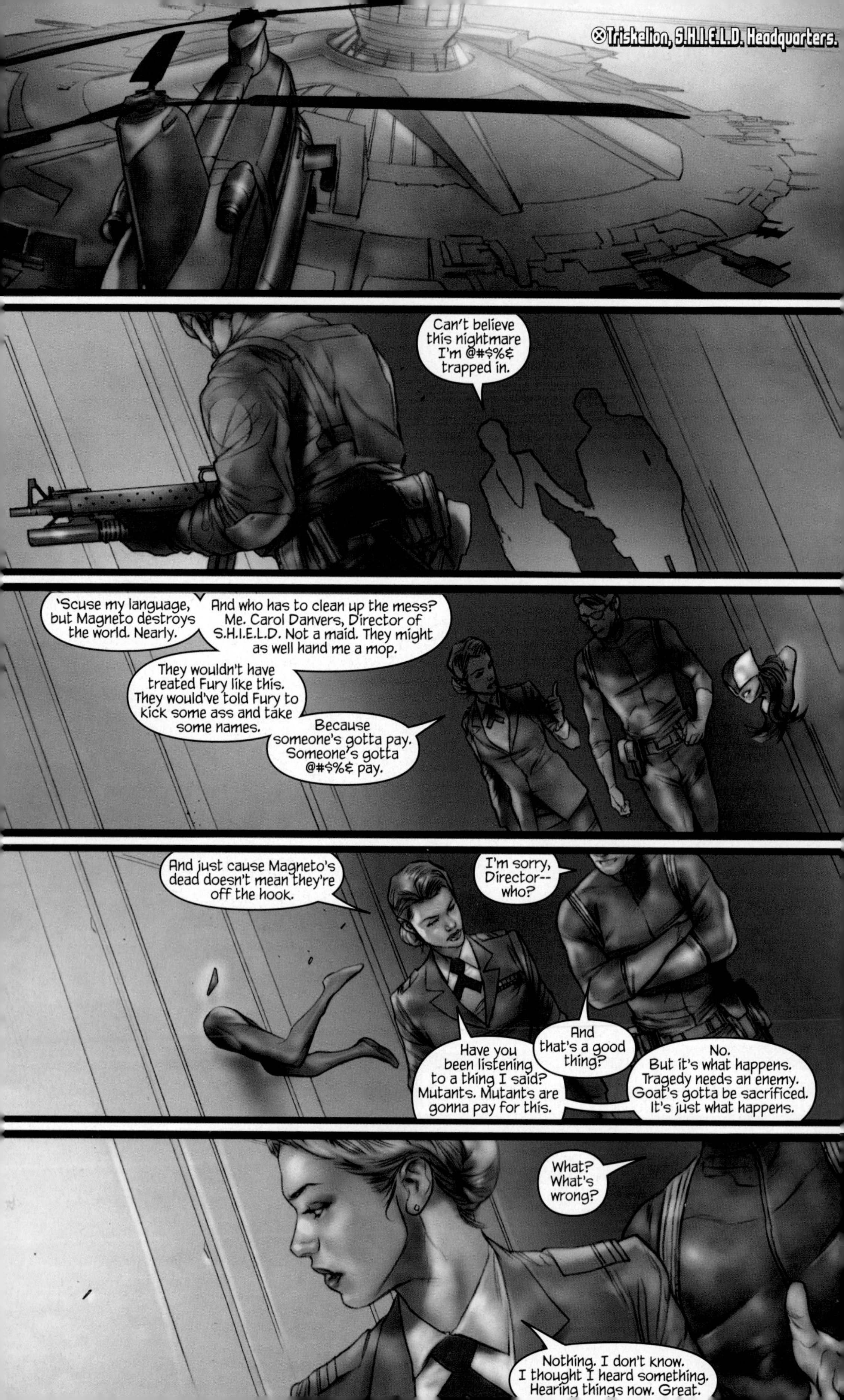
Triskelion, S.H.I.E.L.D. Headquarters.
Can't believe this nightmare I'm @#$%& trapped in.
'Scuse my language, but Magneto destroys the world. Nearly.
And who has to clean up the mess? Me. Carol Danvers, Director of S.H.I.E.L.D. Not a maid. They might as well hand me a mop.
They wouldn't have treated Fury like this. They would've told Fury to kick some ass and take some names.
Because someone's gotta pay. Someone's gotta @#$%& pay.
And just cause Magneto's dead doesn't mean they're off the hook.
I'm sorry, Director-- who?
Have you been listening to a thing I said? Mutants. Mutants are gonna pay for this.
And that's a good thing?
No. But it's what happens. Tragedy needs an enemy. Goat's gotta be sacrificed. It's just what happens.
What? What's wrong?
Nothing. I don't know. I thought I heard something. Hearing things now. Great.

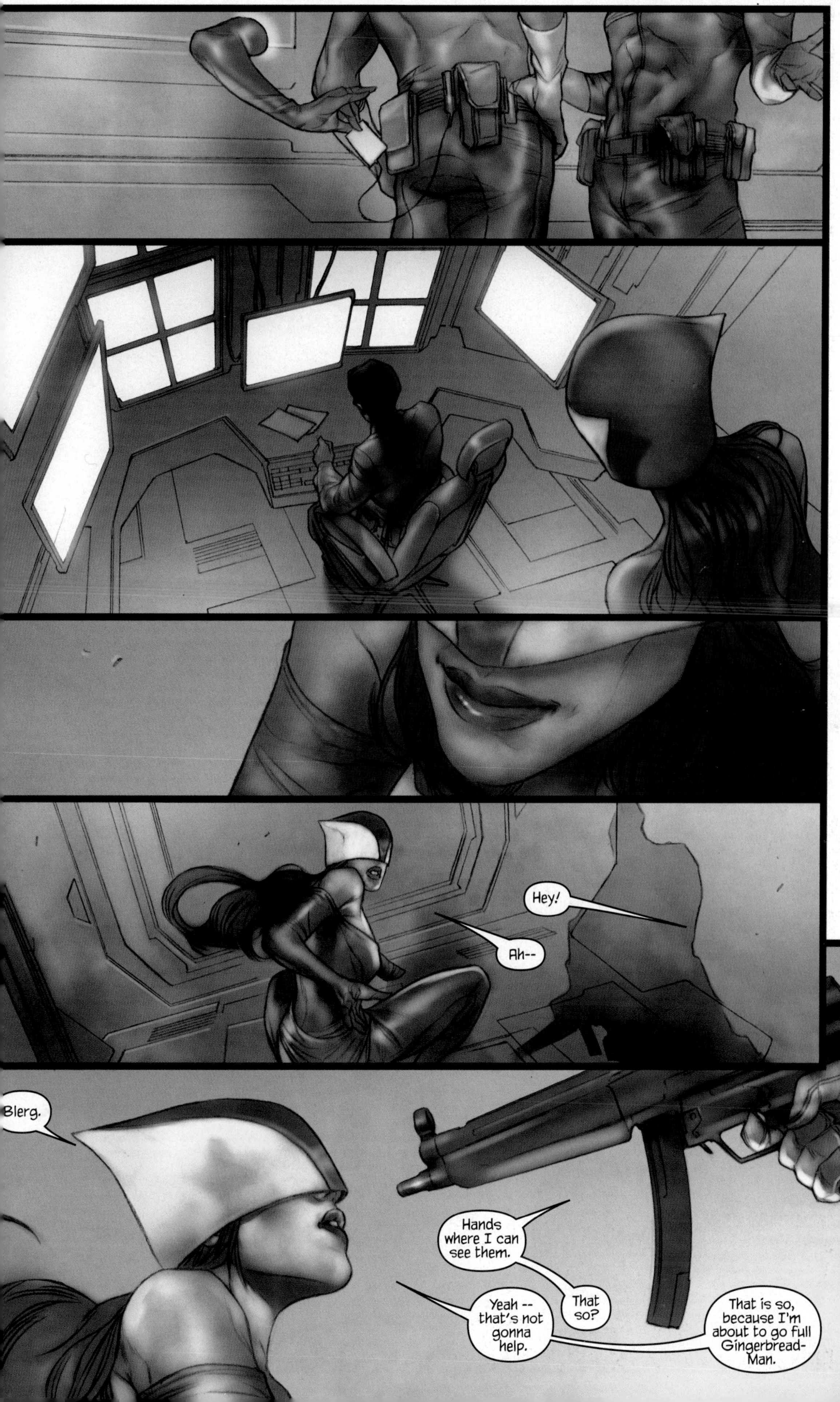
Hey!
Ah--
Blerg.
Hands where I can see them.
That so?
Yeah -- that's not gonna help.
That is so, because I'm about to go full Gingerbread-Man.

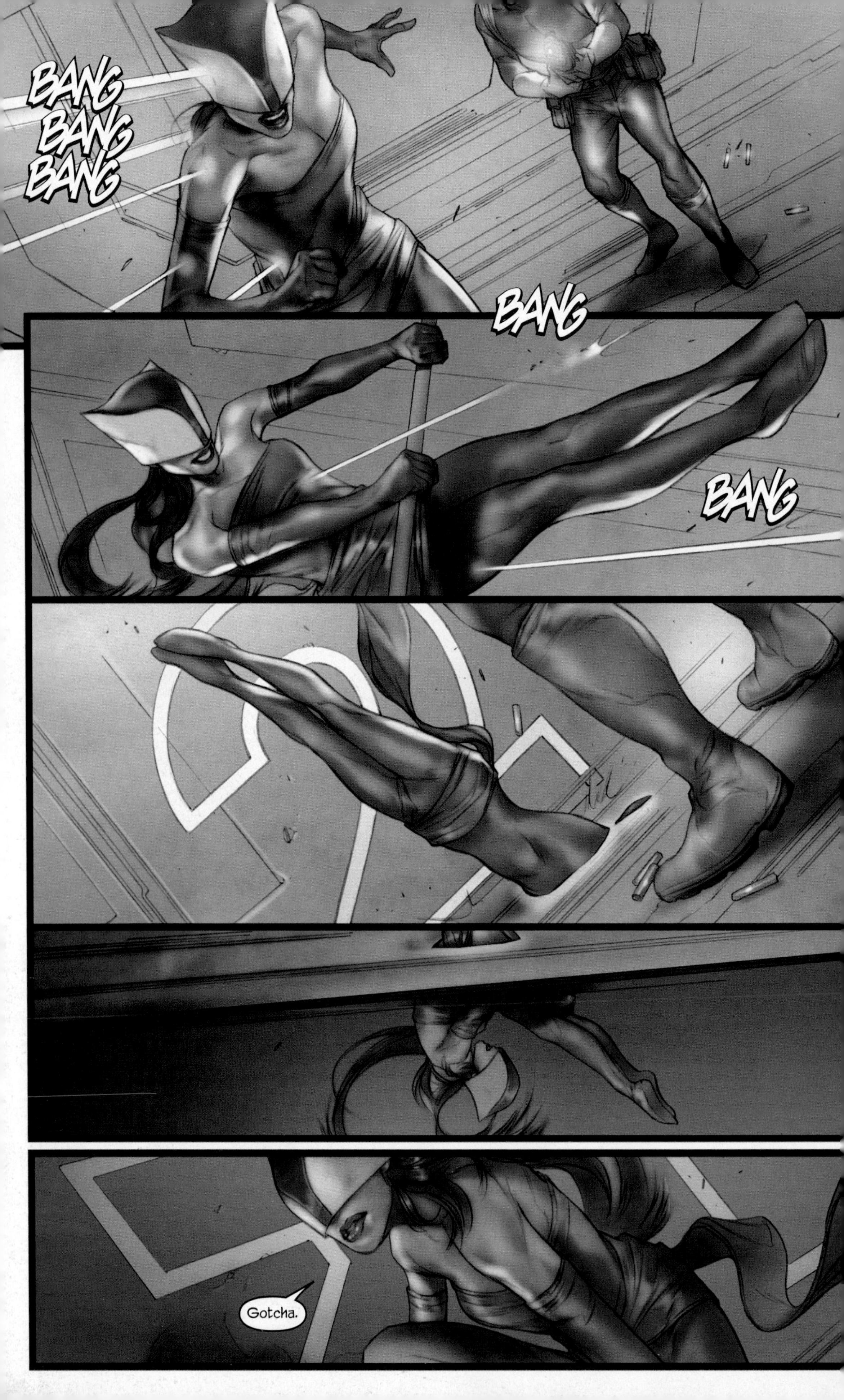
BANG
BANG
BANG
BANG
BANG
Gotcha.

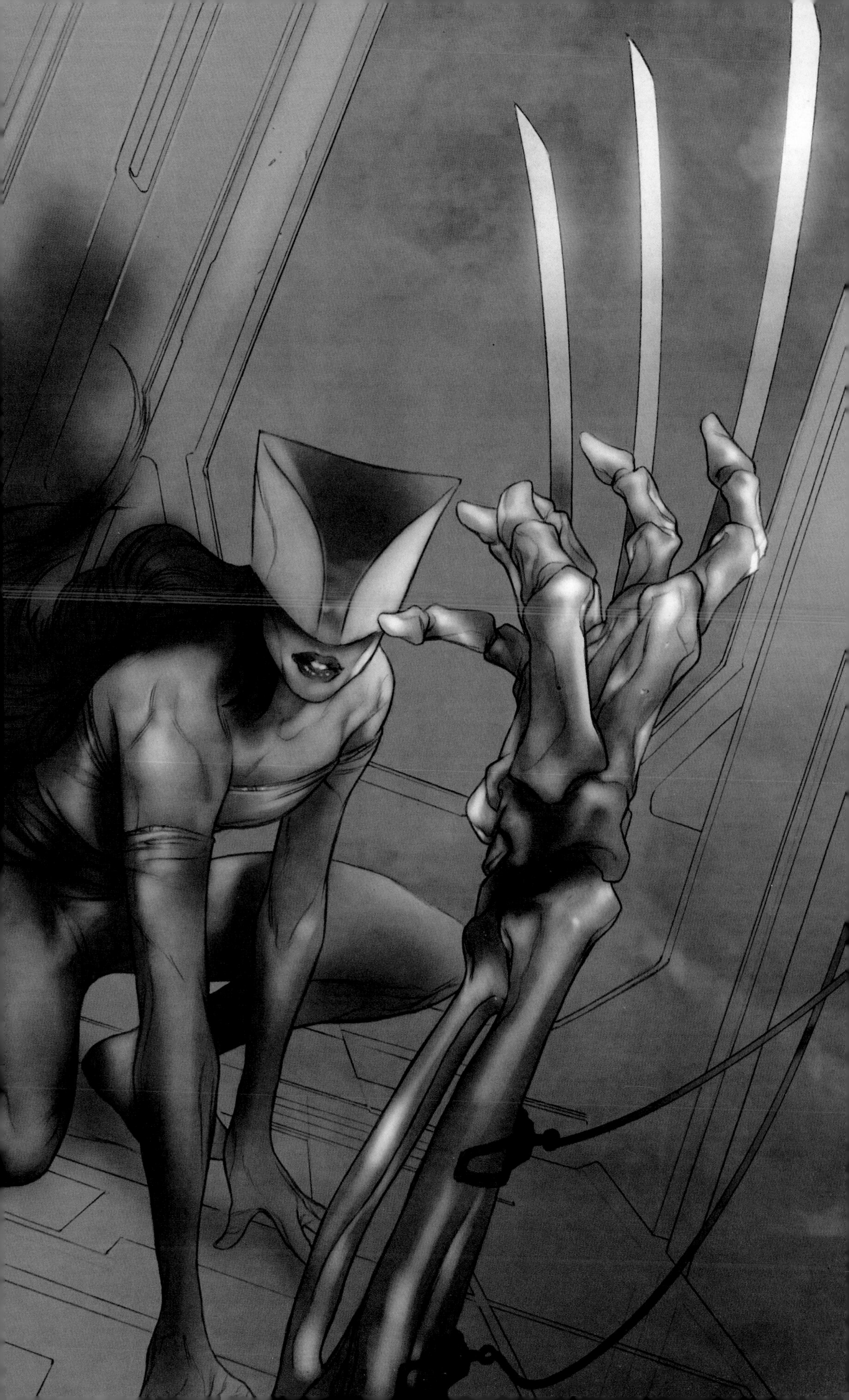

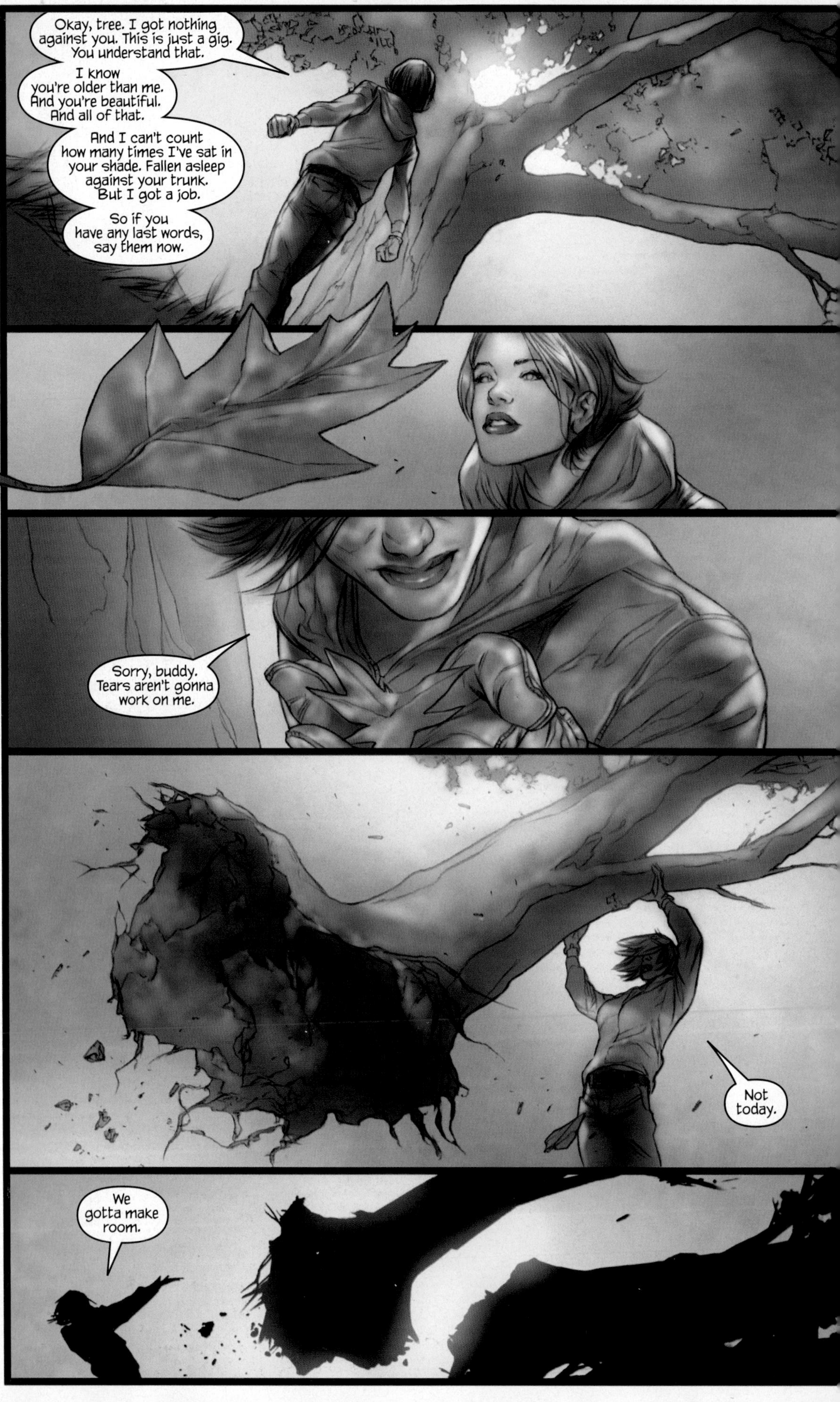
Okay, tree. I got nothing against you. This is just a gig. You understand that.
I know you're older than me. And you're beautiful. And all of that.
And I can't count how many times I've sat in your shade. Fallen asleep against your trunk. But I got a job.
So if you have any last words, say them now.
Sorry, buddy. Tears aren't gonna work on me.
Not today.
We gotta make room.

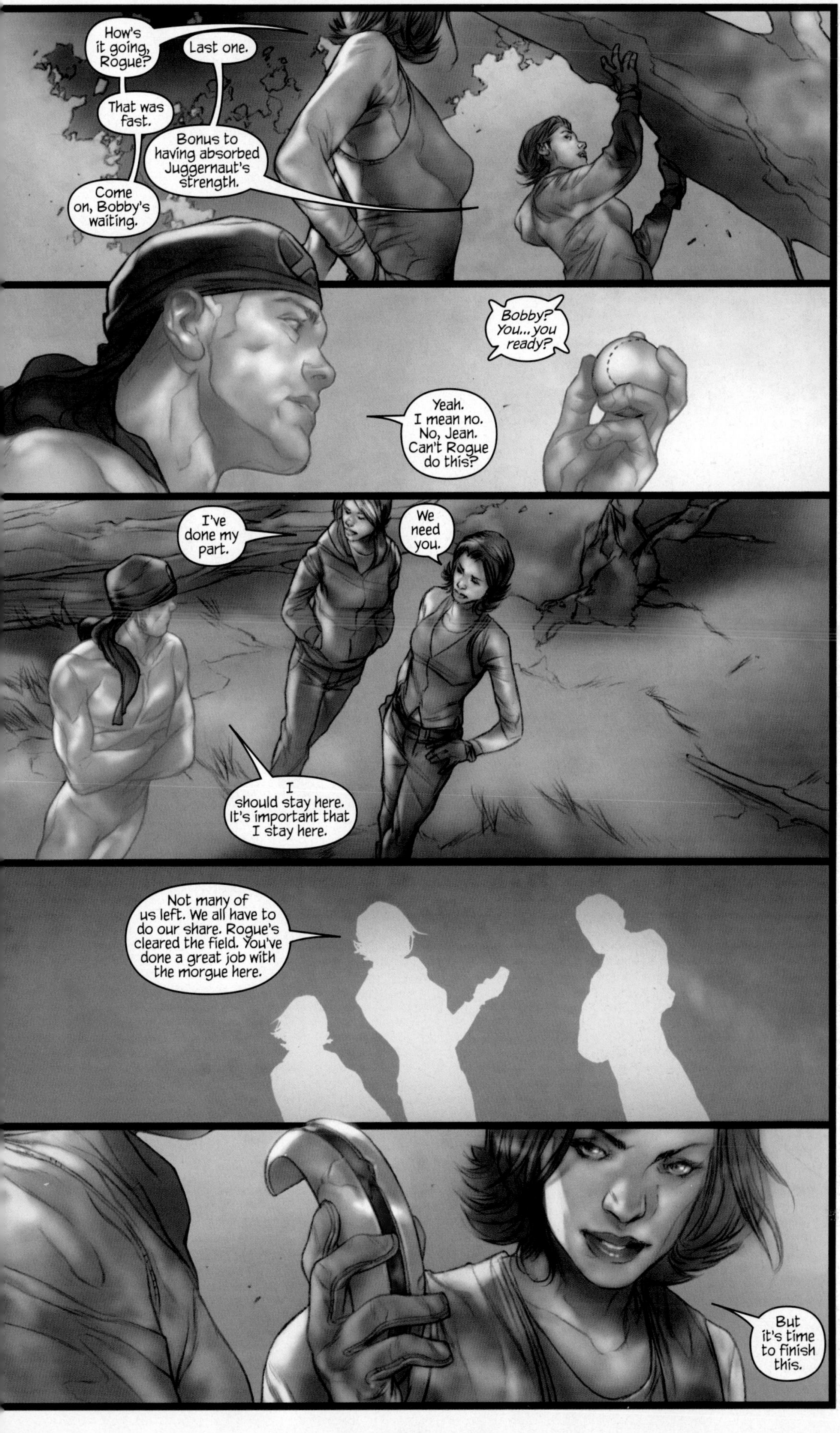
How's it going, Rogue?
Last one.
That was fast.
Bonus to having absorbed Juggernaut's strength.
Come on, Bobby's waiting.
Bobby? You... you ready?
Yeah. I mean no. No, Jean. Can't Rogue do this?
I've done my part.
We need you.
I should stay here. It's important that I stay here.
Not many of us left. We all have to do our share. Rogue's cleared the field. You've done a great job with the morgue here.
But it's time to finish this.

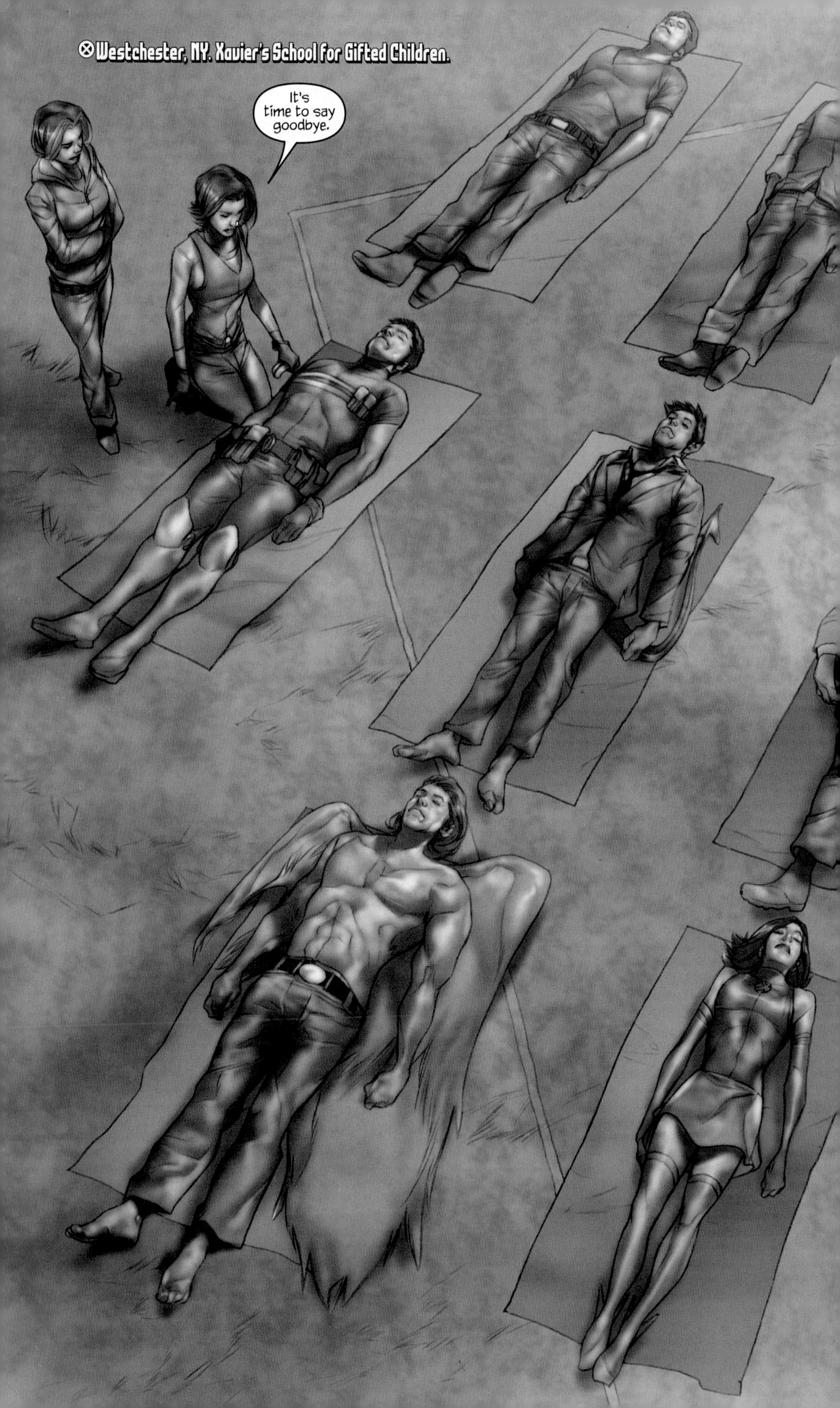
Westchester, NY. Xavier's School for Gifted Children.
It's time to say goodbye.

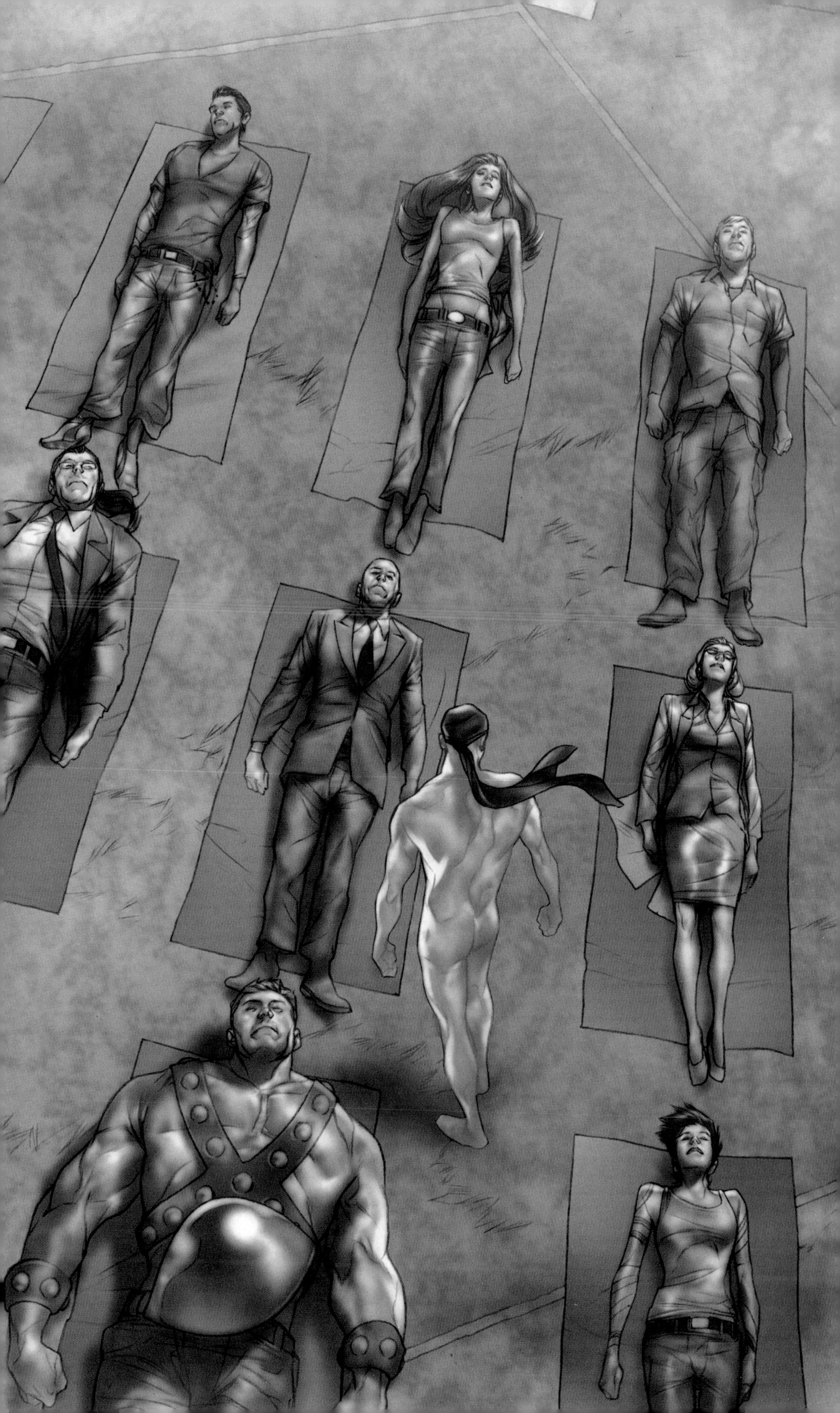

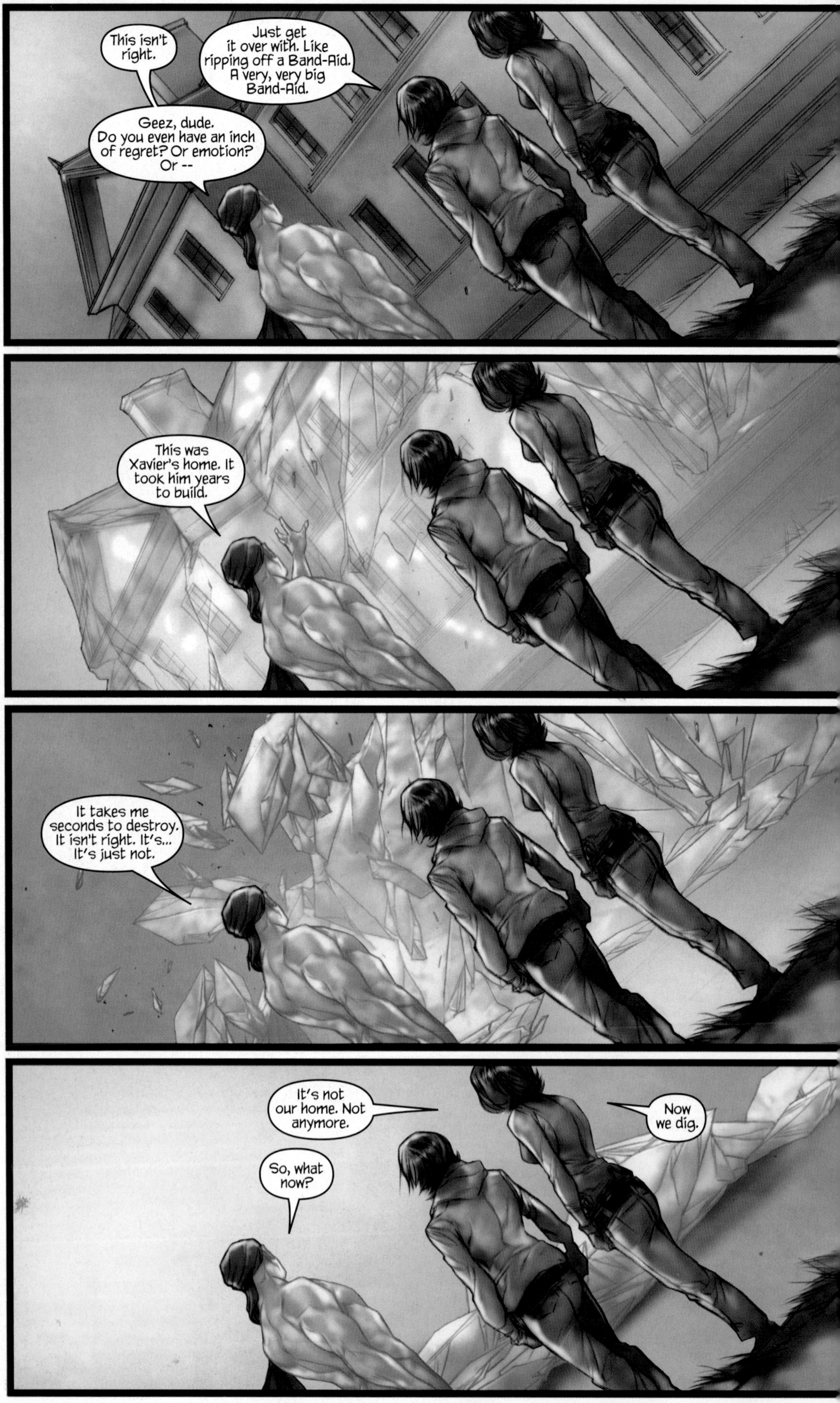
This isn't right.
Just get it over with. Like ripping off a Band-Aid. A very, very big Band-Aid.
Geez, dude. Do you even have an inch of regret? Or emotion? Or --
This was Xavier's home. It took him years to build.
It takes me seconds to destroy. It isn't right. It's... It's just not.
It's not our home. Not anymore.
Now we dig.
So, what now?

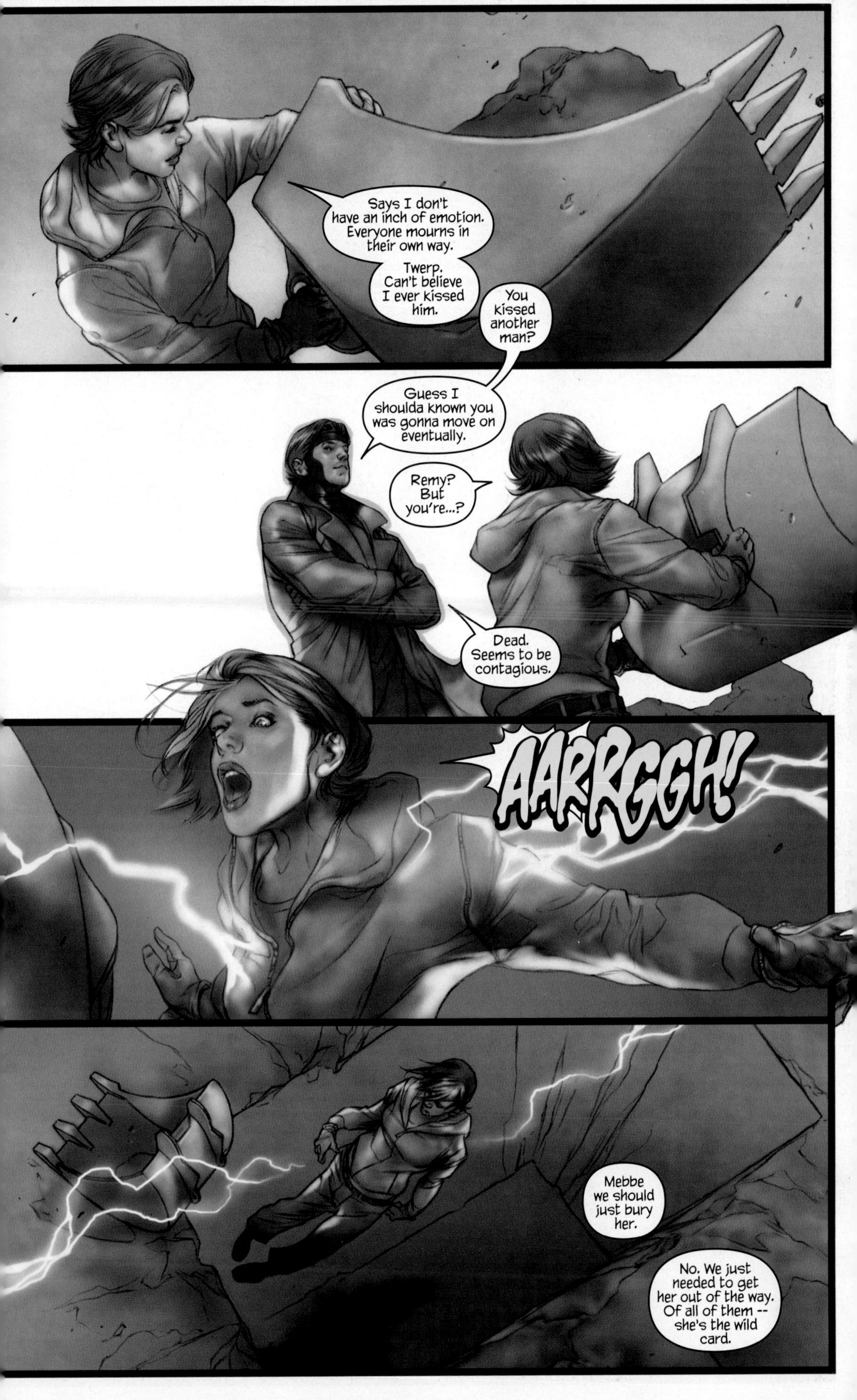

Says I don't have an inch of emotion. Everyone mourns in their own way.
Twerp. Can't believe I ever kissed him.
You kissed another man?
Guess I shoulda known you was gonna move on eventually.
Remy? But you're...?
Dead. Seems to be contagious.
AARRGGH!
Mebbe we should just bury her.
No. We just needed to get her out of the way. Of all of them -- she's the wild card.

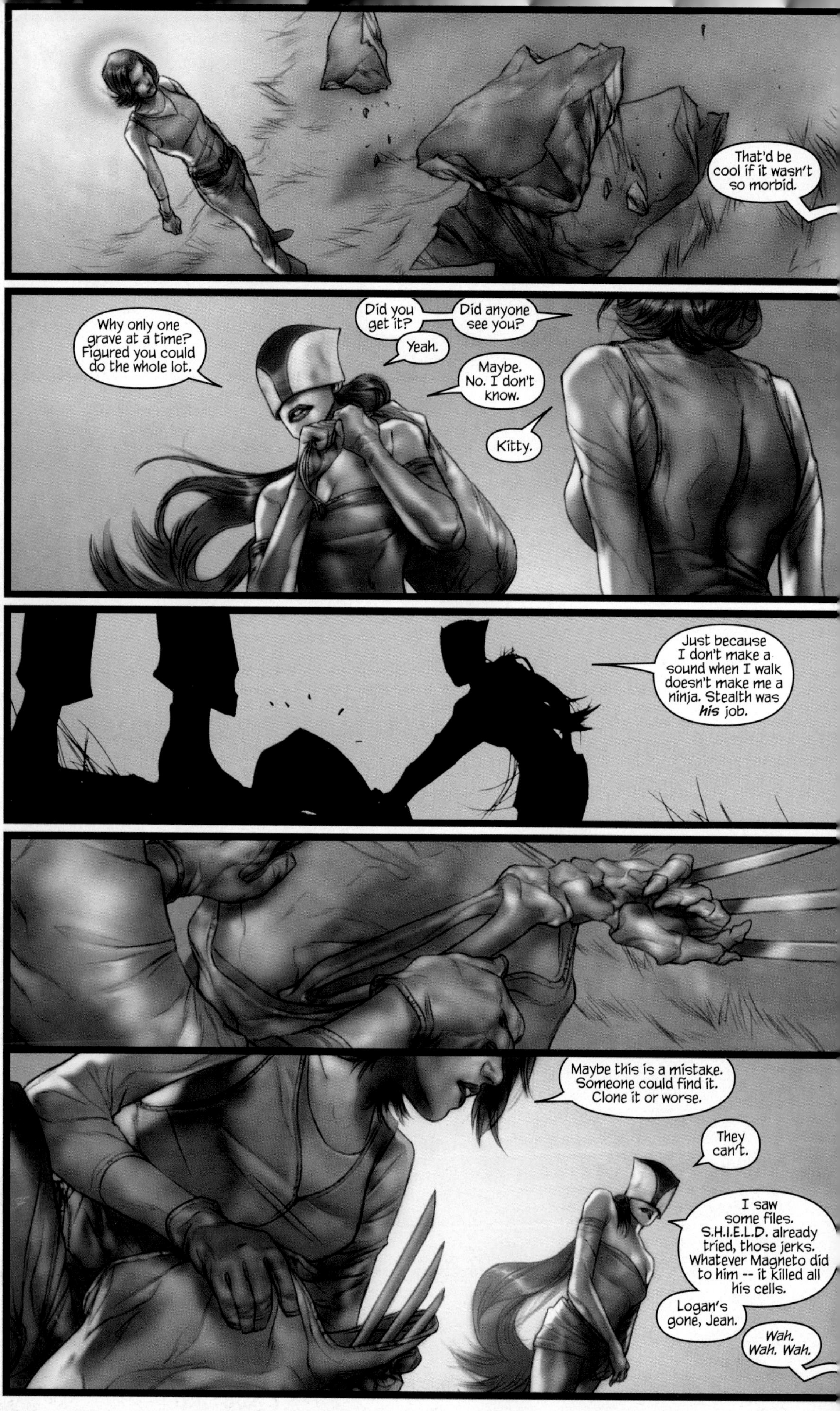
That'd be cool if it wasn't so morbid.
Why only one grave at a time? Figured you could do the whole lot.
Did you get it?
Did anyone see you?
Yeah.
Maybe. No. I don't know.
Kitty.
Just because I don't make a sound when I walk doesn't make me a ninja. Stealth was **his** job.
Maybe this is a mistake. Someone could find it. Clone it or worse.
They can't.
I saw some files. S.H.I.E.L.D. already tried, those jerks. Whatever Magneto did to him -- it killed all his cells.
Logan's gone, Jean.
Wah. Wah. Wah.

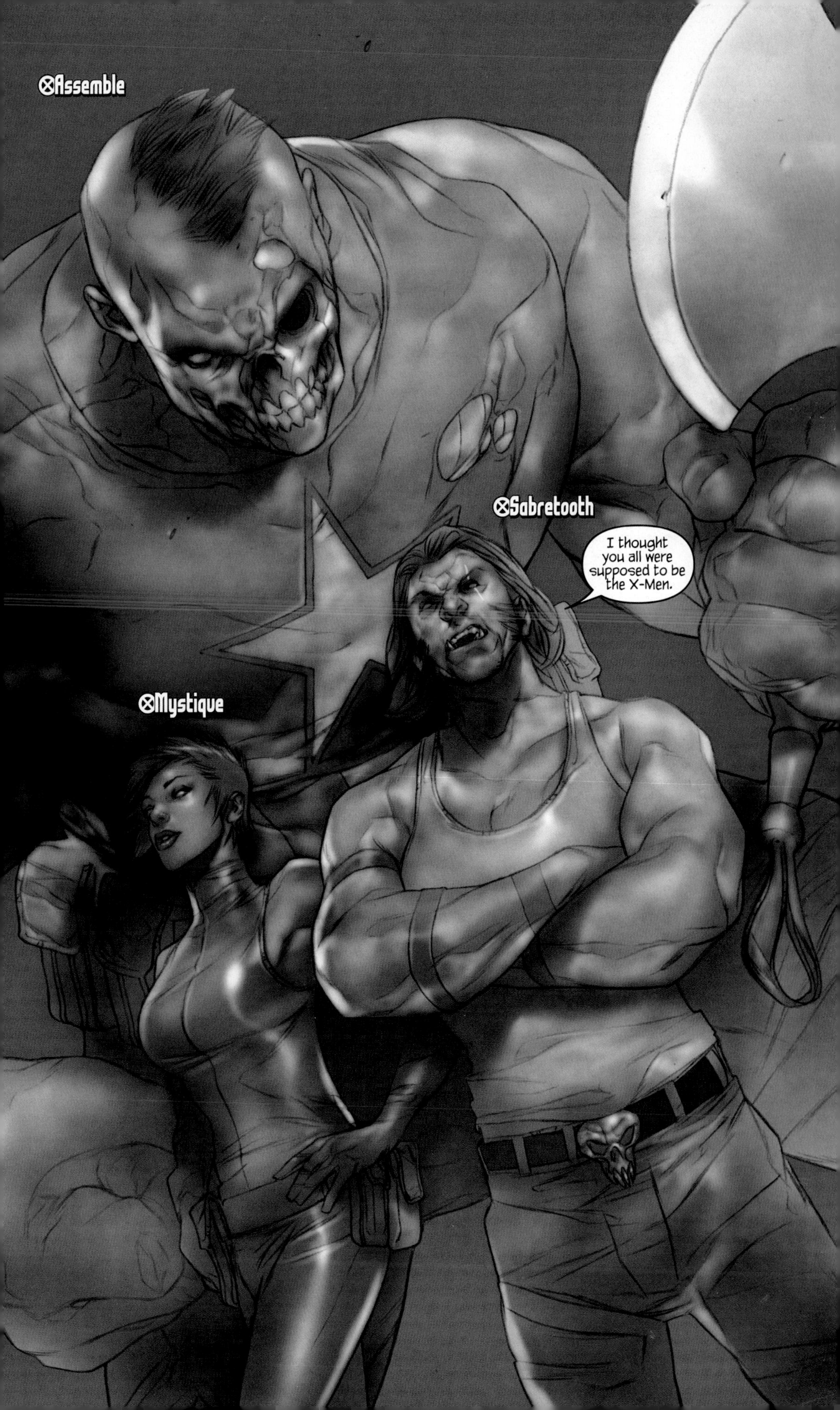
Assemble
Sabretooth
I thought you all were supposed to be the X-Men.
Mystique

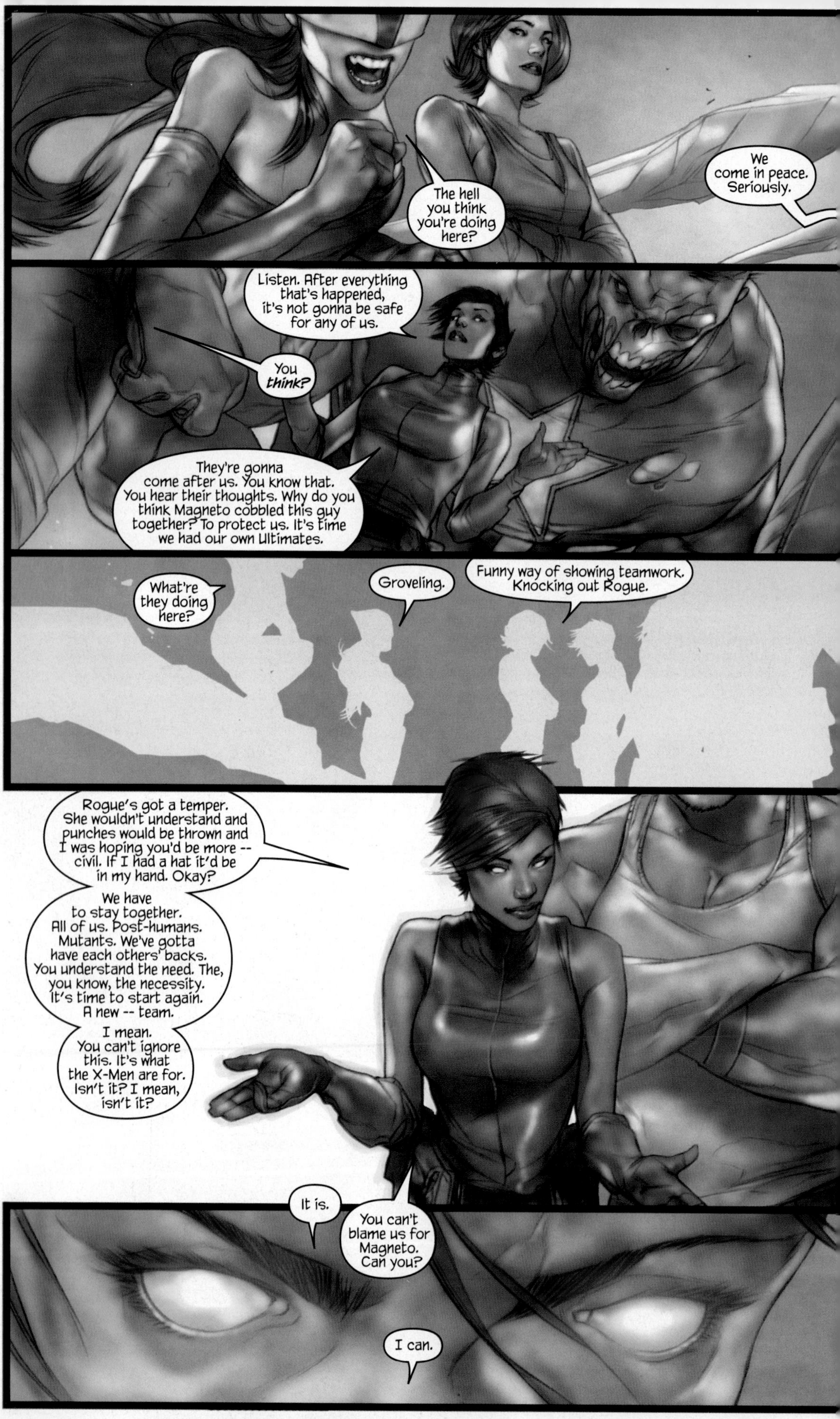

The hell you think you're doing here?
We come in peace. Seriously.
Listen. After everything that's happened, it's not gonna be safe for any of us.
You *think?*
They're gonna come after us. You know that. You hear their thoughts. Why do you think Magneto cobbled this guy together? To protect us. It's time we had our own Ultimates.
What're they doing here?
Groveling.
Funny way of showing teamwork. Knocking out Rogue.
Rogue's got a temper. She wouldn't understand and punches would be thrown and I was hoping you'd be more -- civil. If I had a hat it'd be in my hand. Okay?
We have to stay together. All of us. Post-humans. Mutants. We've gotta have each others' backs. You understand the need. The, you know, the necessity. It's time to start again. A new -- team.
I mean. You can't ignore this. It's what the X-Men are for. Isn't it? I mean, isn't it?
It is.
You can't blame us for Magneto. Can you?
I can.

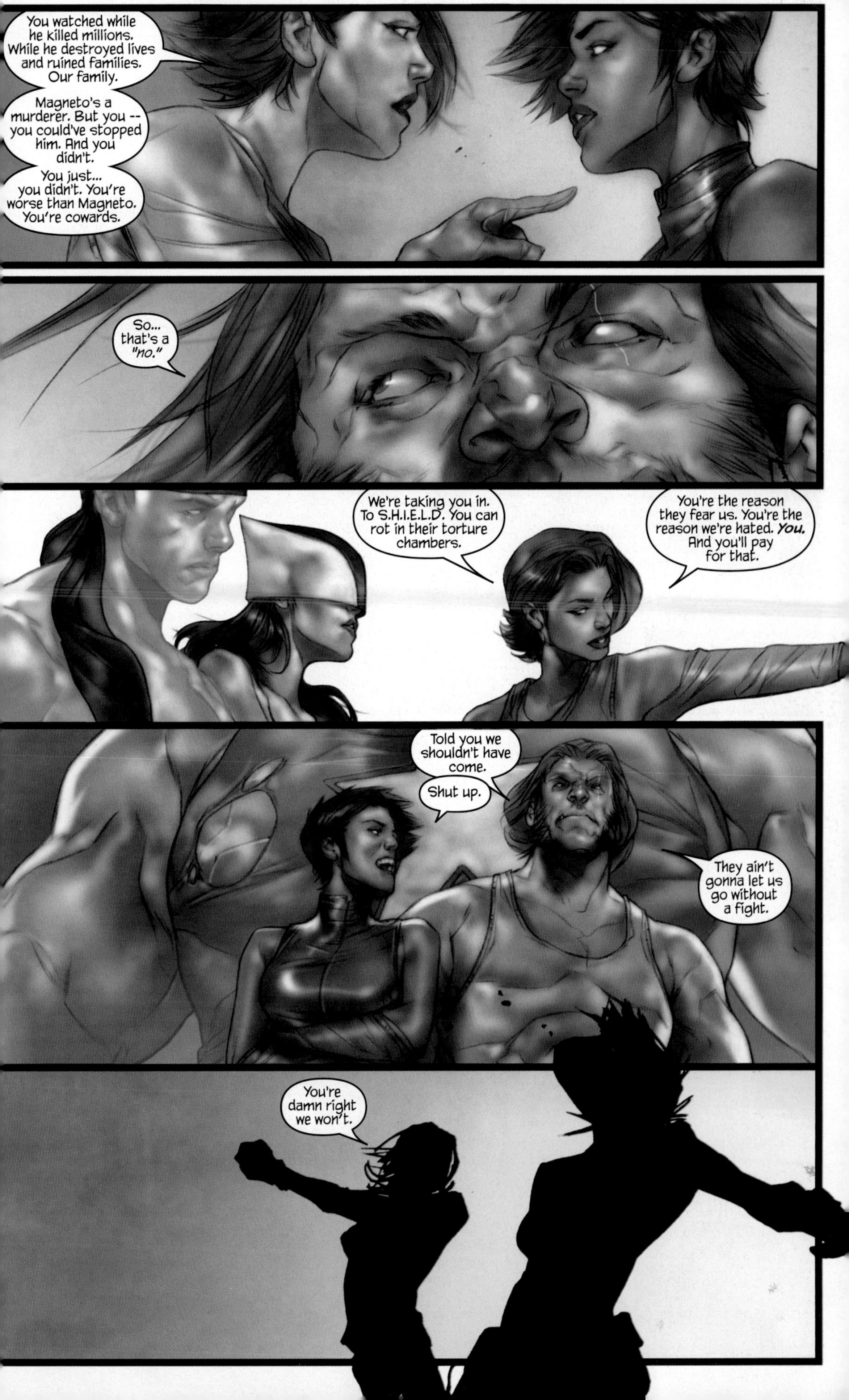
You watched while he killed millions. While he destroyed lives and ruined families. Our family.
Magneto's a murderer. But you -- you could've stopped him. And you didn't.
You just... you didn't. You're worse than Magneto. You're cowards.
So... that's a "no."
We're taking you in. To S.H.I.E.L.D. You can rot in their torture chambers.
You're the reason they fear us. You're the reason we're hated. *You.* And you'll pay for that.
Told you we shouldn't have come.
Shut up.
They ain't gonna let us go without a fight.
You're damn right we won't.

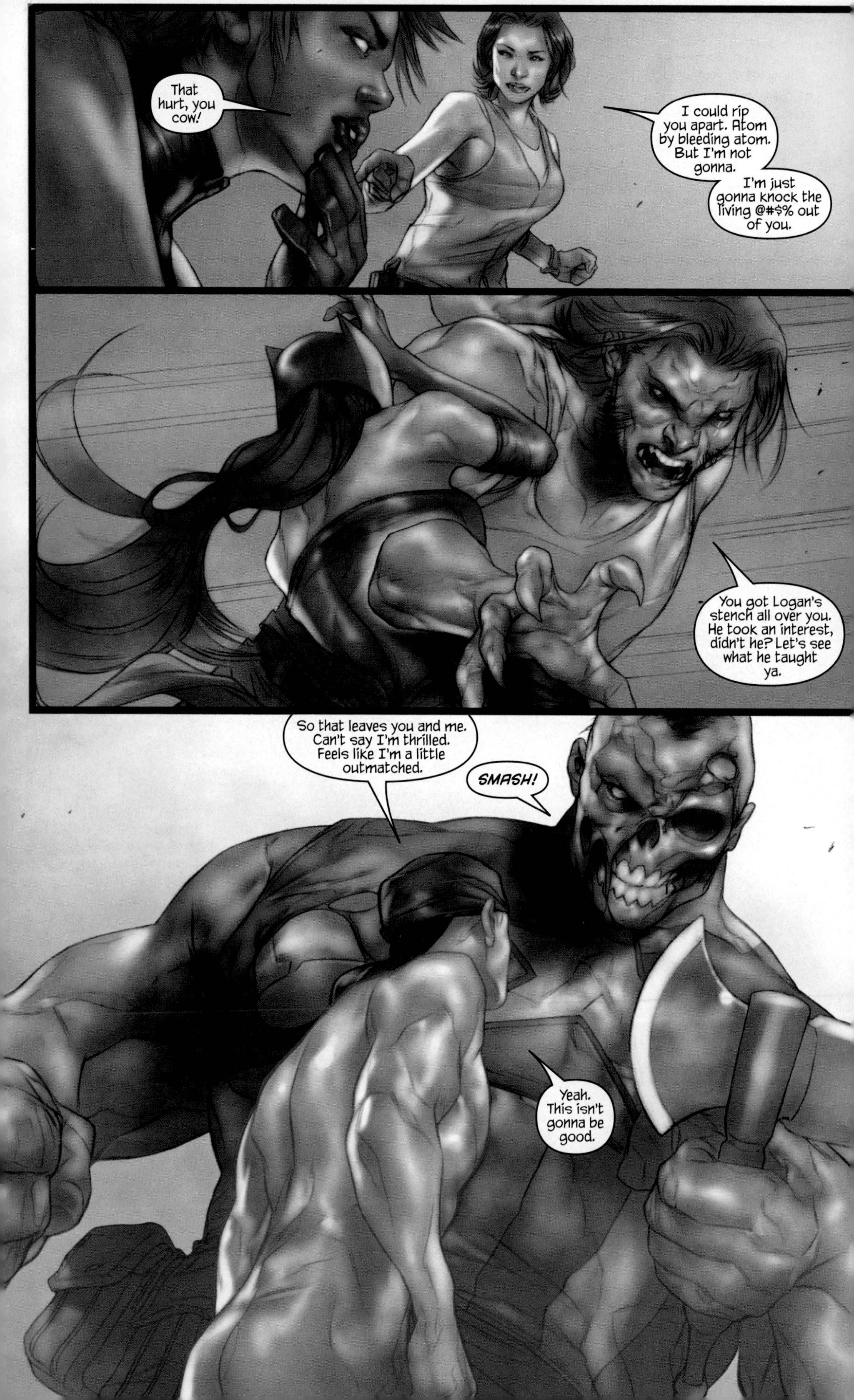
That hurt, you cow!
I could rip you apart. Atom by bleeding atom. But I'm not gonna.
I'm just gonna knock the living @#$% out of you.
You got Logan's stench all over you. He took an interest, didn't he? Let's see what he taught ya.
So that leaves you and me. Can't say I'm thrilled. Feels like I'm a little outmatched.
SMASH!
Yeah. This isn't gonna be good.

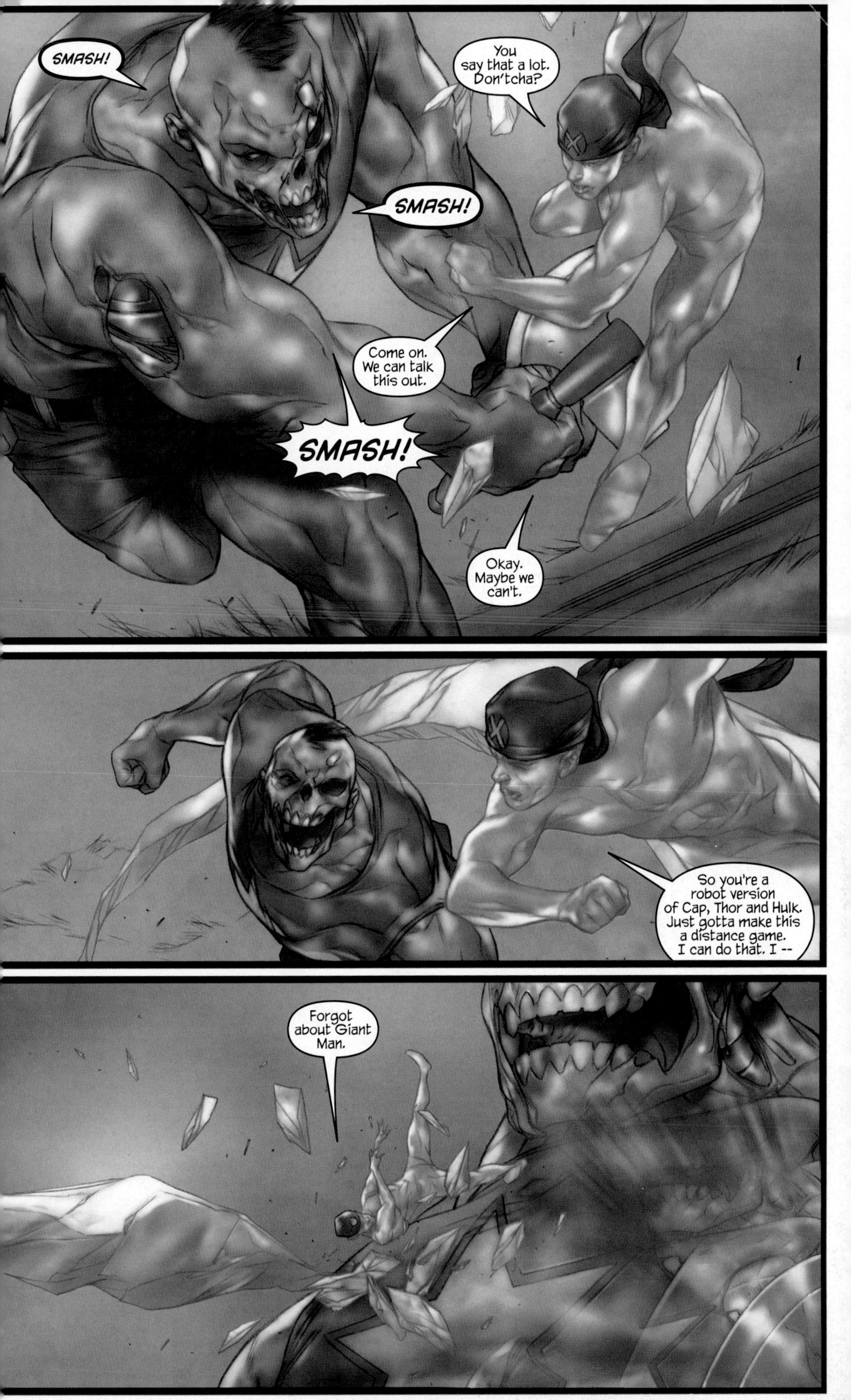
SMASH!
You say that a lot. Don'tcha?
SMASH!
Come on. We can talk this out.
SMASH!
Okay. Maybe we can't.
So you're a robot version of Cap, Thor and Hulk. Just gotta make this a distance game. I can do that. I --
Forgot about Giant Man.

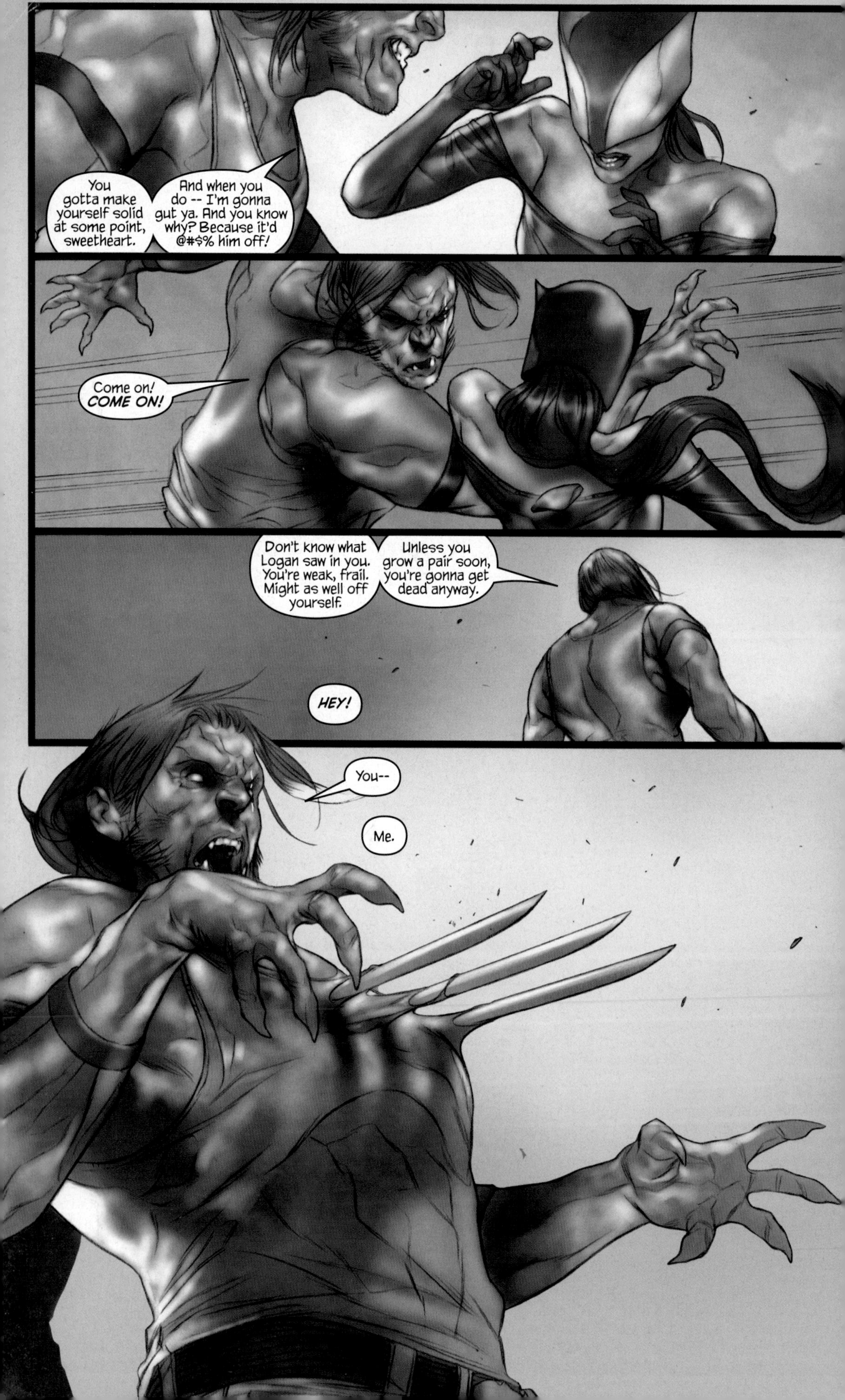
You gotta make yourself solid at some point, sweetheart.
And when you do -- I'm gonna gut ya. And you know why? Because it'd @#$% him off!
Come on! COME ON!
Don't know what Logan saw in you. You're weak, frail. Might as well off yourself.
Unless you grow a pair soon, you're gonna get dead anyway.
HEY!
You--
Me.

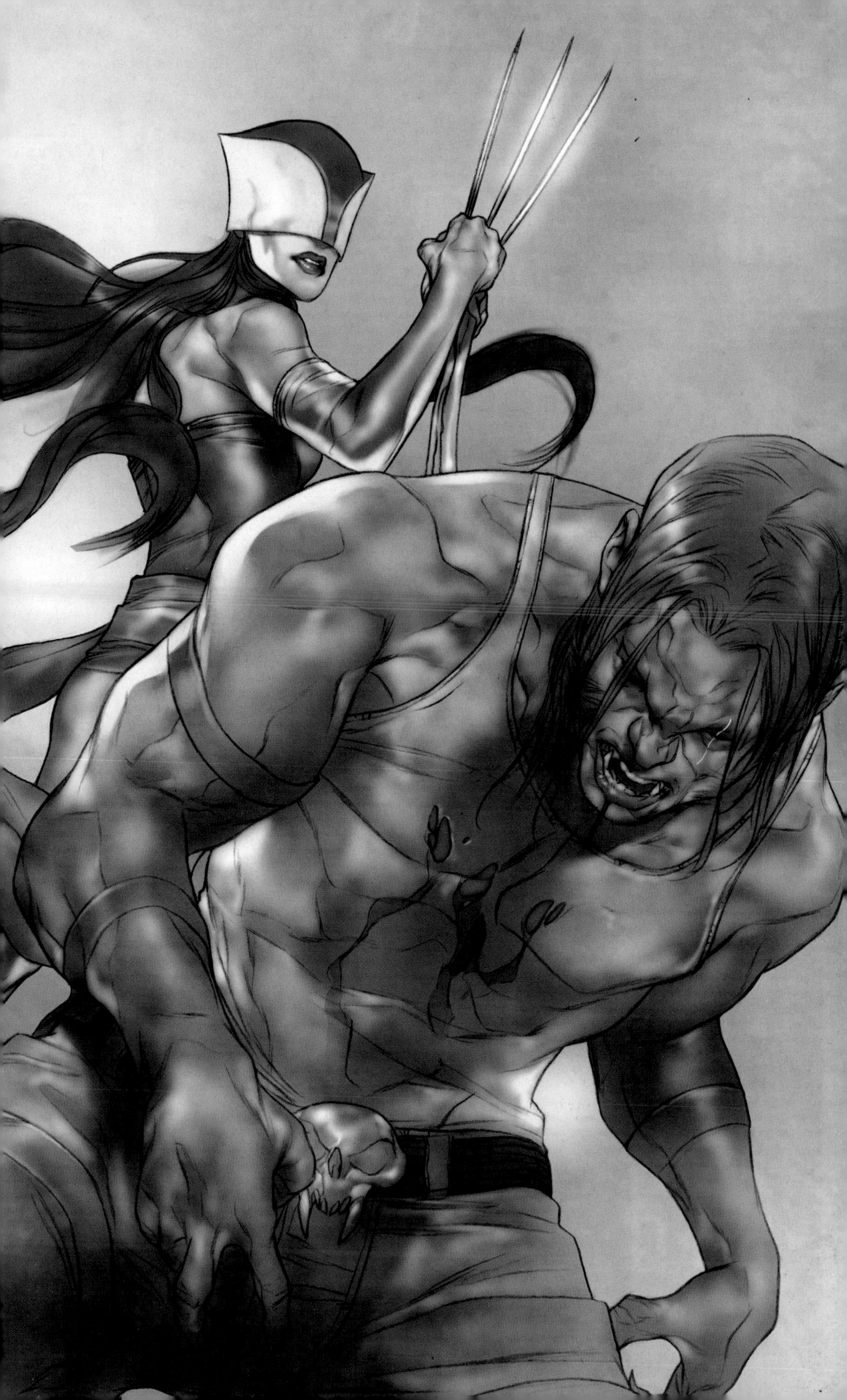

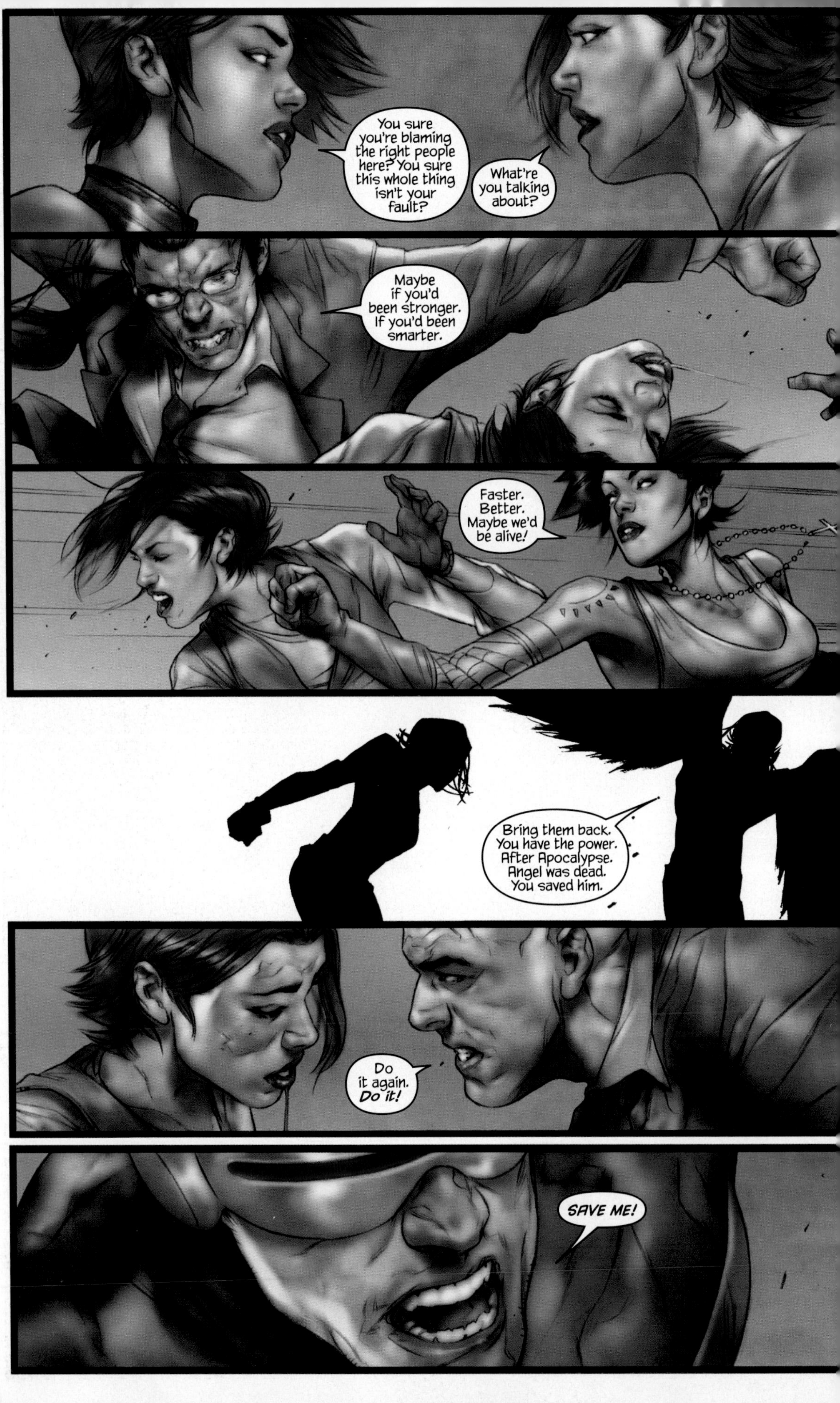
You sure you're blaming the right people here? You sure this whole thing isn't your fault?
What're you talking about?
Maybe if you'd been stronger. If you'd been smarter.
Faster. Better. Maybe we'd be alive!
Bring them back. You have the power. After Apocalypse. Angel was dead. You saved him.
Do it again. Do it!
SAVE ME!

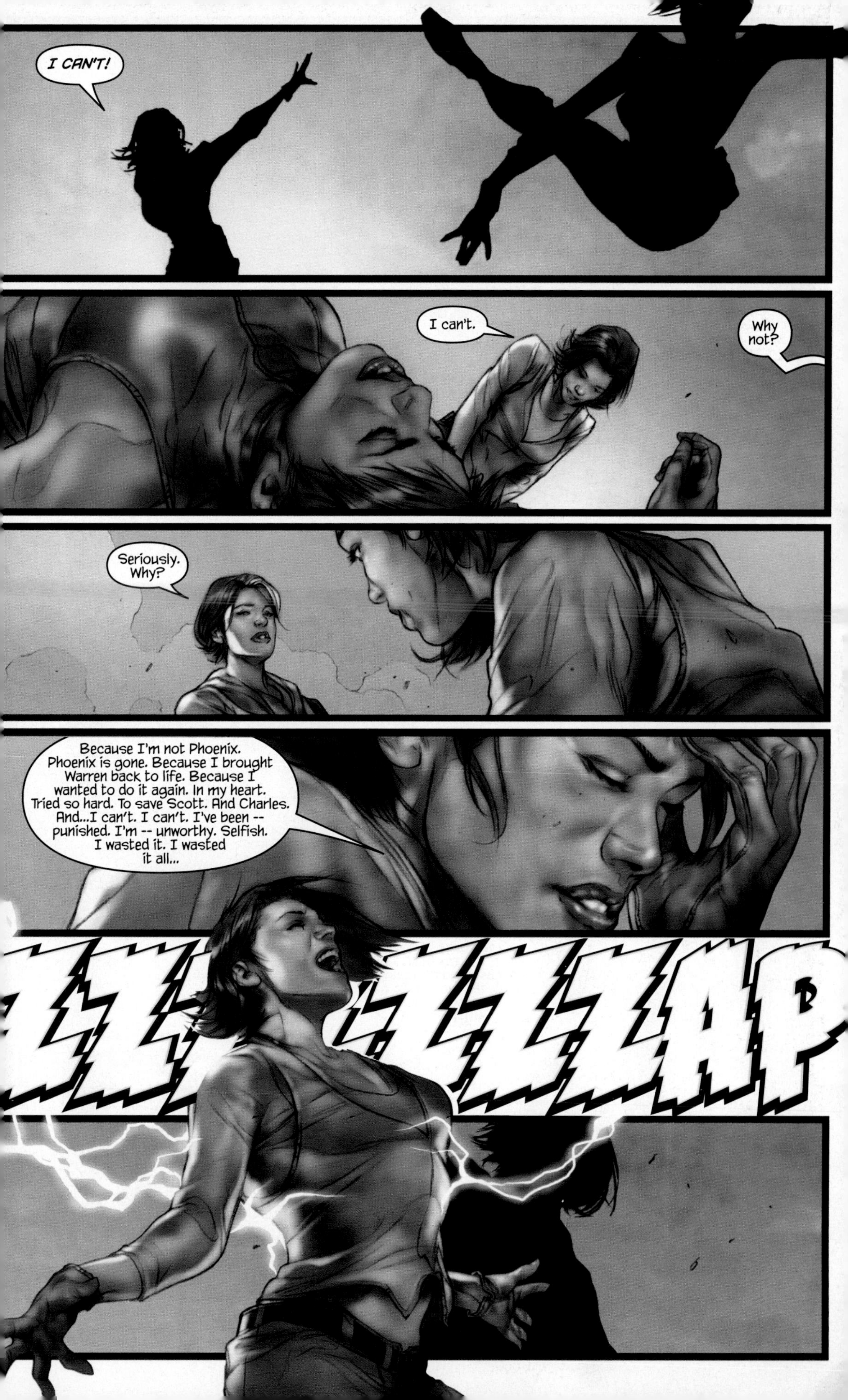
I CAN'T!
I can't.
Why not?
Seriously. Why?
Because I'm not Phoenix. Phoenix is gone. Because I brought Warren back to life. Because I wanted to do it again. In my heart. Tried so hard. To save Scott. And Charles. And...I can't. I can't. I've been -- punished. I'm -- unworthy. Selfish. I wasted it. I wasted it all...
ZZZZZZAP

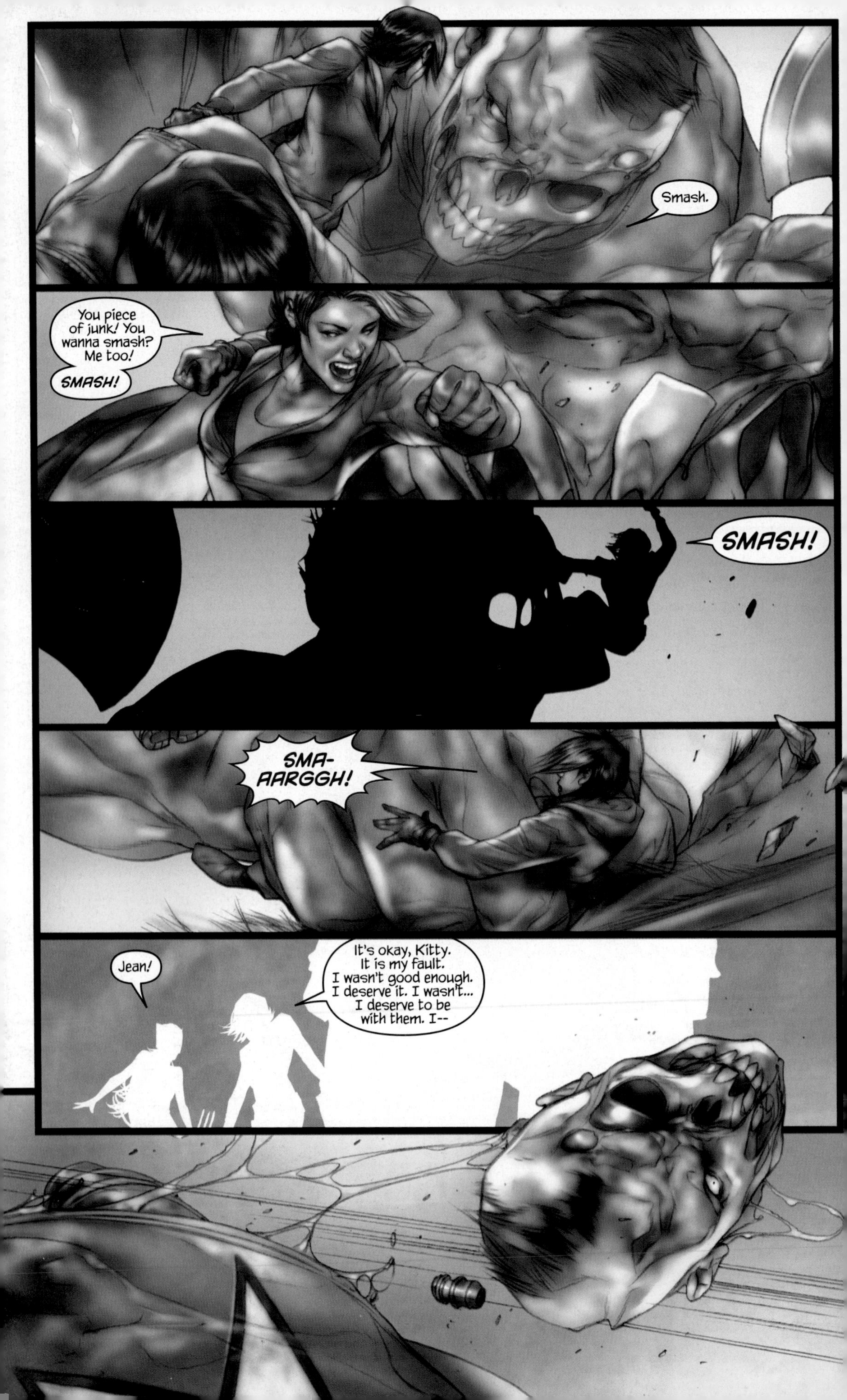
Smash.
You piece of junk! You wanna smash? Me too!
SMASH!
SMASH!
SMA-AARGGH!
Jean!
It's okay, Kitty. It is my fault. I wasn't good enough. I deserve it. I wasn't... I deserve to be with them. I--

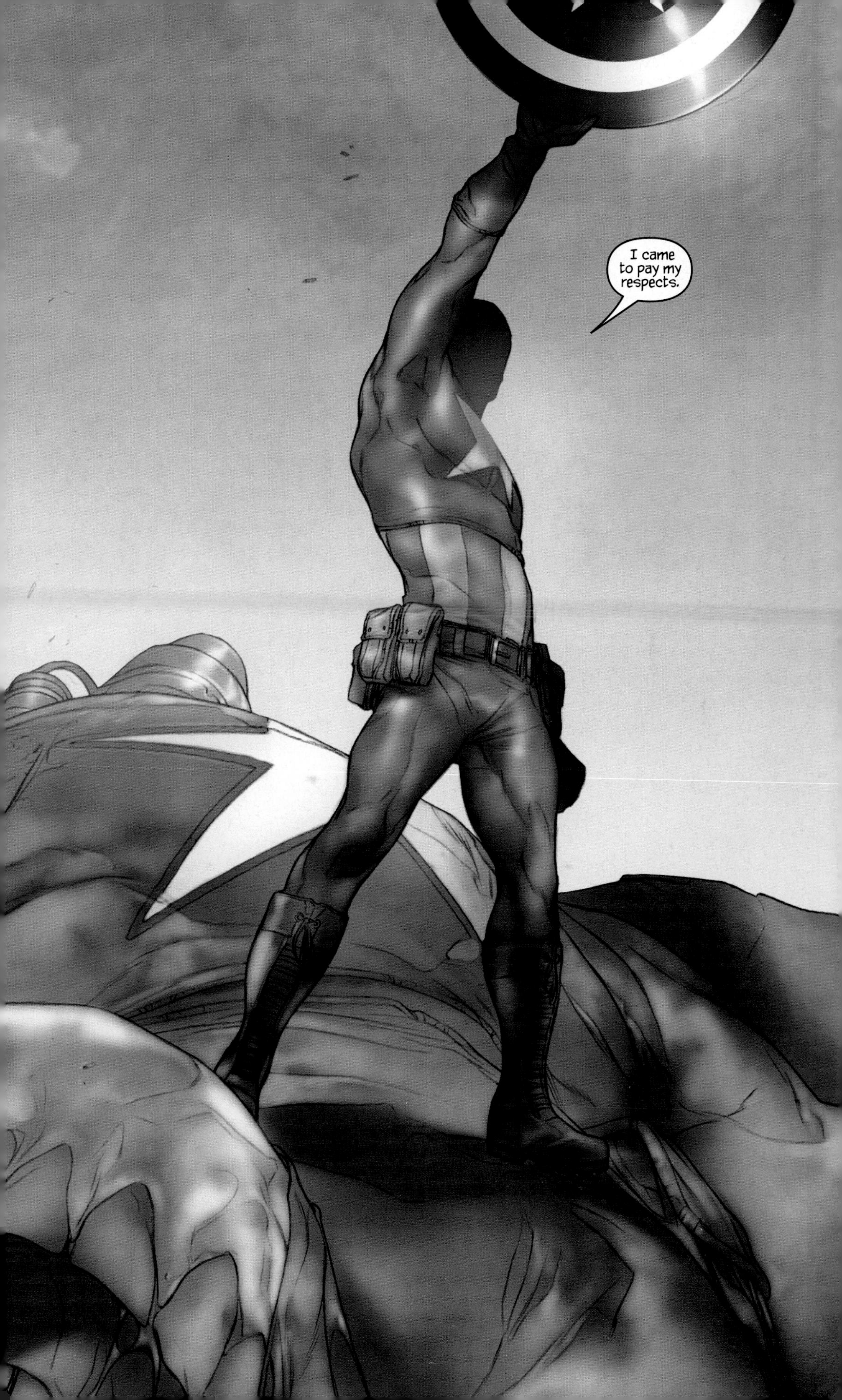
I came to pay my respects.

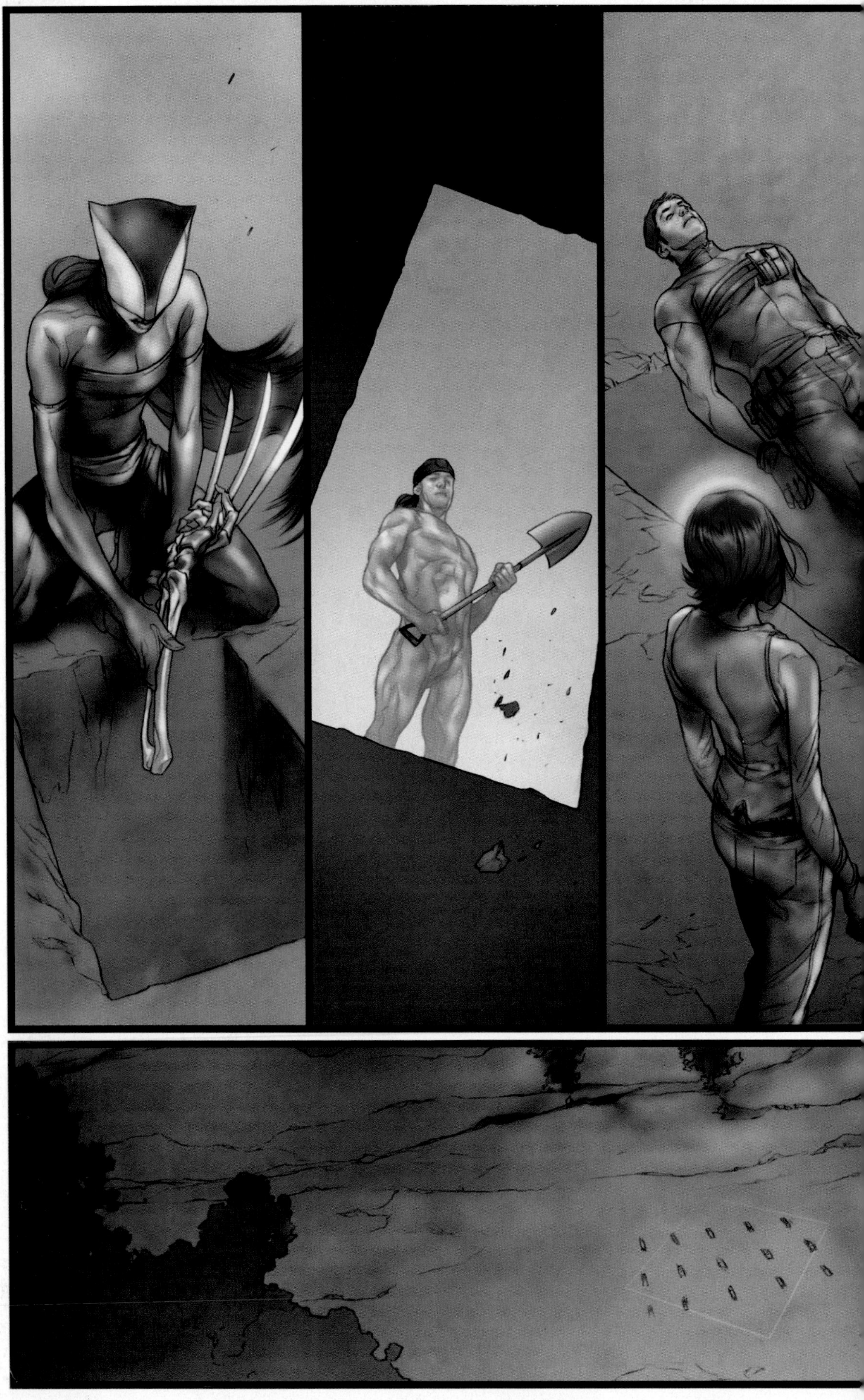

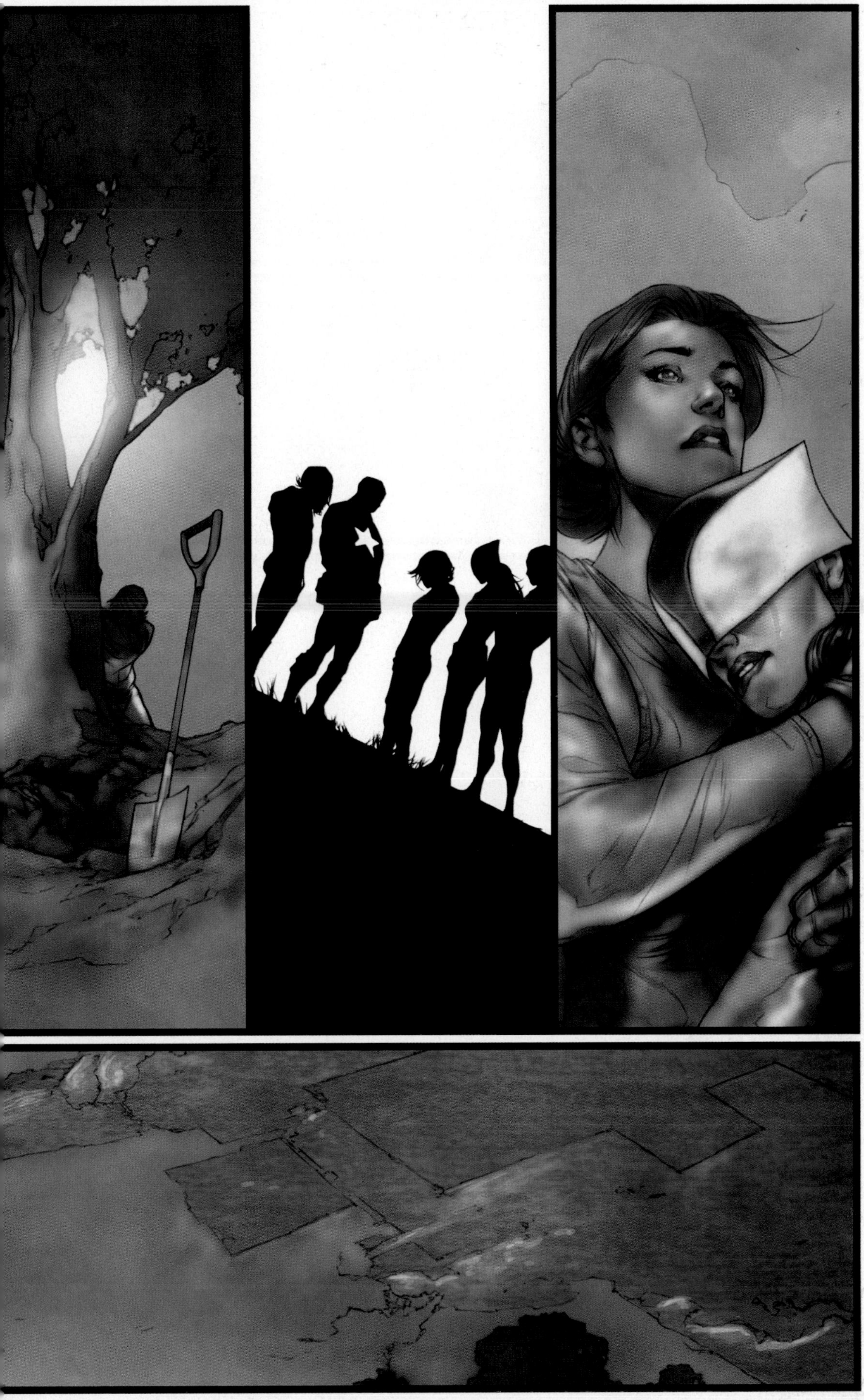

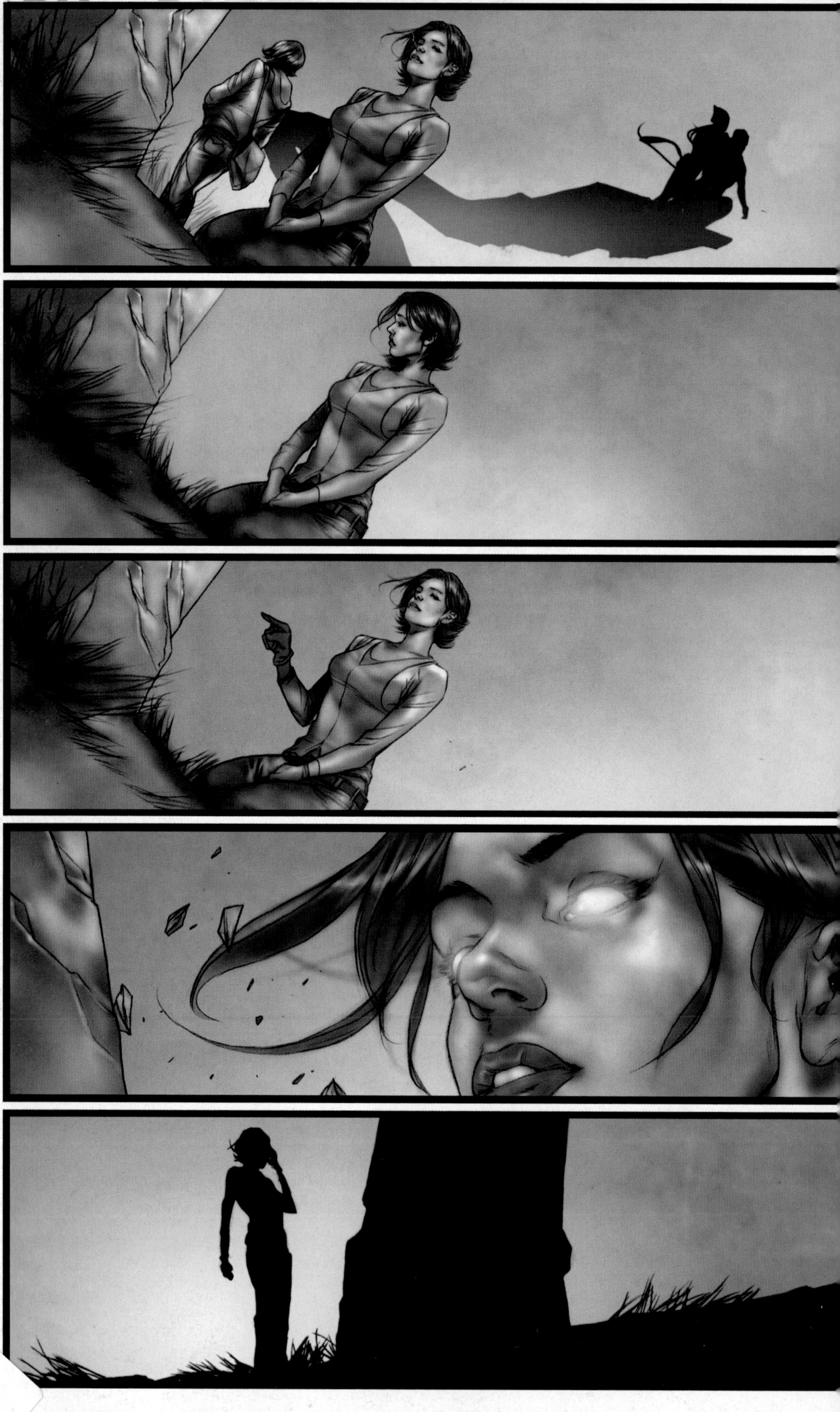

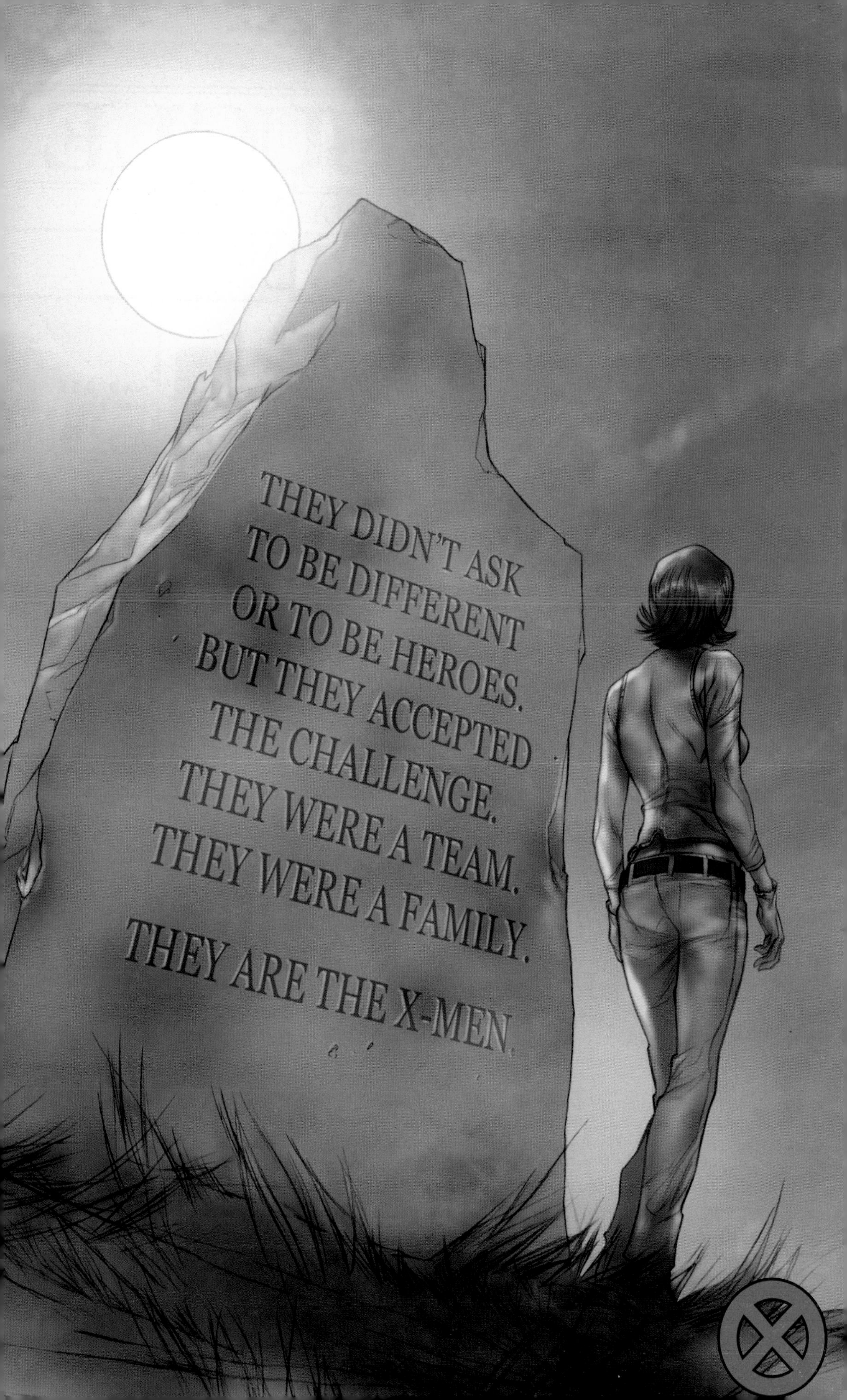
THEY DIDN'T ASK
TO BE DIFFERENT
OR TO BE HEROES.
BUT THEY ACCEPTED
THE CHALLENGE.
THEY WERE A TEAM.
THEY WERE A FAMILY.
THEY ARE THE X-MEN.

DAILY BUGLE

NEW YORK'S FINEST DAILY NEWSPAPER

OBITUARIES

p.

HENRY "THE BEAST" McCOY

Henry McCoy, better known to the world at large as the mutant hero "The Beast," died today. The founding member of the mutant super team known as the X-Men was one of countless casualties in the tidal wave that struck New York. While the death toll is still rising, one thing is certain, that the loss of this hero will have a major impact in this time when the world is in dire need of saving.

Despite being the quarterback of his high school football team, McCoy found adolescence difficult, due to his unusually sized hands and feet. Fortunately, this troubled teen-aged genius found a home among the other mutants at the Xavier Institute, a school that housed and trained mutants. His acumen in the field of genetic research made him an invaluable member of the X-Men. After a critical injury in Times Square shortly after the formation of the X-Men left him near death, it was his own research that helped save his life. Unfortunately, his biological makeup was altered in the process, giving him a truly beast-like appearance.

Recently, McCoy seemingly cured his own pigmentation, returning to a more human-like state. His relationship with fellow mutant and X-Man Storm was also seemingly on the rebound.

Tragically, this young scientist and adventurer drowned in the tidal wave, one of the hundreds of thousands crushed in its wake. The cause of this wave, and the other natural disasters that began at approximately the same time around the world, is unknown. As reports of more deaths come in, it is likely that this hero's passing is only the first to be reported in this developing story. ∎

DAILY ✦ BUGLE

NEW YORK'S FINEST DAILY NEWSPAPER

OBITUARIES

p.

KURT "NIGHTCRAWLER" WAGNER

The death toll continues to rise in the aftermath of the Ultimatum Wave, as Kurt Wagner's name is added to the list of casualties. The mutant known to the world as "Nightcrawler," due to his blue fur and demonic appearance, was actually a troubled young man who often sought solace and stability in his faith.

Due to his deformity at birth, it was easy to tell Kurt Wagner was different…when you could find him. He spent much of his formative years in the Bavarian Alps, where little is known of his youth. In his early teens, he was kidnapped by the Weapon X Program and forced to be a part of their black ops wet-works organization. He was freed by the X-Men and he returned to his native Germany.

His return to the X-Men was marked by trouble and controversy. He quickly developed feelings for fellow teammate Dazzler (also now deceased thanks to the attack that took Kurt's life), but when this attraction proved unrequited, he was thrown into a state of mental instability. He kidnapped the girl and the X-Men were forced to rescue her from his grasp. They helped rehabilitate him, but he left the team to help the Morlocks, a band of mutants whose mutations caused physical deformities much like his own. He found a home there and was made their leader.

It was during an outing with his former teammates that the disaster the world now refers to as the "Ultimatum Wave" hit New York, an attack that has caused massive destruction across the globe in many forms. Nightcrawler's sad ending adds to the already numerous list of lives taken far too soon in this developing story. ■

DAILY ◆ BUGLE

NEW YORK'S FINEST DAILY NEWSPAPER

OBITUARIES

ROFESSOR CHARLES FRANCIS XAVIER

The world was shocked today as news spread the murder of renowned pacifist and mutant ghts activist, Charles Xavier. Although the entity of his killer has not been released to e public, it is widely reported that the man uilty of this crime is none other than his ne-time friend and frequent adversary rik Lensherr, the mutant terrorist known as lagneto.

Charles Xavier devoted his life and his forne to mutants, opening his doors to those orn genetically different and endangered by eir own powers, offering a place of learning nd sanctuary. His highly exclusive Institute or Gifted Children in Westchester, NY, was evealed to be a training ground and headquarers for the mutant super hero team known as the X-Men, of whom he was the leader and founder.

It was his tumultuous past with Lensherr that formed the man Xavier would become. The two shared a common goal in their early years, but a dispute between them led to a massive fallout in which Lensherr left Xavier crippled, abandoning their mutual philosophy of peaceful coexistence of mutantkind and humans. Charles spent his remaining years at odds with the man who would become one of the world's greatest terrorists, thwarting his plans time and again, while furthering the civil rights of mutants.

Found with his neck snapped, the murder of Charles Xavier seems to further indicate that Magneto is indeed the man responsible for not only this death but the deaths of hundreds of thousands in the event the world has come to call the Ultimatum Wave. Although unproven, it would explain the strange weather patterns across the globe, including the tidal wave that destroyed most of Manhattan. The death toll from this attack continues to rise. As a result of these anomalies, combined with the murder of Charles Xavier, Erik "Magneto" Lensherr has become the world's greatest fiend and threat. ■

Mar. 19th, 2009
Early Edition

DAILY BUGLE

NEW YORK'S FINEST DAILY NEWSPAPER

DOZENS OF STUDENTS KILLED IN ULTIMATUM DISASTER!

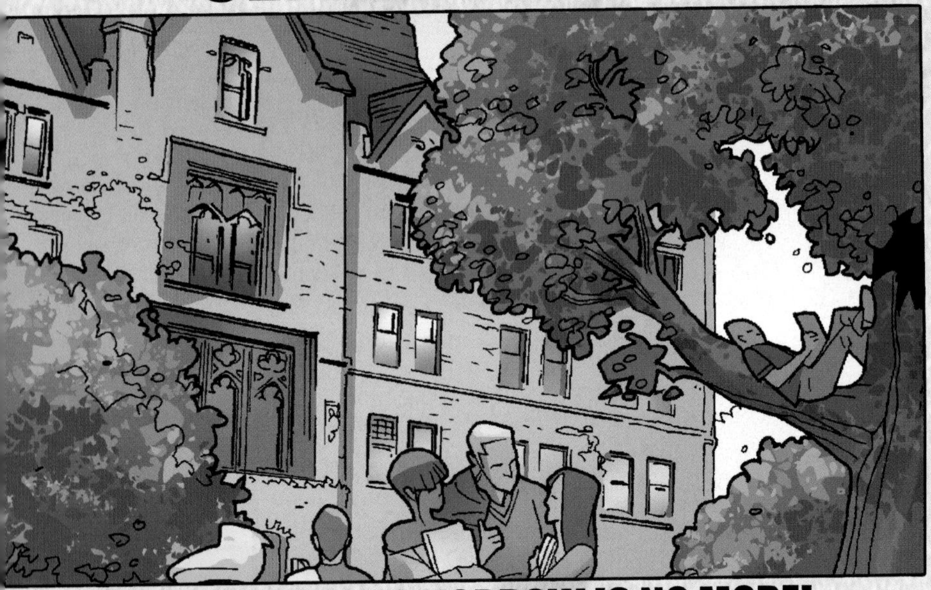

ACADEMY OF TOMORROW IS NO MORE!

In a shocking and incredibly disturbing turn of events, the mutant terrorist known as Magneto has begun targeting his own kind in his quest to wipe out all of humanity and its supporters. In a single act of mutant-on-mutant violence, he has become the greatest threat this world has ever seen, as he unleashed a series of suicide bombers, all duplicates of the mutant known as Jamie Madrox, the aptly named "Multiple Man."

The greatest casualties of this act are being reported from the site of Emma Frost's ***Academy of Tomorrow***, a school designed to be a safe haven for mutants and humans.

Formed as a counter to Charles Xavier's seemingly aggressive, "police force" of mutants, the Academy of Tomorrow opened its doors to all students with gifted abilities, regardless of genetic status. It is perhaps because of this cohabitation that Magneto targeted this school for destruction. It appears that there are no survivors from this horrific attack, although it will take weeks to sift through the remains and identify the casualties. In addition to the founder, Emma Frost, the known deceased include Cannonball, Polaris, Cypher, Sunspot, and dozens of others.■

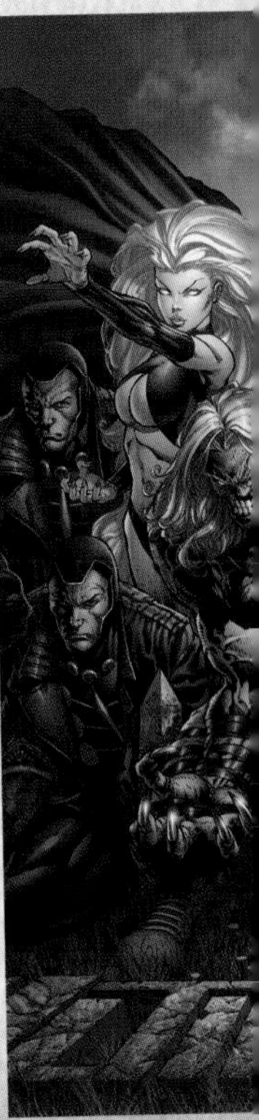

DAILY ✦ BUGLE

NEW YORK'S FINEST DAILY NEWSPAPER

OBITUARIES

FRANKLIN "THE BLOB" DUKES

The mutant terrorist known as the Blob was killed today at the hands of the Ultimates member known as Hank Pym, a.k.a. Yellowjacket. Not much is known of the man outside of his activities in conjunction with the Brotherhood of Mutants. Given that organization's ties to Magneto, it is no surprise that this villain is involved in the disaster gripping our world these past few days, causing death and carnage in his wake.

What little is known of the Blob is disturbing, to say the least. Long rumored to have cannibalistic tendencies, and a mutant power that is strengthened by this, the Blob was seen devouring bodies of the victims of the Ultimatum wave in New York City. It was his latest victim – the Ultimates member Janet Van Dyne, a.k.a. The Wasp – that finally proved to be his last, when Van Dyne's husband came across the Blob feasting on her corpse. Completely lost in grief, Hank Pym killed the man, ending his reign of terror.

Franklin "The Blob" Duncan leaves behind a legacy of evil, but also an innocent child – his daughter, the mutant Liz Allen, a student at Midtown High. Allen believed the man to be her uncle, but was recently exposed to the truth when her own mutant powers developed. It remains to be seen if she will follow in her father's evil footsteps.

Although every death that comes in adds to the tragically growing number of casualties, it is with little mourning that we report on the death of such a heinous monster as The Blob.■

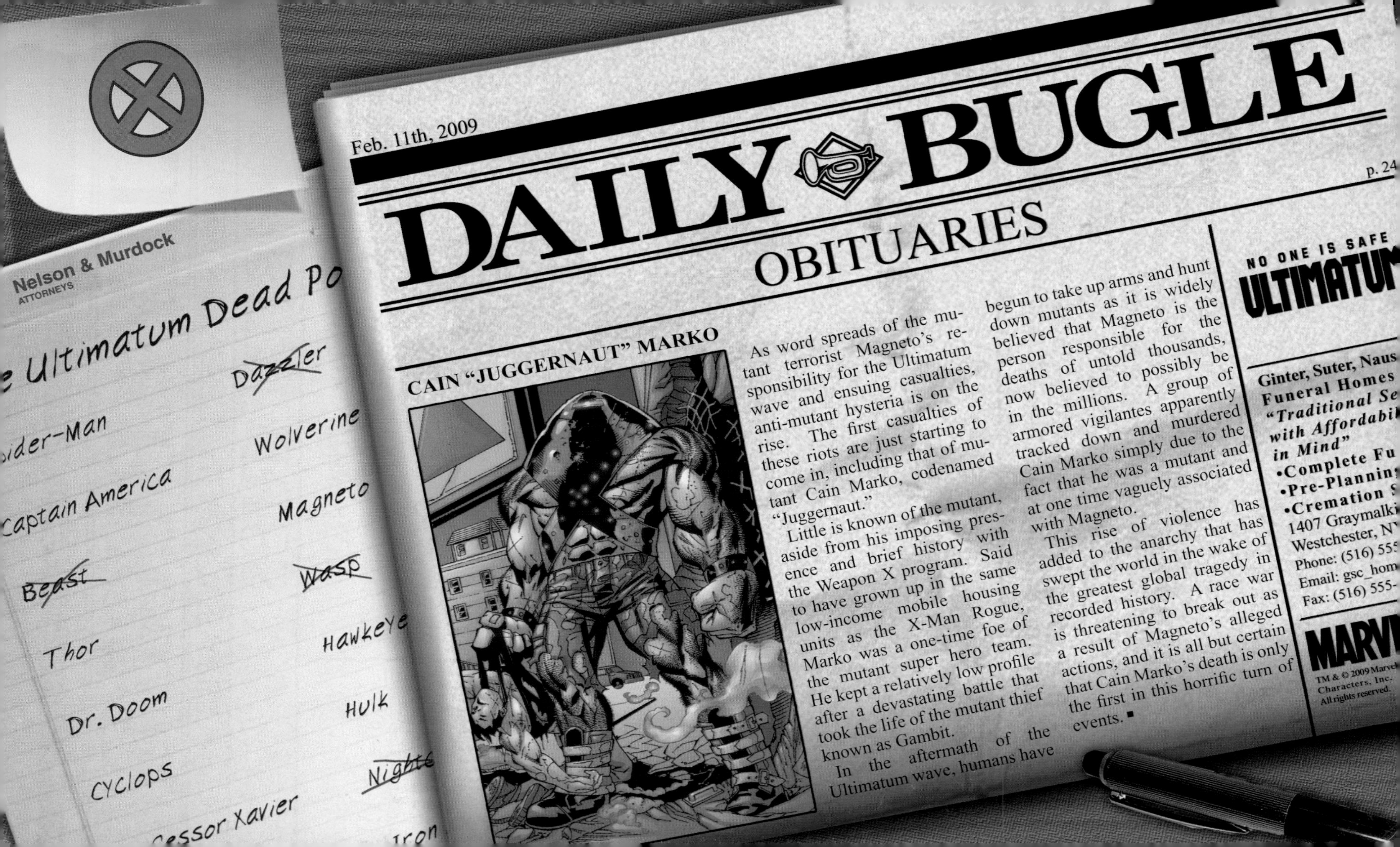

Nelson & Murdock
ATTORNEYS
e Ultimatum Dead Po
Dazzler
pider-Man
Wolverine
Captain America
Magneto
Beast
Wasp
Thor
Hawkeye
Dr. Doom
Hulk
Cyclops
Night
essor Xavier
Iron

Feb. 11th, 2009

p. 24

DAILY BUGLE

OBITUARIES

CAIN "JUGGERNAUT" MARKO

As word spreads of the mutant terrorist Magneto's responsibility for the Ultimatum wave and ensuing casualties, anti-mutant hysteria is on the rise. The first casualties of these riots are just starting to come in, including that of mutant Cain Marko, codenamed "Juggernaut."

Little is known of the mutant, aside from his imposing presence and brief history with the Weapon X program. Said to have grown up in the same low-income mobile housing units as the X-Man Rogue, Marko was a one-time foe of the mutant super hero team. He kept a relatively low profile after a devastating battle that took the life of the mutant thief known as Gambit.

In the aftermath of the Ultimatum wave, humans have begun to take up arms and hunt down mutants as it is widely believed that Magneto is the person responsible for the deaths of untold thousands, now believed to possibly be in the millions. A group of armored vigilantes apparently tracked down and murdered Cain Marko simply due to the fact that he was a mutant and at one time vaguely associated with Magneto.

This rise of violence has added to the anarchy that has swept the world in the wake of the greatest global tragedy in recorded history. A race war is threatening to break out as a result of Magneto's alleged actions, and it is all but certain that Cain Marko's death is only the first in this horrific turn of events. ■

DAILY ◈ BUGLE

NEW YORK'S FINEST DAILY NEWSPAPER

OBITUARIES

p. 26

JAMIE "MULTIPLE MAN" MADROX

The uncountable number of Multiple Man copies suddenly disappeared earlier today from the streets of cities across the world, leaving people everywhere rejoicing at what appears to be the death of the mass-murdering mutant terrorist. While it is unclear how Jamie Madrox met his sudden end, it is likely safe to assume that one of his adversaries in the mutant group the X-Men, took his life in a valiant effort to save the world from further destruction following the recently dubbed "Ultimatum Wave."

Beyond his recent passing and his birth in Madison, WI, little is known about Jamie Madrox. His alter ego(s) on the other hand is slightly better explored. As the mutant terrorist Multiple Man, Madrox was responsible for the death of thousands of innocent civilians along with his cohorts in the mutant terrorist Magneto's Brotherhood of Mutants. Creating numerous copies of himself and strapping bombs to each of their chests, Madrox and his Multiple Man doubles created death and chaos on a global scale, claiming even the life of hero Hank Pym, known to many as Giant Man, and more recently as Yellowjacket.∎

DAILY ◆ BUGLE

NEW YORK'S FINEST DAILY NEWSPAPER

OBITUARIES

p.

ELIZABETH "BETSY" BRADDOCK (PSYLOCKE)

The world cannot help but be devastated at the loss of Elizabeth "Betsy" Braddock. A true hero in every sense of the word, Betsy, known to friends and family as Psylocke, was assaulted and murdered in Charles Xavier's Institute for Gifted Youngsters by a crazed group of human supremacists led by former minister William Stryker, Jr.

Elizabeth Braddock was born to renowned scientist Sir James Braddock, who along with her brother Brian Braddock, a fellow hero known as Captain Britain, were recently killed in a terrorist bombing at Parliament in London. While much of Betsy's early adult life is unknown, what has made its way into the public eye can only be considered a testament to the magnificent person she must have been. When the abomination known by many as Proteus ran rampant through the streets of New York City it was solely through the sacrifice of Elizabeth Braddock that the creature could be brought to a halt, claiming with it the first life of the young hero Psylocke.

While undoubtedly many more tragedies similar to this one will occur in the passing days, one can only hope that Betsy's death will serve as a deterrent to people around the world seized by anti-mutant hysteria. Elizabeth "Betsy" Braddock strove to keep safe all those around her, with no regard to her own life. She died young. She died twice. She died tragically. But most of all she died a hero. ■

DAILY ◆ BUGLE

NEW YORK'S FINEST DAILY NEWSPAPER

OBITUARIES

p. 26

WARREN WORTHINGTON III (ANGEL)

The skies will never be the same as one of Earth's most valiant heroes will never again soar through them. Warren Worthington III, better known amongst both his colleagues and people across the world as Angel, has passed away in what can only be referred to as a heroic struggle with the mutant terrorist Erik Lensherr, better known across the globe by his alias Magneto.

Warren Worthington III was born an only child to multimillionaire Warren K. Worthington Jr. Spending the majority of his life in the Colorado Mountains, Warren was eventually enrolled in the recently deceased Charles Xavier's Institute for Gifted Youngsters. Understandably confused for an angel by people around the world, Warren's début in the public eye will not soon be forgotten. For as much of the religious hysteria regarding his form has passed, as Worthington himself confirmed his wings to be the result of a genetic mutation, upon examining the ordeals he overcame in his lifetime it becomes impossible to deny that Warren possessed a spark of something truly special.

Joining Xavier's X-Men soon after his arrival at the Institute, Warren proved himself countless times to both his comrades and the world that watched him from afar. Soaring into the midst of conflicts that remain to this day unthinkable to many, Warren fought to protect not only mutants like himself, but often the rest of the world that, often violently, shunned him. One cannot help but wonder if such a selfless individual wasn't something more than even he himself realized. Yet all speculation aside, one thing is for sure: Warren Worthington III will always be remembered, by both human and mutant alike, soaring the open skies like an Angel, watching over all those below him from leagues above. ∎

DAILY BUGLE

NEW YORK'S FINEST DAILY NEWSPAPER

OBITUARIES

p.

SCOTT "CYCLOPS" SUMMERS

Teacher. Leader. Hero. Scott Summers, the mutant superhero known as Cyclops was gunned down on the steps of the Capitol Building in Washington D.C. by an unknown gunman before a gathered crowd of thousands of onlookers. The historic moment will undoubtedly be forever etched on the collective memory of the country and serves as a reminder to those who take life and worthwhile causes for granted.

Perhaps best known for his steadfast leadership of Charles Xavier's mutant group the X-Men, Summers fought for the hope that one day mutants and humans would coexist peacefully. With his trademark optic blast, he rallied the combined forces of the X-Men, the government sponsored Ultimates and the Fantastic Four against Magneto, the mutant terrorist responsible for the destruction of New York and the mass murder of thousands of innocent Americans. His valiant efforts put a stop, once and for all, to the threat of the homicidal madman and have paved the way for the dream of mutant/human co-existence to become reality. ■

DAILY ✦ BUGLE

NEW YORK'S FINEST DAILY NEWSPAPER

OBITUARIES

p. 26

JAMES "WOLVERINE" HOWLETT

Little is known about the man known as Wolverine but if the world considers him anything, it is a hero. Once believed to be an assassin in the employ of the mutant terrorist Magneto, James Howlett's life was taken in the horrendous battle that took the lives of countless heroes. No body was ever found.

Before coming to work and live at Professor Charles Xavier's exclusive Institute for Gifted Children in Westchester, NY, much of Howlett's past remained a mystery to him. He served valiantly in the Canadian armed forces with the America's greatest hero - Captain America - as a paratrooper during World War II. His astounding resiliency in the heat of battle earned him the nickname "Lucky Jim" and he continued his service to our country in varying capacities including as part of the notorious mutant group, the X-Men.

Those who knew him will remember his independent nature, his love of beer and his willingness to sacrifice his own safety for the greater good. He died fighting the good fight against a monster who killed thousands with the Ultimatum Wave – he was the best at what he did. ∎

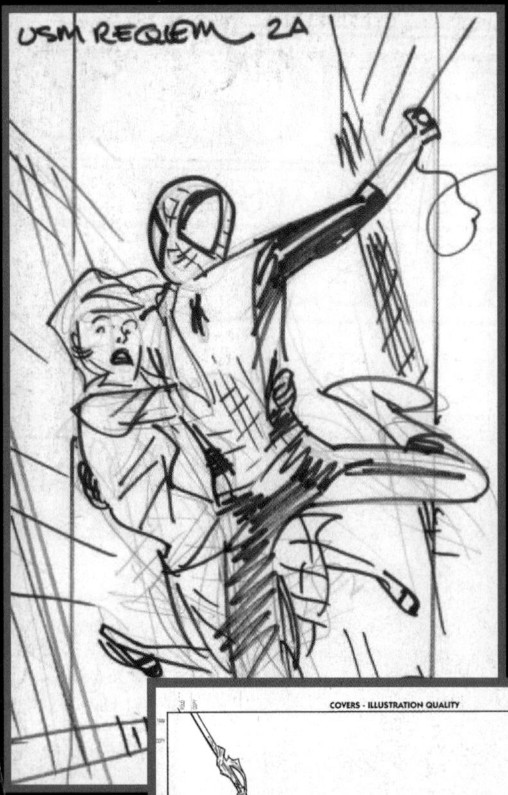
USM REQUIEM 2A
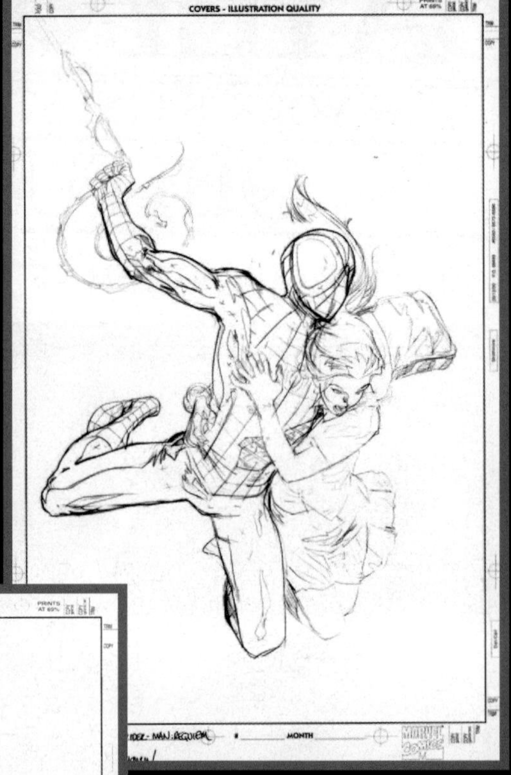
COVERS - ILLUSTRATION QUALITY
PRINTS AT 69%
MONTH
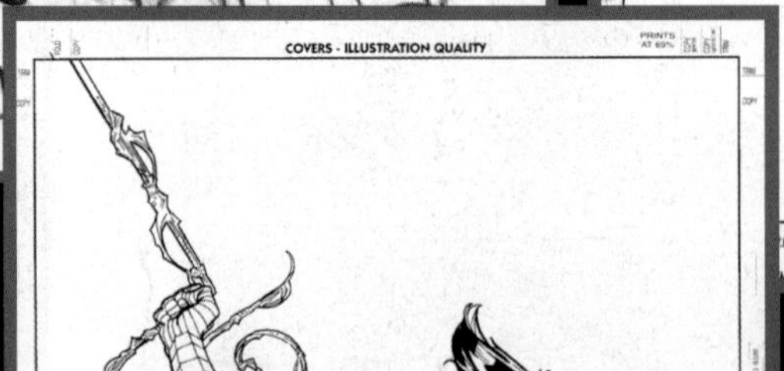
COVERS - ILLUSTRATION QUALITY
PRINTS AT 69%
TITLE ULTIMATE SPIDER-MAN: REQUIEM
MONTH
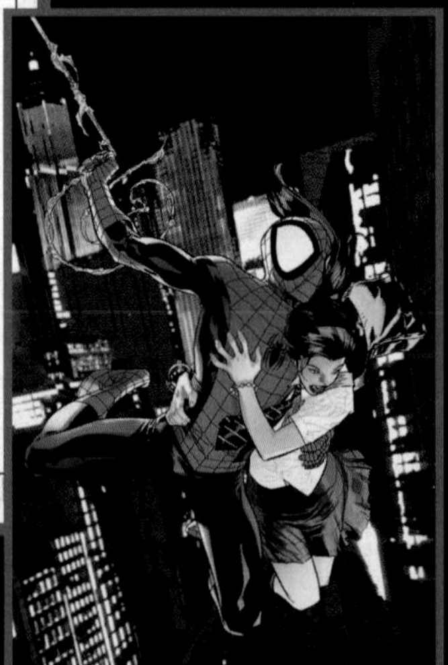

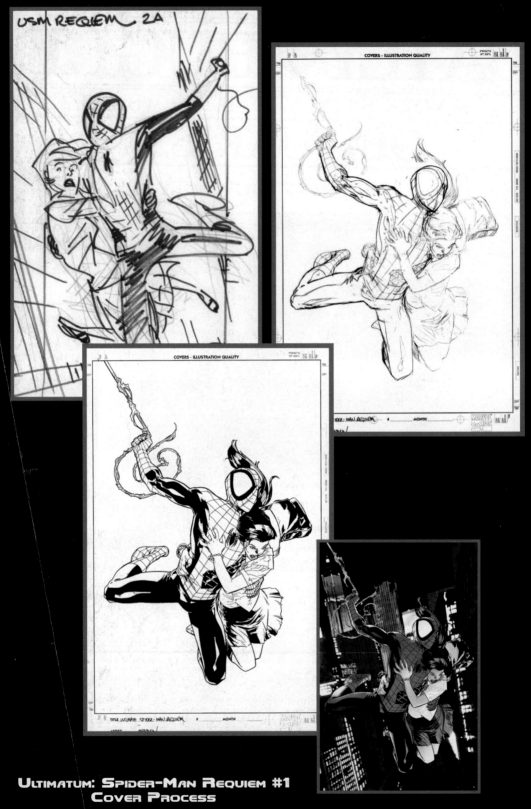

Ultimatum: Spider-Man Requiem #1
Cover Process
by
Stuart Immonen

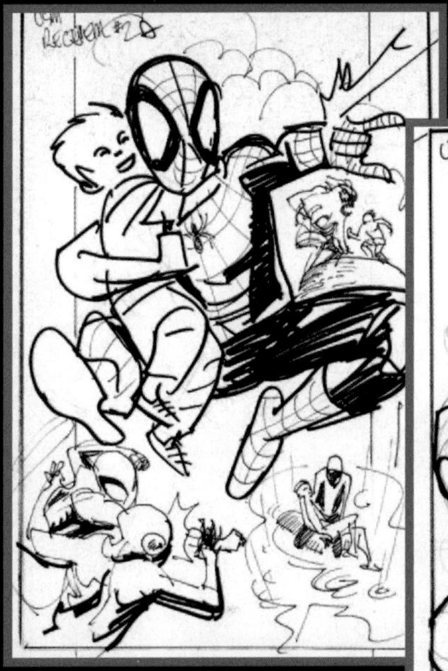
USM
REQUIEM #2 A

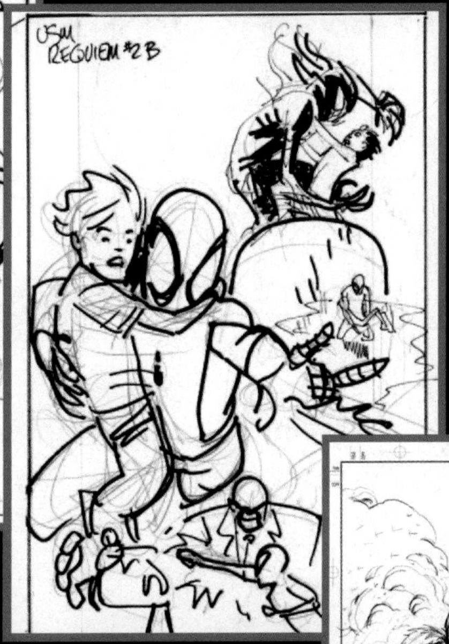
USM
REQUIEM #2 B

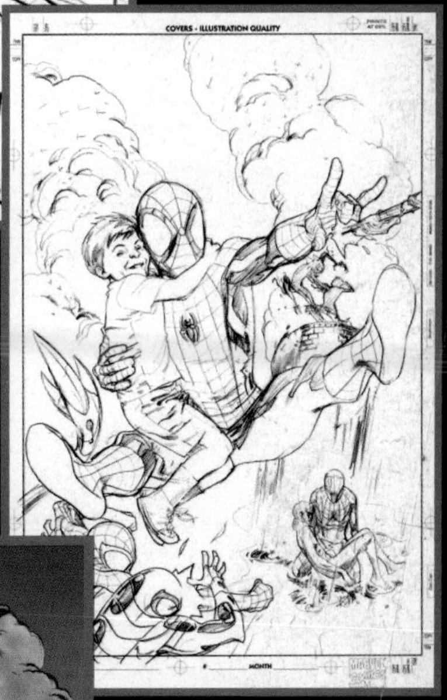
COVERS - ILLUSTRATION QUALITY

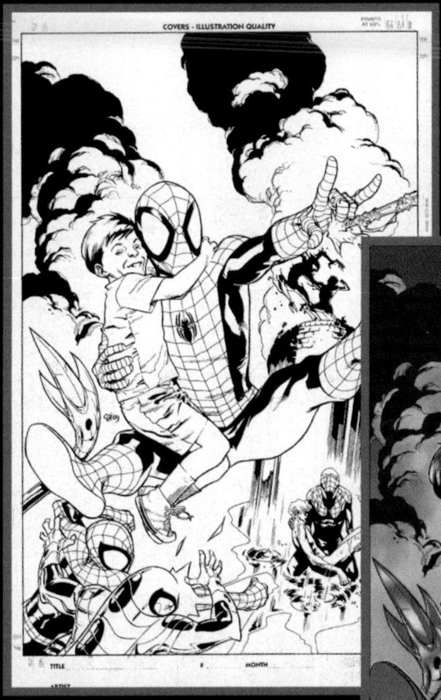
COVERS - ILLUSTRATION QUALITY
TITLE
MONTH

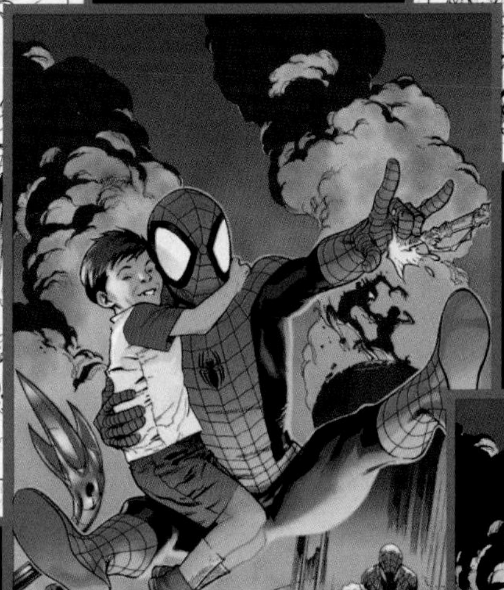

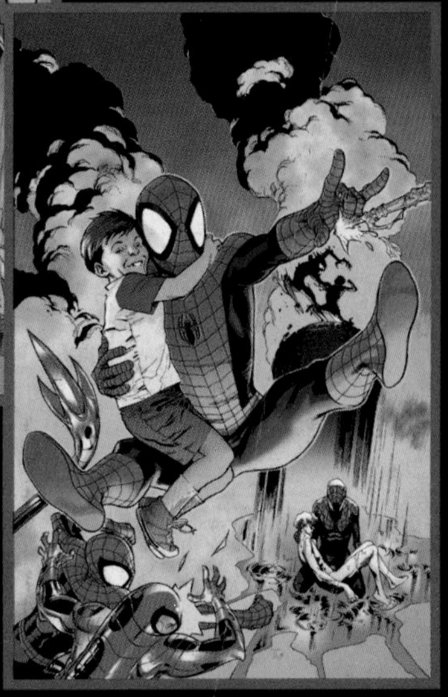

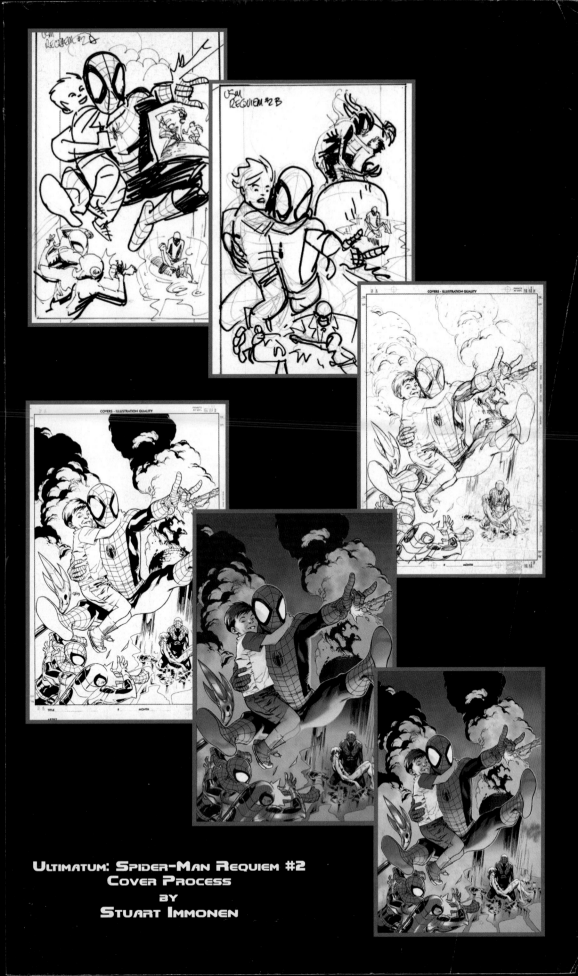

Ultimatum: Spider-Man Requiem #2
Cover Process
by
Stuart Immonen

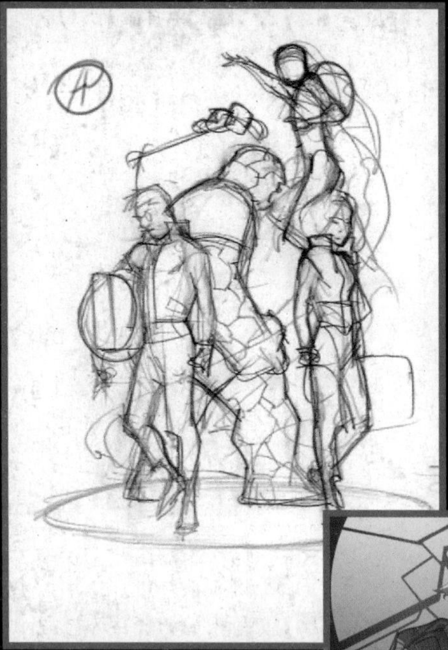

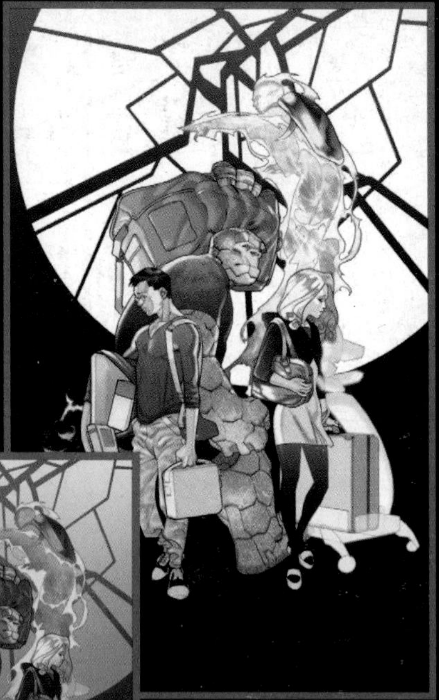

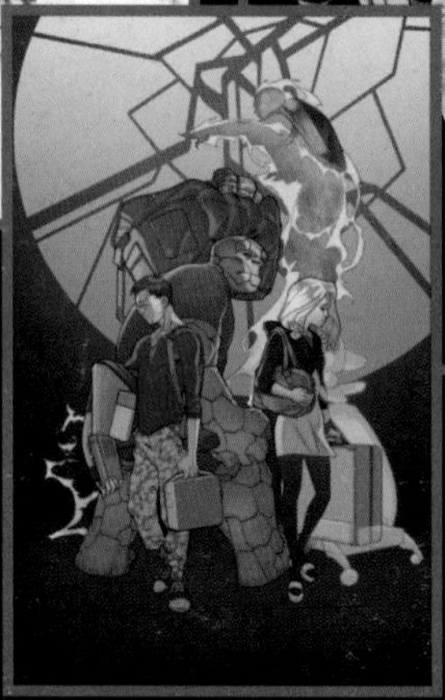

Ultimatum: Fantastic Four
Requiem #1
Cover Process
by
Pasqual Ferry

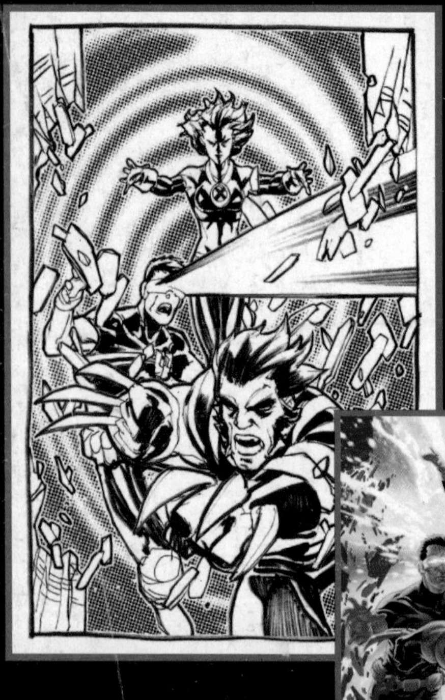

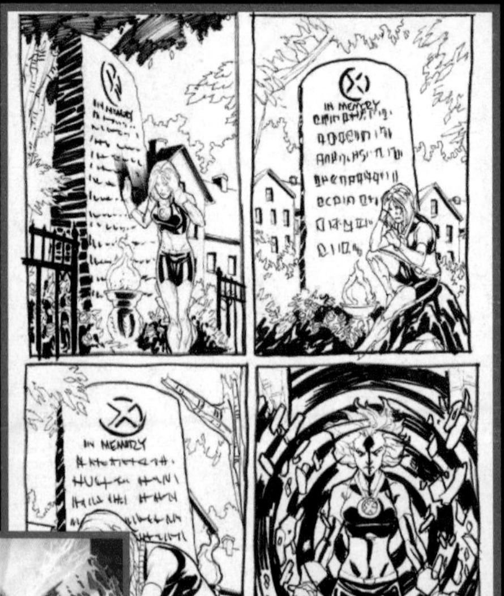

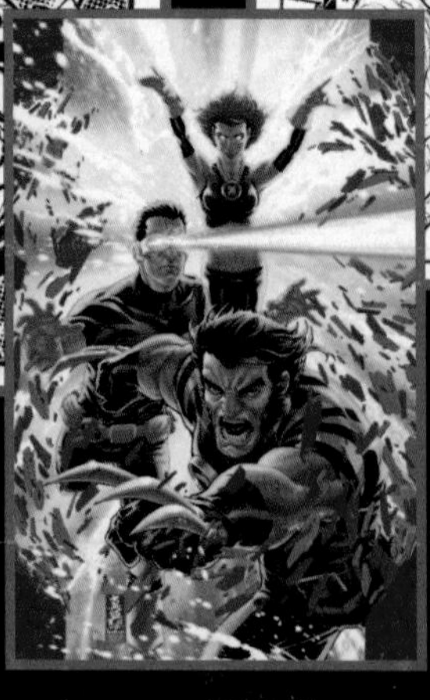

Ultimatum: X-Men
Requiem #1
Cover Process
by
Mark Brooks